# Teaching

## AT POST-16

## Effective Teaching
### IN THE A-LEVEL, AS AND VCE CURRICULUM

edited by
# Lin LE VERSHA & Gill NICHOLLS

# Acknowledgements

I would like to thank my colleagues at Godalming College for sharing their best practice with me, for reading chapters and making suggestions, especially Alan Lyons, Rob Greening, Val Hewitt, Gill Welford, David Adelman and Margaret Hobrough. I would also like to thank my husband Paul and daughter Kate for coping with domestic devastation during the weekends when this book was being produced.

Lin Le Versha

First published in Great Britain in 2003

Kogan Page Limited
120 Pentonville Road
London N1 9JN
United Kingdom
www.kogan-page.co.uk

**British Library Cataloguing in Publication Data**

A CIP record for this book is available from the British Library.

ISBN 0 7494 3348 5

Typeset by Saxon Graphics Ltd, Derby
Printed and bound in Great Britain by Bell & Bain Ltd, Glasgow

# Contents

# Contributors

**Jackie Greatorex** is a Research Officer at the University of Cambridge Local Examinations Syndicate

**Jeanne Holloway** is an independent educational adviser and author

**Lin Le Versha** is Vice Principal at Godalming Sixth Form College

**Simon Lygo-Baker** is a Lecturer in Academic Practice at King's College, London

**Rachel Macdonald Cragg** is a Lecturer in Academic Practice at King's College, London

**Hilary Street** is an Associate of the International School Effectiveness and Improvement Centre at the Institute of Education, London

# Series Editor's foreword

The post-16 environment has undergone and continues to go through major changes. Changes that have been so rapid and demanding of those teaching and working in the post-16 classroom that intense continuing professional development, training and learning has been required by all involved within the sector. This framework of rapid change has required all involved in the post-16 phase to gain formalized teaching qualifications, either by training as teachers or by enhancing any existing teaching qualifications. Those already engaged with teaching in the sector are taking up this challenge. Those entering the profession also need to take up the challenge of achieving teaching qualifications.

Teacher training within the post-16 phase has become more regulated, with competence in teaching and learning areas designated by agencies such as OFSTED introducing inspection based on a competency framework. These factors have increased the need for those learning to teach, as well as those experienced teachers in the sector, to gain teaching qualifications. Expectations of what it is to be a teacher and what a teacher is expected to engage with in the post-16 sector have been increased and highlighted by the external impetus for accountability of teaching quality. Teaching standards have given a framework for those wishing to gain teacher status within the sector; these include:

- knowledge and understanding;
- planning, teaching, and management of the learning environment;
- monitoring, assessment, reporting and accountability;
- professional values;
- continual professional development.

This book aims to guide the trainee and new teacher through each category, with the anticipated help of their mentor or critical friend. The underlying principle of the book is that teaching is an art as well as a science. Teaching is one of the most creative and satisfying professions to be involved in. Yet as in any profession there are key elements, skills, practices and standards that have to be achieved if effective and efficient practitioners are to be developed. This book addresses all the key areas within the post-16 teaching and learning environments. In some chapters this is made more explicit than others. Throughout it is assumed that the trainee or new teacher will have a copy of the requirements and standards for teachers within the sector and will gain, with the help of the book, a good working knowledge and understanding of them, in order to become an effective and competent teacher in the post-16 environment.

The book, through its tasks and overall design, is aimed at helping trainee and new teachers to develop their skills, knowledge and pedagogic practice so that they not only meet the demands of the post-16 teaching standards, but also develop and nurture their own philosophy of teaching.

Every teacher-training course starts trainees on their way. Learning the art and craft of teaching is a process, one that lasts a career – from trainee to newly qualified teacher to experienced teacher. The book attempts to address this learning process by involving the mentor or critical friend in the trainee's or new teacher's training and learning.

*Gill Nicholls*

# Introduction

Lin Le Versha

Curriculum 2000 has provided the first opportunity for 50 years to reconstruct the qualifications framework and the experience of 16- to 19-year-old students. Over the last five years the development of the framework has stimulated discussions on routes and pathways, structures and systems and modes of assessment, which have involved government, professional associations and teachers in their schools and colleges. The implementation of the framework has moved the spotlight from questions on its construction to those that challenge the teacher – how do we use the new qualifications as a means to improve our teaching and our students' learning?

The extent of the discussions has also prompted university departments of education to become aware of the paucity of educational research in this sector and to recognize that the specific needs and characteristics of 16- to 19-year-old students deserve more attention. Their research is moving from statistical surveys on retention and achievement to the classroom and the ways in which we can successfully stimulate, motivate and support students and prepare them for higher education or employment.

This book moves from theory to practice and it is intended for students who are studying PGCE/A courses and for newly qualified teachers who wish to learn more about working with 16- to 19-year-old students. The first section provides a context for the qualifications framework, its assessment and ways of supporting and developing students personally and academically. The second section moves into the classroom and explores practical strategies to manage students and their learning. These practical approaches are rooted in theory but have been used successfully in classrooms by post-16 teachers, and the systems described are those actually used to manage learning in colleges and sixth forms. Tasks are included in all chapters to stimulate development activities and discussion, and to involve the reader in the debate that is still taking place in the post-16 sector.

The authors hope that their views and strategies will support a creative, confident approach to 16- to 19-year-old education, one that is based on self-reflection and the desire to improve learning.

# Part 1

# Exploring the theory and context of the post-16 framework

# 1 How did the post-16 qualifications framework develop?

Lin Le Versha

The post-16 qualifications framework was introduced to the first year (Year 12) of sixth forms in England and Northern Ireland in September 2000, following 20 years of discussion, vision and attempts to revolutionize post-compulsory education for 16- to 19-year-olds. After two major consultations, the Dearing Report (1996) and *Qualifying for Success* (DfEE, 1997), under successive Conservative and Labour governments, we now have a framework that incorporates the academic and vocational and has at its core the desire to improve retention and widen participation at 16.

The assessment of learning through examinations was initially established to test the vocational competencies of those engaged in particular professions. Among the first examinations were those set for apothecaries in 1815, followed by one for solicitors in 1835 and then for accountants in1880. General education was assessed through inspectors' visits to elementary schools, such as that famously described by Dickens in *Hard Times* where Gradgrind wants 'nothing but facts', and for those in predominantly fee-paying secondary schools through the School Certificate at 16 or the Higher School Certificate at 18. The School Certificate, introduced in 1917, was structured around a baccalaureate approach and generated much criticism, as generations of able students who failed one component were, for that reason, denied progression to higher education.

This baccalaureate style was radically altered when in 1951 examinations were set to assess separate subjects in the General Certificate of Education (GCE). The GCE was examined at two levels, Ordinary (O) levels taken at the age of 16 and Advanced (A) levels taken at 18. From the 1940s until the 1960s the brightest children were selected at the age of 11 to go to grammar schools to follow an academic curriculum, which usually led to an arts/science divide at 14 or 16.

The 80 per cent of 11-year-olds who failed their 11-plus examination went to secondary modern schools and left school without taking examinations. The Beloe Report in 1960 recommended the introduction of the Certificate of Secondary Education (CSE) as an incentive for these students to stay in education until 16 and to leave with some qualifications. CSEs offered students the possibility of assessment through a wider range of learning styles than O levels as they could submit coursework for academic as well as practical subjects. This did not, however, increase the staying-on rate at 16 as secondary modern school students did not wish to cross the divide established at 11 to join grammar school sixth forms.

During the second half of the 20th century successive governments were concerned about the number of pupils leaving school without qualifications and how few students were progressing to post-16 education. Until 1939, 88 per cent of children left school at 14, and the Crowther Report (1959) recorded that only 10 per cent of 17-year-olds were in full-time education. In the middle of the swinging 60s almost half the school population left school with no formal qualifications. The raising of the school-leaving age from 15 to 16 in 1974, linked with the development of the comprehensive school system, meant that 87 per cent of pupils then took either O levels or CSEs before leaving school. In the mid-1980s, 53 per cent of students left school after taking these examinations but 40 per cent of students still left school without qualifications (HMSO, 1968, 1986). At this stage only 20 per cent returned to the sixth form for a further year's study. Staying-on rates improved with the advent of the GCSE in 1986 when O levels and CSEs were merged into a single examination and the path to sixth form education was widened.

The 1980s saw a number of papers calling for post-16 reform, among them the Higginson Report (1988), suggesting a broadening of the 16–18 curriculum, which was rejected in favour of the 'gold standard' of the existing A levels. Rather than tamper with the academic pathway, a new vocational route was established in 1986 by the National Council for Vocational Qualifications (NCVQ) and, by 1990, 130 lead bodies existed to validate National Vocational Qualifications (NVQs). These competence- or skill-based examinations were considered to be too narrow for schools and colleges to include in their full-time 16–19 curriculum as NVQs were to be assessed in the workplace.

So a broader course, based on underpinning vocational knowledge and skills, known as the General National Vocational Qualification (GNVQ) was introduced to schools and colleges in *Education and Training for the Twenty First Century* (DFE, 1991). Following pilot studies in 1992 GNVQs were rapidly available to all schools and colleges from September 1993.

As GNVQ assessment was based on portfolios of coursework and multiple choice answer tests, they offered students who did not succeed in traditional examinations an alternative way of study and assessment at post 16. University courses, particularly in 'new' universities, were set up to receive this particular style of learning and offer these students access to degree-level study. The GNVQ was seen as providing a new pathway between the academic A levels and the vocational NVQs.

The debate about parity of esteem between GNVQs and A levels raged throughout the early 1990s and was fuelled by the National Audit Office report *Unfinished Business* (OFSTED/National Audit Office, 1993). The Audit Office reported that between 30 and 40 per cent of students who started A level courses failed to complete them and then left the sixth form with no qualifications beyond their GCSEs.

This concern with retention, improving the staying-on rate at 16 and the growing number of examinations that students could take at 16-plus led to three reports in 1995–96. The Beaumont (1995) and Capey (1996) Reports looked at NVQs and GNVQs respectively and suggested modifications to both. NVQs were to have core and optional units and to remove the jargon from their specifications and GNVQs, although applauded for offering a more 'independent' style of learning post 16, were criticized for being difficult to complete in the two years offered in the sixth form, with two-thirds of candidates failing to do so.

The consultations for the Dearing Report were conducted in parallel with those for Beaumont and Capey, and all three political parties supported the three-track system in 1996. The House of Commons Education Committee (1996) wanted to find ways to 'enhance the rigour of assessment of A Levels, GNVQs and NVQs'. Dearing was to rationalize the 20,000 qualifications available to 16-year-olds, to impose coherence and control but to include diversity and choice.

This tension and the support for the three tracks that had emerged over the previous decade led to a system that several commentators have compared to Plato with his gold, silver and bronze levels of education (Stanton and Richardson, 1997; Tomlinson, 1997): the gold citizens of the highest class should receive the liberal education, those in the silver or middle class would benefit from a vocational education while those in the bronze layer should be socialized and acquire basic vocational skills.

Instead of a three-track class system, the framework incorporated three pathways: the A level route, which developed the knowledge, understanding and skills rooted in specific subjects; the applied pathway of GNVQ, which developed the broad range of skills and underpinning knowledge associated with a vocational area; and a third or vocational track where students could become competent in a trade or a profession at an appropriate level in the workplace. Thus at the end of the 20th century we saw the gold, silver and bronze of Plato's *Republic* embodied in the proposals for the post-16 qualifications framework.

The debate surrounding the Dearing Report came to a halt in 1997 as a general election led to a New Labour government. The vision of the Labour Party manifesto *Aiming Higher*, published a week before the Dearing Report, and the reality of the reforms following the *Qualifying for Success* (DfEE, 1997; QCA, 1998) consultations once New Labour was in government are well documented by Hodgson and Spours (1999). The academic/vocational divide was blurred structurally by the rationalization of the regulating body for academic qualifications (SCAA) and the NCVQ into a single body, the Qualifications and Curriculum Authority (QCA), along with the merger of all academic examination boards and vocational accreditation bodies into three awarding bodies (Edexcel, AQA and OCA) and the Education and Employment departments into a single ministry.

The qualifications framework, or Curriculum 2000, was developed alongside this structure. A levels were broken down into two blocks each comprising three units, called AS and A2, with a corresponding structure and grading in GNVQs, which were to become AVCEs (Advanced Vocational Certificate of Education). Key skills in communication, application of number and information technology were to be accredited, while the 'soft' key skills of problem solving, working with others and improving one's own learning and performance were to be developed later. Work was to begin on an overarching certificate and diploma – the National Certificate at level 2/GCSE and the National Advanced Diploma at level 3/Advanced level – but neither was to be implemented until at least 2001. Coursework was limited to 20–30 per cent, as was the number of resits that could be taken, in an attempt to ensure that the rigour, or 'gold standard', of A levels was preserved.

# What is the qualifications framework?

The 20,000 qualifications for 16- to 19-year-olds that were publicly funded in 1996 have been categorized in five levels along three tracks. Students at all levels from the most basic at Foundation level or level 1 to postgraduate at level 5 can study courses and seek accreditation along the three tracks of academic, applied or vocational. Those at level 3 attract points that can build up a profile or tariff for university entrance.

The consultations on the framework had at their centre the creative tension of how to broaden the A level programme while maintaining its standard, to widen participation of 16- to 19-year-olds in full-time education and, once they were attracted to study, to retain them. The standard of vocational programmes was to rise so that they would enjoy 'parity of esteem' with the traditional 'gold standard' of A levels and form part of a coherent framework that higher education and employers could understand (see Figure 1.1).

## Increase in subjects

From September 2000 students selecting their level 3/Advanced level course have selected four or five AS subjects leading to three examinations or modules assessed at the end of the first year. Following the issuing of AS results in August they return for a second year of study to follow three or four A2 courses in the subjects taken at AS. Students have the opportunity to tailor their course to build on their success in the AS or to change direction and add additional AS courses to their programme.

## Vertical flexibility

Unlike the traditional A level course, where usually three subjects were chosen at the beginning of year one and the examinations taken at the end of the second year, the framework offers the flexibility that students and their tutors have welcomed. After the stable, common core of subjects offered by the National Curriculum until Key Stage 4

| Level of qualification | General | Vocationally related | Occupational |
|---|---|---|---|
| 5 | Higher-level qualifications | | Level 5 NVQ |
| 4 | | | Level 4 NVQ |
| 3<br>Advanced level | A level | Vocational A level (Advanced GNVQ) | Level 3 NVQ |
| 2<br>Intermediate level | GCSE grade A*-C | Intermediate GNVQ | Level 2 NVQ |
| 1<br>Foundation level | GCSE grade D-G | Foundation GNVQ | Level 1 NVQ |
| Entry level | Certificate of (educational) achievement | | |

**Figure 1.1**   The qualifications framework

(GCSEs), students were often trapped in two-year A level courses that did not meet their expectations or which they found very different and at a much higher standard than suggested at GCSE.

They had two choices: to continue struggling with a subject they did not like and understand or to drop out and start again. Many students just dropped out of education altogether at the end of the first year, as the Audit Commission discovered in 1993. Now these students can choose which of their subjects to drop or to replace with another AS if they wish to continue in education. If they choose to leave education they have a qualification that they can convert to A2 later in their life or they can use their AS certificates as access to higher education at HND or Foundation Year level.

## Horizontal flexibility

Not only has the flexibility been built into vertical progression but it has also been built in horizontally, as students are now able to select from three-module AS and A2 courses and similarly from three- or six-module Vocational Certificate of Education (VCE), formerly known as the General Vocational Certificate of Education (GNVQ). This was primarily designed as a two-year full-time programme with the equivalent time and outcome of two A levels. Another A level could be added alongside it but for many students the GNVQ, in for example business or leisure and tourism, was their main course.

Now students can select from double VCEs of 12 units, the equivalent of two AS/A2 subjects, or a single VCE six-unit award, which has the same volume and value as one AS/A2 subject. This can be broken down even further: students could take a three-module award in some VCEs over one year as they would an AS subject. This has the effect of offering students a choice between two different modes of assessment and learning styles in, for example, business studies. The AS/A2 in business studies is examined primarily in the examination room with data response and essay questions, while the VCE offers the student a much greater coursework option and short-answer questions on applied knowledge and understanding.

## Mix and match

Figure 1.2 shows the possibilities for mixing and matching.

## Key skills

For the first time all students following post-16 programmes of study are expected to be following courses in the three 'hard' key skills of communication, application of number and information technology. In addition to a portfolio of work for each key skill, students also take examinations in them at level 1, 2 or 3. The successful acquisition of key skills at level 3 could earn the student points towards university entry on the UCAS tariff introduced for university admissions in September 2002.

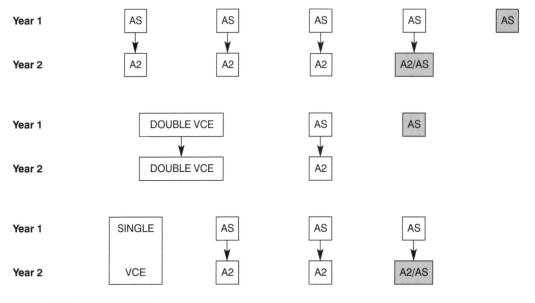

Note: Possibilities are in shaded boxes.

**Figure 1.2** Mixing and matching

## A voluntary framework

The Dearing Report in 1996 suggested the way to ensure breadth in the A level programme was to establish an overarching certificate or basic matriculation requirements at levels 2 and 3. Level 2 would reflect the broad programme already studied at Key Stage 4 but it would mean that students at level 3/Advanced level would continue studying subjects across the range of art, science, humanities and mathematics with key skills. This would reflect the baccalaureate approach of many of the systems in Europe and prevent the specialism at Advanced level that is criticized in the English system.

The qualifications framework introduced in September 2000 is perceived as 'soft' as there is no firm compulsion to combine particular subjects or even to take a basic minimum. During the first year of Curriculum 2000 key skills were delivered primarily by FE and sixth form colleges, as they received funding to teach them. Schools made individual decisions on whether key skills would be part of their post-16 curriculum. The number of AS subjects taken by students also varied across colleges and schools. Colleges encouraged students to sit at least four AS subjects while in many local authority schools students have taken three subjects. In the independent sector the pattern appears to be similarly idiosyncratic as some schools are offering students four AS followed by four A2 subjects while others suggest four AS reducing to three A2 subjects.

The framework could become 'firm' if the government were to impose an overarching certificate suggesting the rules of combination and number of subjects to be taken to achieve level 3. Another force on the framework is its currency in the eyes of the universities. If admissions tutors in the universities that *select* their students, such as the Russell Groups, and medical and veterinary schools, continue to ask for three passes at grade A in a narrow range of subjects, then students and their parents will question the wisdom of taking a broader range of subjects, additional examinations and key skills that could well lower their grade profile. The success of the framework in achieving its aims will depend on the long-term stance taken towards its development by the government, schools and colleges and, at the receiving end, the universities and employers.

## An alternative

Governments may have been making changes to post-compulsory education over the last 20 years but so have schools themselves. Alongside the discussions that have generated Curriculum 2000, proposals for a British baccalaureate have also been developed (Finegold *et al*, 1996). Some schools have turned towards the International Baccalaureate as an alternative for their students and in the following box Robert Tibbott, Deputy Headteacher of Dartford Grammar School, describes the award that has been offered at the school since 1995 and is now taken by 50 per cent of the sixth form.

---

## The International Baccalaureate Diploma

Courses leading to the award of the International Baccalaureate Diploma (IB) are an attractive alternative to GCE Advanced level.

The IB Diploma is an internationally recognized school-leaving qualification. It involves a two-year programme of study for 16- to 19-year-olds and British universities welcome students with the diploma.

The IB curriculum is genuinely broad and balanced. Students study in six disciplines:

- the home language;
- a second language (modern or classical);
- a humanity (history, geography, business studies, IT, classical civilization, etc);
- a science (or design technology);
- mathematics; and
- *either* art, music *or* theatre arts etc, or a further language, humanity or science.

Through this curriculum virtually all career paths can be safeguarded, while each student follows a pathway that is broad enough for academic balance and to allow the possibility of change between the sixth form and university. An aspiring medical student will take two sciences along with mathematics, for example; a candidate keen to read law at university will find it easy to choose a balanced course from the options available.

A student normally studies three subjects at higher level (A level equivalent) and three at standard level (between GCSE and AS level).

---

Underpinning this part of the curriculum are three areas of core activity:

- The theory of knowledge – an interdisciplinary course intended to stimulate critical reflection on knowledge and experience gained inside and outside the classroom. Students are challenged to question the bases of knowledge and to appreciate other cultural perspectives.
- The extended essay – with staff support, students investigate and write up a topic of special interest. This is a useful preparation for university work.
- CAS – students receive accreditation for work in the fields of creativity, action and service. By this means, it is hoped that students become responsible, compassionate citizens.

The final examination, taken after five terms of study, is assessed at seven levels: 7 points represent the highest grade (above grade A at A level); 3 or fewer points represent an unsatisfactory level of performance. Each student, therefore, has a potential total score of $6 \times 7 = 42$ IB points on the six selected subjects. To this may be added a maximum of 3 bonus points for a distinguished performance in the theory of knowledge and the extended essay. The absolute maximum points per student is thus 45.

Although there are timetabling, administrative and financial issues raised by the prospect of introducing the IB, none of these offers any real obstacle. Our satisfaction with the IB as a curriculum for the sixth former of the 21st century is considerable.

The International Baccalaureate Organization is based in Switzerland. Its office in Great Britain is at Peterson House, Malthouse Avenue, Cardiff Gate, Cardiff CF23 8GL.

## Has Curriculum 2000 delivered?

According to QCA research (2002) using OFSTED and UCAS statistics, the answer would seem to be yes. The curriculum has greater breadth and is more flexible:

- The breadth of the curriculum offered is satisfactory or better in the large majority of schools, with over half being good or better.
- Students are able to follow their chosen combination of subjects in the large majority of schools (OFSTED, quoted in QCA, 2002: 3).

A UCAS survey in 2001 shows that the academic divide is being blurred, as 86 per cent of sixth form colleges and 56 per cent of all schools and colleges are combining GCEs and VCEs. Students are broadening their programme and the volume of their study with 66 per cent of students taking four AS subjects in Year 12 (excluding general studies) and 13 per cent adding a new AS subject in Year 13; and 42 per cent of students are resitting at least one GCE unit in Year 13 so almost half of the cohort are working to improve their grades at AS before entering the examination room for their A2 subjects. Add to this the 13 per cent of Year 13 students who claim that they are studying a different A2 subject to that originally planned and it would appear that Curriculum 2000 is indeed offering the breadth and flexibility hoped for in its design.

So it would appear that students now have the real opportunity for the first time to cross the gold/silver divide and move towards a framework where flexibility and programmes of study can be tailored to an individual style of learning. They can explore two and in some cases all three of the pathways as they develop an integrated curriculum that meets their individual needs. In the 21st century we have made the first step away from the discrete metals of the Platonic divide and instead moved towards a creative alloy that is forged within the individual student.

# References

Beaumont, G (1995) *Review of 100 NVQs and SVQs: A report submitted to the DfEE* (The Beaumont Report), DfEE, London

Beloe Report (1960) *Secondary Schools Examinations other than the GCE*, HMSO, London

Capey, J (1996) *Review of GNVQ Assessment* (The Capey Report), National Council for Vocational Qualifications, London

Central Advisory Committee for Education (1959) *Fifteen to Eighteen (Crowther Report)*, HMSO, London

Dearing, Sir Ron (1996) *Review of Qualifications for 16–19 Year Olds* (The Dearing Report), SCAA, London

Department for Education (DFE) (1991) *Education and Training for the Twenty First Century*, HMSO, London

Department for Education and Employment (DfEE) (1997) *Qualifying for Success: A consultation paper on the future of post-16 qualifications*, DfEE, London

Finegold, D *et al* (1996) *A British Baccalaureate*, Institute for Policy Research, London

Higginson Report (1988) *Advancing A Levels*, HMSO, London

HMSO (1968, 1986) *Education Statistics for the UK Stationery Office*, HMSO, London

Hodgson, A and Spours, K (1999) *New Labour's Educational Agenda*, Kogan Page, London

House of Commons Education Committee (1996) *Education and Training for 14–19 Year Olds*, First Report, House of Commons, London

OFSTED/National Audit Office (1993) *Unfinished Business: Full time educational courses for 16–19 year olds*, HMSO, London

QCA (1998) *Qualifying for Success: Report on the consultation about the future of post-16 qualifications*, QCA, London

QCA (2002) *Developing Provision for Curriculum 2000*, Circular No 155, QCA, London

Stanton, G and Richardson, W (1997) *Qualifications for the Future: A study of tripartite and other discussions in post-16 education and teaching*, FEDA, London

Tomlinson, S (1997) *Education 14–19: Critical perspectives*, Athlone, London

# 2 Examination and assessment in Curriculum 2000

Jackie Greatorex

*Disclaimer: The opinions expressed in this paper are those of the author and are not to be taken as the opinions of the University of Cambridge Local Examinations Syndicate (UCLES) or any of its subsidiaries.*

## General qualifications in Curriculum 2000

The aim of this chapter is to explore the similarities and differences between Advanced Subsidiary (AS) qualifications, A2, A levels and Vocational Certificates of Education (VCE), which are all Advanced qualifications.

General Certificate of Education (GCE) A levels were introduced in 1951 for a small, elite group of students preparing for single honours study at universities (Young and Leney, 1997). By 2000 nearly 50 per cent of students under 21 years of age had achieved an A level qualification. The government's target is that by 2003 this would grow to 60 per cent (DfEE, 1999). Hodgson and Spours described these as dramatic changes and added that: 'Advanced level provision now includes a significant proportion of vocational study alongside more traditional academic subjects' (2000: 2).

Prior to Curriculum 2000 there were two types of A levels: 'linear A levels' and 'modular A levels'. For linear A levels, students followed a syllabus of study for two years and then took a series of examinations (sometimes known as terminal examinations) at the end of the two years. The terminal examinations allowed some linear A levels to include a synoptic element in the assessment. The modular A level syllabuses were divided into modules, and candidates were examined at the end of each module, but there was a minimum of 30 per cent assessment through terminal examination (Hodgson and Spours, 1997). Students generally studied three A levels over two years of full-time education. Prior to Curriculum 2000 there were also General National Vocational Qualifications (GNVQs) in the 16 to 19 sector, which were designed to prepare students for employment in a broad occupational area as well as being an accepted route to higher education. GNVQs were based on the idea that students should demonstrate competence to achieve the award. GNVQ assessment relied heavily on project work and collecting a portfolio of evidence to demonstrate competence although there were some examinations (Hayward, 1995). GNVQs in the 16 to 19 sector were generally available in schools and colleges from September 1993 (Wolf, 1997).

A level students in the systems in England, Northern Ireland and Wales have had a narrow and specialized educational experience compared with students at the same level in other European countries. Today's global market demands that learners demonstrate a broader range of skills in work and everyday life but, like many other curricula, the Advanced curriculum has been characterized by an academic/vocational divide. Vocational qualifications have been devalued and there has been little mixing of academic and vocational study (Hodgson and Spours, 2000).

The Dearing Committee's (1996) review of 16 to 19 education outlined proposals for reform. Hodgson and Spours (2000) argued that the Dearing Report was the main influence on the present New Labour government's approach to this education sector. For example, it recommended the new six- and three-unit VCEs, which were adopted in *Qualifying for Success* (*QfS*), a DfEE consultation paper on the future of post-16 qualifications. The New Labour government's plans for the 16 to 19 qualifications came to fruition in September 2000 when Curriculum 2000 was launched.

In summary the changes to the curriculum were that new three-unit GCE Advanced Subsidiary (AS) qualifications were introduced as the first part of an A level. Students could then take a three-unit A2 to transform their AS to an A level. The AS qualifications aim to be:

assessed and graded to match the levels of attainment expected from students halfway through an advanced course of study... [They] focus on the skills, knowledge and understanding developed during the first half of an advanced course of study... The conceptually less demanding material will tend to be assessed in AS units. The more demanding A2 units will be assessed and graded at a higher standard.

(Stobart, 2000: 17)

The AS standard is meant to be below A level but above GCSE. The full A level should be of equivalent standard to the old A levels.

The 12-unit Advanced level GNVQ became the Advanced Vocational Certificate of Education (Double Award). A new vocational qualification, the Advanced Vocational Certificate of Education (AVCE), or Vocational A level, has now been introduced along with the three-unit Advanced Subsidiary Vocational Certificate of Education (ASVCE). ASVCE is currently only available in business, engineering, health and social care, and information and communications technology. All these Advanced Vocational qualifications are deemed to be of equivalent standard to A levels and as a group of qualifications they are known as VCEs. Recently the Qualifications and Curriculum Authority (QCA) launched a national qualifications framework. QCA is a government body that regulates qualifications. The national qualifications framework 'is a way of organising and quality assuring qualifications in England, Wales and Northern Ireland. It is like a map that shows how qualifications relate to each other, and the quality of the qualifications in it will be guaranteed' (QCA, 2000a: 2). GCEs, VCEs and National Vocational Qualifications (NVQs) have been incorporated into the national qualifications framework but NVQs are not considered in detail in this chapter.

The new Curriculum 2000 qualifications, AS and A levels, are administered by five awarding bodies: Assessment and Qualifications Alliance (AQA), Oxford, Cambridge and RSA Examinations (OCR) and Edexcel in England; Council for Curriculum, Examinations and Assessment (CCEA) in Northern Ireland; and Welsh Joint Examinations Council (WJEC) in Wales. A2 units are also administered by these awarding bodies. The A2 is not a qualification in itself; it is only part of an A level. VCEs are administered by AQA, Edexcel and OCR but are not currently offered by CCEA or WJEC. The awarding bodies compete in terms of the differences between the specifications (formerly known as syllabuses) that they provide for each qualification and the services that they can provide. QCA monitors the practice of the awarding bodies in England and publishes a Code of Practice (QCA, 2002) to which they must adhere. Qualifications and Curriculum Authority for Wales (ACCAC) is the regulating organization in Wales, and CCEA is self-regulating.

## Similarities and differences between VCE, GCE and other Advanced qualifications (AS and A levels)

In this section the objective is to identify similarities and differences between VCE and other Advanced qualifications. There are issues that need to be considered:

- *curriculum* – purposes, standards, unitization factors (ie size of qualifications, choices between units, resits, the cashing in of units), key skills and pedagogy;
- *assessment* – internal and external assessment, grading issues (ie the grades available, award meetings, uniform mark scales) and the assessment specification (ie quality of written communication, synoptic assessment).

VCEs equip candidates with general skills and are relevant to a broad employment area. By contrast A levels provide students with access to specialist knowledge and associated concepts and skills. Both VCEs and GCEs are routes to higher education.

'Unlike GCE where AS units are not at full A level standard, all units in Vocational A level are assessed at the same standard. The units are intended to be more difficult than GCE AS units but less difficult than GCE A2 units' (QCA, 2001a: 17). The old A level standard is often considered to be the 'gold standard' that should be maintained over time. There has, however, been some debate about modular A levels (from before Curriculum 2000). Some authors deemed modular A levels to be harder than linear A levels because the candidate may need to achieve an A level standard early in the course and the system requires a commitment to hard work throughout a two-year course rather than just a spurt at the end. On the other hand, it has been argued that modular A levels were easier than linear A levels because they did not assess the candidate's synoptic grasp of the subject (Hodgson and Spours, 1997). Both these points were heeded in the development of the new A levels in Curriculum 2000, which now must contain a synoptic component and also an Advanced Subsidiary GCE, assessed at a standard expected to be reached at the end of the first year of a two-year Advanced GCE course. AS is now considered to be of a lower standard than A level and a higher standard than GCSE. This might be deemed more appropriate than the old modular A level and VCE approach as they were assessed at A level standard from the beginning of Advanced study. Some students taking ASVCEs in January 2002 would have taken GCSEs in the summer of 2001: less than two terms later they were expected to have reached A level standard in their VCE units, but they were never required to reach A2 standard in any GCE unit. The new system of taking AS qualifications at a lower standard than A levels, and then taking an A2 to make up an A level, recognizes that it might take some students time to reach A level standard.

Developments are under way to introduce a VCE AS at the GCE AS standard. This would mean a major redevelopment of the existing VCEs. It has been recommended that revised qualifications are introduced for teaching from September 2004. This would allow time for the regulatory bodies, awarding bodies and centres (schools and/or colleges) to prepare for the implementation of revised qualifications (QCA, 2001a).

Curriculum 2000 is a unitized system: both the new A levels and VCEs are unitized qualifications. The old modular A levels were in a system similar to a unitized system but linear A levels were not part of either a modular or a unitized system.

VCE qualifications come in three sizes – three-, six- and 12-unit qualifications. In Curriculum 2000 AS qualifications normally combine three units, A2s combine three units and A levels six units. There are some minority subject areas where the AS is one unit and the A level is two units (QCA, 2000b). For a full list of the subjects that do not conform to the three-/six-unit pattern, see Stobart (2000).

The six-unit and the three-unit ASVCEs are equivalent in size to A level and AS respectively.

ASVCEs consist of three compulsory units. In six- and 12-unit VCEs and the Double Award there are compulsory and optional units. In general, for a six-unit VCE there are at least three compulsory units and a maximum of three optional units. In some six-unit VCEs there are over 10 optional units and there are rules about which combinations are permitted. Generally for a 12-unit VCE there is a minimum of six and a maximum of eight compulsory units, meaning that there is a maximum of six optional units. Generally all units in an A level are compulsory. However, in a minority of A levels there is a choice between units. Some A levels involve choice between questions on papers and choice between different components within a unit.

## Resits and cashing-in process

Candidates are allowed to resit each unit once. When a resit has been taken the better of the two results contributes to the final grade of the AS and the full A level. Therefore resitting a unit never disadvantages a student. The shelf life of candidates' results from units is limited by the lifetime of the specification (UCAS, 2001).

'Cashing in' is defined by QCA (2001a) as: 'the process whereby schools and colleges ask awarding bodies (by submitting requests towards the end of the spring term) to generate qualification certificates for their students. Once a qualification certificate is awarded, the asssessment units are used-up (cashed-in) and cannot be reused for the award of the same qualification.'

Certificates are issued twice a year, after the June examination session and, for some specifications, also after the January examination session. Between receiving examination results and the award of the qualifications, centres have a short period of time to cancel requests to cash in (QCA, 2001a).

QCA (2001a) report that there is uncertainty about whether candidates will be advantaged or disadvantaged by cashing in the AS *en route* to the A level. They add that the uncertainty arises from conflicting messages from the Universities and Colleges Admissions Service (UCAS) and individual universities about whether or not they expect to see AS grades on UCAS forms. UCAS is the central organization through which applications are processed for entry to higher education.

## Key skills

Formerly key skills were a compulsory part of the GNVQ: candidates had to pass the key skills assessments to gain the GNVQ qualification. The new key skills (KS) qualifications draw upon evidence from a candidate's wider programme of study, including AS, A levels and VCEs (Hodgson and Spours, 2000). The KS qualification is optional, like all qualifications in Curriculum 2000. The key skills are:

- application of number;
- communication;
- information technology;
- improving learning and performance;
- problem solving;
- working with others.

In the national qualifications framework there are five levels of qualifications: level 1 is the lowest and level 5 is the highest. Level 3 qualifications are Advanced level qualifications, eg A levels. There are key skills qualifications available at levels 1 to 4 for application of number, communication and information technology (UCAS, 2001). These qualifications utilize both internal and external assessment. The key skills of improving learning and performance, problem solving and working with others are certificated on the basis of internal assessment. Originally Curriculum 2000 included a key skills qualification that combined communication, application of number and information technology. Subsequently this was removed, as it unintentionally created inflexibilities in programme design (QCA, 2001a).

Opportunities to derive evidence for key skills are 'signposted' in the A level, AS and VCE specifications. Additionally there are some qualifications that can be used to gain exemption from aspects of the key skills specifications. These qualifications are called 'proxy qualifications'. For example, if students have grade A to E English language A level then they are exempt from the level 2 and level 3 tests for communication, but not from the portfolio part of the assessment. For a full list of these qualifications, see the QCA Web site.

## Assessment

The classroom experience for candidates doing different qualifications will also be different. The VCE approach to learning for art and design, and travel and tourism involves practical work, assignments and independent research (OCR, 2000a, 2000b). In travel and tourism it is also expected that some candidates might undertake group work for their centre-assessed assessments although the work of the candidate must be clearly identified separately from the group work for assessment (OCR, 2000b). By contrast, for old A levels, teaching activities were characterized by teacher-led explanations, student note-taking, question/answer exchanges and revision work (McEwen, McGuiness and Knipe, 1999). Modular A levels had end-of-module examinations, so the teaching and national assessment experience was possibly more integrated than for other qualifications. There would also be a good deal of revision for examinations. The pedagogy of the new A levels may have changed slightly from that of old linear A levels. Teaching of old linear A levels was more holistic with an emphasis on skills of inquiry, evaluation and debate. By contrast, when teachers have taught the new AS specifications some have adopted a more didactic style or have engaged in 'over-teaching' to ensure students cover everything (QCA, 2001b).

*External assessment* is an assessment that an awarding body sets or defines. It is often in the form of tests or examinations. The awarding body specifies the conditions under which the assessments are to be taken, eg supervision and time allowed, and assesses candidates' responses. *Internal assessment* is an assessment that does not fit the definition for external assessment for general qualifications. Internal assessment is generally assessed by the candidate's teacher/tutor. In the case of GCEs, internal assessment is often called *coursework*.

In VCE the type of assessment is not necessarily determined by whether the unit is optional or compulsory. There also tends to be one type of assessment per unit (Stobart, 2000). The majority of A levels and ASs have one form of assessment per unit, but there are some, for example, where a choice between coursework and another form of assessment, usually a written examination, is offered.

VCE is assessed using a variety of different types of assessment. Some units are assessed by collecting a portfolio of evidence. For example, in the OCR specifications launched in September 2000, art and design VCE employed written work, artwork and written papers, and travel and tourism VCE employed unseen case studies, a case study and written paper and short scenarios.

Similarly, the external assessments for A levels use a variety of approaches to assessment; for example, English literature employs essay-based examination papers requiring a levels-of-response ('banded') mark scheme, whereas mathematics uses a points mark scheme. Levels-of-response mark schemes specify level descriptors, that is a description of the kind of answer that will receive a mark from within a given band. For example, a level descriptor might read: 'good understanding across the breadth of the material and some depth; this directly synthesizes the material to provide an answer to the question: 7 to 10 marks' (adapted from Elander and Hardman, 2002). Points mark schemes distinguish between the tasks that candidates can do and cannot do, and marks are given according to the tasks that the candidate completes correctly.

For VCE, AS and A level, candidates do not need to pass every assessment to gain a pass at the qualification level. The marks that are gained on each internal and external assessment all contribute to the qualification grade.

In general, two-thirds of VCE assessment is portfolio assessment and one-third is external assessment (QCA, 2000c; Stobart, 2000). But there are some subjects that do not conform to this rule of thumb, such as OCR art and design AVCE taught between September 2000 and June 2002 where either two-thirds or 83 per cent of the qualification is centre-assessed, depending on the options taken by a candidate. In Curriculum 2000, GCE AS and A levels 'normally contain a proportion of coursework up to 30 per cent, (though some practical or creative subjects have more)' (QCA, 2000c: 1). These figures illustrate that VCE is almost the reverse of new A levels in the balance between internal and external assessment. This means that there is a big difference between the kind of assessment and the different skills candidates must exhibit to gain the same grade on an A level compared to a VCE.

VCE, AS and A level internal assessments are all moderated. This can involve postal moderation and/or a moderator visiting the centre, depending upon the nature of the coursework. For A level coursework and VCE portfolios, centres are asked to ensure that the rank ordering of the internally assessed units is correct. The role of a moderator is to ensure that a mark awarded for work of a given standard is the same from centre to centre. Moderators do not award a grade.

In all of the assessment systems, the teacher is involved in teaching and assessing the candidate's work. However, the amount of direct influence that teachers have over the candidate's grade throughout their involvement in national assessment is higher for VCE than for A levels.

GCE and VCE AS, and GCE A level in Curriculum 2000 have grades A to E available at the qualification and unit levels. The 12-unit VCE qualifications are graded on a Double Award scale, ie AA, AB, BB, BC, etc. If candidates do not achieve EE or E, they will receive U (unclassified).

## Award meetings

For VCE externally assessed units, grades E and A are awarded by an awarding committee (senior examiners) using professional judgement and statistical evidence. Intermediate grade boundaries (ie B, C and D grade boundaries) are determined arithmetically (QCA, 2002). The same process is used for both externally and internally assessed AS and A2 units (QCA, 2002). For internally assessed units the fundamental difference is that GCE coursework is graded at the award meeting, while internally assessed VCE units (usually portfolios) have pre-set boundaries based on marking criteria.

For GCEs and VCEs, raw marks at the unit level are converted to a common scale or uniform mark scale (UMS). UMSs are used because of the following situations:

- Although examiners aim to set comparable assessments in each examination session (January and June), sometimes one assessment is more or less demanding than expected. These differences need to be accounted for so that the grades awarded are comparable.
- There may be a range of choices candidates can take in unitized schemes, with the result that once the boundaries are aggregated from all the different combinations there might be a variety of qualification-level grade boundaries.

The maximum marks available per unit and the standardized (predetermined) grade boundaries on the UMS scale are found in the qualification specifications.

The raw marks that candidates achieve on each unit are converted into points on a UMS. The UMS points from the AS units are added together to give the overall mark for the AS qualification, and the marks are then converted into grades. The maximum UMS marks available for the GCE and VCE AS qualification are 300, and the minimum UMS marks required for each grade are: A 240, B 210, C 180, D 150, E 120. If a candidate has a total of 157 UMS marks that candidate will have achieved grade D. The UMS marks available for each GCE AS unit vary with the weighting of the different units. For VCE there are 100 UMS marks available for each unit. The minimum UMS marks required for each VCE unit grade are: A 80, B 70, C 60, D 50, E 40.

For GCE the sum of the UMS points for the AS and A2 units for a candidate gives the candidate's total UMS mark for the A level. For AVCE the sum of the UMS points for six units that constitute an AVCE gives a candidate's total UMS mark for the AVCE. The minimum UMS marks required for GCE and Vocational A level at the qualification level are A 480, B 420, C 360, D 300 and E 240 (twice those for the AS qualification-level grades). If a candidate has 400 UMS marks at the qualification level that candidate has achieved a grade C.

There is a maximum of 1,200 UMS marks available for the VCE Double Award and the minimum UMS marks required for each grade are AA 960, AB 900, BB 840, BC 780, CC 720, CD 660, DD 600, DE 540, EE 480. As for the other qualifications, the UMS marks from the unit are added together to determine the candidate's final mark, which is translated into a grade.

## Statement of results

UMS points are given with other information on the 'statement of results' that awarding bodies issue to candidates via their centre after each examination session. An example of a statement of results is given in Figure 2.1.

On his statement of results Robin has the outcomes of the two qualifications and the Advanced units that he took in the same examination session.

Robin sat three mathematics AS units, pure maths 1, pure maths 2 and mechanics, in this session. There were 100 UMS points available for each of these units, and each unit was worth 33.33 per cent of the AS qualification. He achieved 95 UMS points for pure maths 1, 76 for pure maths 2 and 96 for mechanics. The minimum UMS points required for each grade for an AS unit where 100 UMS marks are available are: A 80, B 70, C 60, D 50, E 40. With 95 points for pure maths 1 he gained a grade A; he gained a grade B with 76 points for pure maths 2; and he gained a grade A with 96 points for mechanics. When the total numbers of UMS points from the AS mathematics units are added together they give 267 of the 300 points available. This information is given on the statement of results. The minimum UMS points required for each grade for the AS qualification are: A 240, B 210, C 180, D 150 and E 120. Robin achieved 267 points and therefore a grade A for AS mathematics. This information is given on the statement of results.

## Assessment specifications – synoptic assessment

Hodgson and Spours (1997) argue that one reason why modular A levels were seen to be easier than linear A levels was that there was no terminal examination check of candidates' synoptic grasp of the subject. This view was heeded in the development of

## Statement of Results

## June 2002

| Centre Name | Centre Number | Candidate Number |
|---|---|---|
| **PITMASTON COMPREHENSIVE SCHOOL** | **99999** | **9999** |

| Candidate Name | Date of Birth | UCI |
|---|---|---|
| **ROBIN GRIFFITHS** | **3/07/1985** | **99999999999V** |

| Code | Title | Grade | Uniform Mark |
|---|---|---|---|
| **Advanced GCE** | | | |
| 3842 | Mathematics | A(a) | 267/300 (max) |
| 7841 | Law | A(a) | 497/600 (max) |
| | | | |
| **Advanced GCE Unit** | | | |
| 2573 | Criminal Law 1 | a | 78/90 (max) |
| 2574 | Criminal Law 2 | c | 57/90 (max) |
| 2575 | Criminal Law Special Study | a | 101/120 (max) |
| 2633 | Pure Mathematics 1 | a | 95/100 (max) |
| 2635 | Pure Mathematics 2 | b | 76/100 (max) |
| 2639 | Mechanics 1 | a | 96/100 (max) |

| Page 1 | THIS IS NOT A CERTIFICATE | Date of issue 03/08/02 |
|---|---|---|

*Note*: The awarding body logo has been omitted so that the statement could be from any awarding body. The candidate, centre, results and units details are all fictitious.

**Figure 2.1**   Statement of results

A levels in Curriculum 2000, which 'all involve a synoptic assessment that must be taken terminally and constitutes one or two units' (QCA, 2000c: 1). The synoptic assessment varies in nature for different subjects, and might be through centre and/or external examination. It contributes at least 20 per cent of the overall assessment. There is no synoptic assessment in VCEs or GCE AS; synoptic assessment is confined to the A2 units in GCE A levels.

# Comparability of qualifications

The standard of VCEs is required to be the same as the standard of GCE A levels, and they are also deemed to have parity of esteem. Similarly, different A levels taken in the same subject over time are of the same standard. It is expected that concurrent Advanced qualifications at the same level should be of a comparable standard, although the qualifications reward very different knowledge and skills. Additionally, there is a QCA Code of Practice requirement that standards must be maintained over time, that is that the standards of A levels and VCEs must be the same as in previous years. This is more easily said to be the case – by deeming qualifications to be of the same standard – than demonstrated through research evidence. There are two ways of making research-based comparisons: statistical comparisons and comparisons made by expert judges. In both cases the comparisons are only meaningful when we are comparing like with like. It is difficult to compare:

- concurrent qualifications such as VCE engineering and A level media studies given that they are testing such different knowledge and skills;
- qualifications over time when a mathematics A level from 20 years ago might have more calculus and a mathematics A level in Curriculum 2000 might include a lot of statistics. Again, the different qualifications are testing different knowledge and skills, which are difficult to compare. Indeed the greater the difference in time between the qualifications, the greater the difference between the knowledge and skills tested, and the more meaningless the comparison.

The use of direct statistical comparisons between the percentages of people passing different qualifications is very limited. A direct statistical comparison would be the example given by Tysome (2002). For the first cohort who took AVCE, there was a pass rate of 74.6 per cent compared with a pass rate of 94.3 per cent for GCE A levels. In the same cohort 4.3 per cent of AVCE students gained a grade A and 20.7 per cent of GCE A level candidates gained a grade A. Therefore, arguably, Vocational A levels are tougher than A levels (Tysome, 2002). This approach is limited, as the students taking A levels and AVCEs could be different groups. It is probable that the candidates who took A level had higher mean GCSE grades than those taking AVCEs. Therefore we would expect that more candidates would pass A levels than AVCEs if the qualifications are of the same standard. There are many statistical techniques, some of which are very sophisticated, that can be used to compare the standards of different qualifications. For more information, see Newton (1997a, 1997b), Cresswell (2000a, 2000b), Pinot de Moira (2000), Bell, Bramley and Raikes (1998) and Bell and Dexter (2000).

Another approach to comparing standards is to use expert judges. Most of the techniques employed involve senior examiners making judgements about:

- the relative quality of work undertaken by candidates from different qualifications;
- the relative difficulty of the tasks and/or programme of study candidates are asked to complete;
- which aspects of different qualifications are comparable and/or equivalent.

For more details about these techniques see Coles and Matthews (1996), Jones (1997), Bell and Greatorex (2000), Greatorex (2001) and Elliott and Greatorex (2002). Jones (1997) and later Greatorex (2001) argue that senior examiners can make mental compensations for some differences between qualifications that cannot be accounted for by statistical techniques. They also argue that the most rigorous approach to making comparisons is to use a combination of statistical approaches and expert judgements.

# Summary

In Curriculum 2000 GCE A levels and Vocational A levels are required to be the same standard as one another. GCE A levels in Curriculum 2000 are required to be of the same standard as GCE A levels from previous years. However, it is difficult to make meaningful comparisons between dissimilar qualifications that are rewarding different knowledge and skills.

There are differences between GCEs and VCEs in terms of the assessment specifications, pedagogy and the knowledge and skills that are rewarded. For instance, GCE A levels are assessed mostly through examinations, while VCEs involve a good deal of portfolio-based assessment.

The following task is aimed at helping you assess your own understanding of the post-16 examination framework.

## Task 2.1

Discuss the following questions in small groups:

*Question 1* In the new UCAS tariff system two AS levels of the same grade are given the same points as an A level at the same grade. Given the definition of AS and A level standards given above, is this tariff appropriate?

*Answer to question 1* AS and A levels are at the same level in the national qualifications framework and an AS is half the size of an A level. This suggests that it is reasonable to give an A level twice as many UCAS tariff points as an AS. However, AS is a lower standard than A level standard and therefore two AS qualifications for the same number of UCAS tariff points as an A level might be seen as an 'easy' route into higher education. The impact of this limitation of the UCAS tariff system is limited by universities requiring that candidates must achieve particular grades in specified A levels, rather than just offering a place on the number of UCAS tariff points achieved.

*Question 2* Given the features of the synoptic unit(s) in A levels, why could performance on the unit(s) be different from performance on the other AS and/or A2 units in the same A level?

*Answer to question 2* Synoptic units test the candidates' holistic understanding of the whole A level. Other units tend to focus on particular aspects of the specification, eg organic chemistry, statistics, etc. The results of the non-synoptic units demonstrate candidates' knowledge and skills in these focused areas. However, a holistic understanding of the subject and making connections between the different aspects of the specification, eg statistics and pure mathematics, is considerably different. This might be illustrated in the different results achieved in different types of units.

*Question 3* What does a candidate have to do to obtain the same grade in the same subject on both an AS and an A2 unit?

*Answer to question 3* The candidate must reach a higher standard of achievement for the A2 unit than for the AS unit.

*Question 4* A candidate inspects his/her scripts and finds that the final mark is different from the one of the statement of results. Why?

*Answer to question 4* The marks on the scripts are raw marks. These are converted to UMS points, which appear on the statement of results. This might explain any discrepancies.

*Question 5* The awarding committee set an E grade boundary for one VCE unit at 49 raw marks and the E grade boundary for another unit at 33 raw marks. How many UMS points would a candidate have if he/she was on the E grade boundary for each unit?

*Answer to question 5* The E grade boundary for VCE units is always 40 UMS points.

*Question 6* Given the features of internally and externally assessed units, why might a given candidate have a higher grade for coursework than for examinations or vice versa?

*Answer to question 6* Candidates have individual strengths and weaknesses. Some are better at coursework and others at examinations, while some are just as good at both, and this is reflected in the A level results.

# References

Bell, J F and Dexter, T (2000) Using multilevel models to assess the comparability of examinations, Paper presented at the Fifth International Conference on Social Science Methodology, 3–6 October

Bell, J F and Greatorex, J (2000) *A Review of Research into Levels, Profiles and Comparability: A report to QCA*, QCA, London

Bell, J F, Bramley, T and Raikes, N (1998) Investigating A level mathematics standards over time, *British Journal of Curriculum and Assessment*, **8** (2), pp 7–11

Coles, M and Matthews, A (1996) *Fitness for Purpose: A means of comparing qualifications – a report to Sir Ron Dearing to be considered as part of his review of 16 to 19 education*, SCAA, London

Cresswell, M J (2000a) The role of public examinations in defining and monitoring standards, in *Educational Standards*, ed H Goldstein and A Heath, Oxford University Press, New York

Cresswell, M (2000b) Defining, setting and maintaining standards in curriculum-embedded examinations: judgemental and statistical approaches, in *Assessment: Problems, developments and statistical issues*, ed H Goldstein and T Lewis, John Wiley and Sons, Chichester

Dearing, R (1996) *Review of Qualifications for 16 to 19 Year Olds*, SCAA, London

DfEE (1999) National learning targets for England for 2002, DfEE, London

Elander, J and Hardman, D (2002) An application of judgement analysis to examination marking in psychology, *British Journal of Psychology*, **93**, pp 303–28

Elliott, G and Greatorex, J (2002) A fair comparison? The evolution of methods of comparability in national assessment, *Educational Studies*, **28** (3), pp 253–64

Greatorex, J (2001) Can vocational A levels be meaningfully compared with other qualifications?, Paper presented at the British Educational Research Association Annual Conference, University of Leeds, 14–15 September

Hayward, G (1995) *Getting to Grips with GNVQs: A handbook for teachers*, Kogan Page, London

Hodgson, A and Spours, K (1997) (eds) *Dearing and Beyond: 14–19 qualifications, frameworks and systems*, pp 40–56, Kogan Page, London

Hodgson, A and Spours, K (2000) *Qualifying for Success: Towards a framework of understanding – the first report from the project Broadening the Advanced Level Curriculum: Institutional Responses to Qualifying for Success*, Institute of Education/Nuffield Project, London

Jones, B E (1997) Comparing examination standards: is a purely statistical approach adequate?, *Assessment in Education, Principles, Policy and Practice*, **4** (2), pp 249–63

McEwen, A, McGuiness, C and Knipe, D (1999) Comparing teaching and learning in A levels and Advanced GNVQs, *General Educator Journal of the NATFHE General Education Section*, **56**, pp 12–15

Newton, P (1997a) Measuring comparability of standards between subjects: why our statistical methods do not make the grade, *British Educational Research Journal*, **23** (4), pp 433–49

Newton, P (1997b) Examining standards over time, *Research Papers in Education*, **12** (3), pp 227–48

OCR (2000a) *OCR Advanced Vocational Certificate of Education in Art and Design (7760), Advanced Vocational Certificate of Education (Double Award) in Art and Design (7780)*, OCR, Cambridge

OCR (2000b) *Advanced Vocational Certificate of Education in Travel and Tourism (7775), Advanced Vocational Certificate of Education (Double Award) in Travel and Tourism (7795)*, OCR, Cambridge

Pinot de Moira, A (2000) *A Comparability Study in GCSE English: Statistical analysis of results by board*, Organized by AQA on behalf of the Joint Forum for GCSE and GCE, AQA, Guildford

QCA (2000a) *Finding Your Way Around: A leaflet about the national qualifications framework*, www.qca.org.uk

QCA (2000b) *Regulations for Entry, Aggregation and Certification: GCE AS/A level examinations for first certification in 2001/2002*, www.qca.org.uk

QCA (2000c) *Level 3 Qualifications*, www.qca.org.uk

QCA (2001a) *QCA's Review of Curriculum 2000: QCA's report on phase two*, www.qca.org.uk

QCA (2001b) *Review of Curriculum 2000: QCA's report on phase one*, www.qca.org.uk

QCA (2002) *GCSE, GCE, VCE and GNVQ Code of Practice 2002*, QCA, London

Stobart, G (2000) *Changes to Post-16 Qualifications: A briefing for higher education on changes to the post-16 curriculum in England, Wales and Northern Ireland*, UCAS, Cheltenham

Tysome, T (2002) Vocational A level tougher, colleges warn, *Times Higher Educational Supplement*, 16 August, **1551**, p 3

UCAS (2001) *Changes to Post-16 Qualifications*, UCAS, Cheltenham

Wolf, A (1997) *GNVQs 1993–1997, A National Survey Report: The evolution of GNVQs – enrolment and delivery patterns and their policy implications*, Further Education Development Agency, Bristol

Young, M and Leney, T (1997) From A levels to an advanced curriculum of the future, in *Dearing and Beyond: 14–19 qualifications, frameworks and systems*, ed A Hodgson and K Spours, pp 40–56, Kogan Page, London

# 3 Key skills in Curriculum 2000

Lin Le Versha

Young people and adults need certain skills to develop and maintain their employability... They are as relevant on the shop floor as they are in the board room.

(DfEE, 1998: 65)

The rate of change is so great that employers need their staff to have the skills necessary for adaptability and innovation.

(QCA, 2001a: 5)

I am committed to developing a high standard of rigorously assessed provision... I agree that it will be important to highlight opportunities for developing key skills content within A/AS syllabuses where that is appropriate. I accept also that funding mechanisms should encourage schools, colleges and training providers to offer Key Skills... to consider the ways in which inspectors can focus on the delivery of Key Skills and I accept that the new UCAS profile and tariff could provide critical reinforcement.

(Baroness Blackstone, Minister of State, letter to Sir William Stubbs, Chair of QCA, in QCA, 1998)

A belief in the value of the concept of Key Skills has been undermined for staff and students by pressure on time, over-complex assessment and the varied response of HE.

(QCA, 2001b: 24)

So what are these key skills that the government and employers consider crucial to the labour market? Where did they come from and why was their introduction unsuccessful?

## What are key skills?

There are six key skills:

- communication;
- application of number;

- information technology;
- working with others;
- problem solving;
- improving own learning and performance.

These skills are the foundation for education, employment and indeed life. We need to be able to communicate effectively with other people – face to face, on the telephone or in writing. We need to be able to analyse and interpret numerical information when working out change in a shop, estimating the space needed for a piece of furniture and under-standing graphical and statistical information in newspaper reports. Now IT skills are at the core of most jobs – gas fitters have laptops in their tool bags, journalists set up their articles on their computer screen and in most companies management information is primarily acces-sible on computers. These three 'hard' key skills – communication, application of number and information technology – are now assessed and lead to the key skills qualification available from the age of 14.

The 'soft' or wider key skills, also essential for employability, have been delivered for some time as part of a sixth form programme in enrichment, general studies or personal and social education. Working with others is a vital skill for employment and working as a successful member of a team is usually high up on the person specification of any job description. Having the ability to analyse ways of approaching a work or personal problem, using different means to find a solution and then analysing your success is a valuable skill for employment or indeed survival within a family! Finally, learning how to set targets and monitor them to evaluate your progress is essential if you are to become an autonomous student or a successful employee and is embodied in 'improving own learning and performance'.

## Where did key skills originate?

Core skills were introduced in 1995 as part of the General National Vocational Qualification (GNVQ). Communication, numeracy and information technology were assessed alongside the vocational units but their delivery was 'embedded' in the subject matter. So, for example, instead of learning the structure and form of how to write a good business letter in isolation, students would learn to write a letter so that they could organize an event, such as a visit to a theme park in leisure and tourism, or to invite outside speakers to a business GNVQ lesson.

Skills in communication and IT were relatively easy to teach as part of the subject matter. With some parts of numeracy, however, it became more difficult. One example was the teaching of Pythagoras' theorem to students on a health and social care course where the only application some ingenious assignment writer could produce was to work out the angle of the ramp needed to push a wheelchair into an ambulance!

In 1996 'key skills' was a term adopted by Sir Ron Dearing in his report on the post-16 qual-ification framework to describe 'a range of essential skills which are key to developing effective learning and performance in a range of contexts'. He noted that the three hard key skills had already been incorporated into the national education and training targets for 2000.

The second target was: '75% young people to achieve Level 2 competence in communication, numeracy and IT by age 19 and 35% to achieve level 3 by age 21'.

He placed the prime responsibility for the development of the three key skills with schools during compulsory education from 5 to 16 but commented that schools, colleges and training bodies should provide 'opportunities for all young people to develop the key skills and to have them assessed and recognised'. The notion of assessment of key skills led to his suggestion of a 'new AS in key skills', which would attract a numerical score in the proposed UCAS tariff.

In the further consultations undertaken by the Labour government in *Qualifying for Success* (QCA, 1998) it was recommended that key skills should form a normal part of all student post-compulsory education and training. The explicit comment on key skills by inspectors was supported by 62 per cent of respondents in the consultation; 59 per cent considered that general studies A level would be a suitable vehicle for key skills delivery; and 60 per cent considered that financial incentives for institutions would be vital for success. The formal certification of the wider key skills was supported by employers and further education (60 per cent) but received a lukewarm reception from schools and teachers (40 per cent).

The consultation led to the following recommendations:

- A free-standing key skills qualification should be available to all learners.
- Key skills should be 'decoupled' from GNVQ.
- The level of each skill should be 'signposted' in each qualification and programme of learning.
- An overarching Advanced certificate could be the vehicle for requiring level 3 attainment in the 'first three' key skills.

# Key skills in the classroom

In September 2000, despite some unenthusiastic reports from the pilot studies the previous year, most post-16 colleges introduced key skills to their 16–19 curriculum, as they were included in the funding allocated for each student. In schools, where no financial support was provided, fewer institutions responded to the enthusiastic urgings of Baroness Blackstone.

The mode of delivery varied from discrete teaching for all three key skills to embedding them in examination subjects, delivering them through general studies AS/A2 or enrichment and tutorial programmes. Some institutions adopted a combination of the two approaches with 'focus days or other large scale events' to supplement their delivery (QCA, 2001b: 24).

In the new AS/VCE specifications, key skills were indeed 'signposted'. In drama and theatre studies GCE (Edexcel, 2002), application of number level 3 may be found in the areas shown in Table 3.1.

In this example drama students acting as costume, set or lighting designers in the practical units 2, 4 and 5 would have little difficulty in producing evidence for all three elements, as they would be undertaking the activities as a natural part of their work. For students who chose to be assessed as actors the range of activities is more limited and the

**Table 3.1** Application of number in drama and theatre studies

| Key Skills Portfolio Evidence Requirement | AS/A Unit | Opportunities for Development or Internal Assessment |
|---|---|---|
| **N3.1** Plan and interpret information from two different types of sources, including a large data set. | Units 2, 4 and 5 | Collecting and interpreting data for performance spaces, performers' measurements and the technical characteristics of sound and lighting equipment could contribute to the evidence for this skill. |
| **N3.2** Carry out multi-stage calculations to do with: A amounts and sizes; B scales and proportions; C handling statistics; D rearranging and using formulae. | Units 2, 4 and 5 | Collect and use data about the actual space used for the performance to develop approaches to setting and design. Use statistics and detailed calculations to make performers' costumes, masks, make-up or puppets where appropriate. In the process of designing, carry out calculations about the theatrical space, costumes, movement of performers etc, and use these calculations to realize design. In preparing a role, consider the use of space, blocking and choreography etc, using specific measurements of the acting area. |
| **N3.3** Interpret results of your calculations, present your findings and justify your methods. You must use at least *one* graph, *one* chart and *one* diagram. | Units 2, 4 and 5 | Plan and justify a budget for a design, giving detailed costings in the form of charts or diagrams. As performers, use diagrams to represent in visual terms the relationships between roles or characters. Evaluate how the audience will experience the performance using diagrams of, for example, sight-lines and charts of the stage-pictures. During the rehearsal process, consider the ways in which dramatic tension is established or the emotional journey of the role is developed, using graphs and diagrams. |

*Evidence*
Student evidence for application of number could include:
copies of students' plans;
records of information obtained;
justification of methods used;
records of calculations showing methods used;
reports of findings.

(Edexcel, 2002: 75–76)

application of number assignments would have to be completed in addition to the structured records they produce as part of the process. The suggested opportunities for generating the evidence, however, are imaginative and would teach students to apply numerical skills in a dramatic context.

These 'signposts' have been used as part of a mapping exercise to check on the coverage of the key skills specification for a particular student. As with the experience of GNVQ core skills, it has been relatively straightforward to find ways of embedding communication and IT in mainstream AS/VCE specifications but even for mathematicians and scientists the requirements of application of number have sometimes been difficult to meet.

## Task 3.1

- Look at the specification for your subject. Plan three activities, each one incorporating a different 'hard' key skill, which you could use to support students to produce work for their portfolio.
- Consider the three 'soft' key skills. Think of three activities in your subject where you could develop students' skills in working with others, problem solving and improving their own learning and performance.
- Which of the six key skills are most relevant to your subject? Choose one and make a list of reasons why it is so important to success in your area.

# What is the qualification?

The qualification offers communication, application of number and IT at levels 1 to 5, increasing the complexity of the activities and techniques and demanding greater autonomy on the part of the student as s/he progresses through the levels. Students can work at the key skill level appropriate to their individual need and not necessarily at the same level as their learning programme. For example, a student might be following a programme of English, French, drama and psychology at level 3 and also take communication and IT at level 3 but follow level 2 in application of number.

The three 'hard' key skills are assessed through short tests and the production of portfolios of evidence. There are 'proxy' qualifications, which mean that students may be exempted from the external tests if they have already achieved a GCSE (level 2) or AS (level 3) in mathematics, English or information technology. To achieve the qualification they need only to produce the portfolios of evidence.

The 'soft' or wider key skills (working with others, problem solving and improving own learning and performance) are also certified by awarding bodies but they are not yet part of the national qualifications framework. A portfolio of evidence for these skills is produced and assessed internally and then the assessment is moderated or quality-assured by the awarding body.

UCAS points are awarded under the tariff for the achievement of key skills units, with a level 2 attracting 10 points and level 3 earning 20 points. For each unit, students have to pass an external assessment and to complete a portfolio of evidence that is internally assessed and then externally moderated.

At all levels the specification is divided into:

Part A: what you must know – the knowledge and techniques students need for each unit;
Part B: what you must do – the ways of applying skills;
Part C: the activities leading to the evidence that might be provided in the portfolio.

Edexcel, one of the awarding bodies offering the qualification, advises practitioners that they should encourage students to work through the learning cycle shown in Figure 3.1.

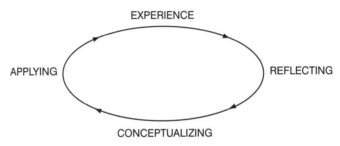

**Figure 3.1** Learning cycle

Following this model opportunities should be provided for:

- learning activities that develop students' underpinning knowledge, skills and understanding;
- practising activities that check learning;
- structures review and reflection, to draw out learning points;
- further exploration, to conceptualize and practise the underpinning knowledge, skills and understanding;
- application of the new 'learning', through assignments and work-based activities. (Edexcel, 2000: 32)

To explore this in more detail, let us follow through the process in the specification of another of the awarding bodies. In level 3 communication for AQA (2001), under the heading of 'Discussion' there are the following expectations and requirements for students:

*Part A*
You are expected to know how to:
– vary how and when you participate to suit your purpose (eg to present a complicated line of reason) and the situation (eg formality, nature of the group);
– listen and respond sensitively (eg acknowledge gender and cultural aspects, how others might be feeling) and develop points and ideas;
– make openings to encourage others to contribute (invite others to speak, ask for follow-up questions to encourage people to develop points).

*Part B*

You must do the following:

– Contribute to a group discussion about a complex subject.

Evidence must show that you can:

– make clear and relevant contributions in a way that suits your purpose and situation;
– listen and respond sensitively to others, and develop points and ideas; and
– create opportunities for others to contribute when appropriate.

*Part C*

Examples of activities you might use:

– carrying out an investigation and reporting finding;
– exchanging information and ideas with other students.

Examples of evidence:

– a record from an assessor who has observed your discussion and noted how you met the requirements of the unit, or an audio-/videotape of the discussion.

## Task 3.2

- Plan a series of lessons in which your students have the opportunity to learn, demonstrate and collect evidence for level 3 discussion as an integral part of your AS/A2/VCE course.
- Consider ways in which you could differentiate in the classroom to ensure that all students, whatever their level of confidence and experience, would be able to achieve level 3 discussion.
- What skills or exercises might be explored in preparation for this work, such as questioning techniques, chairing a meeting or listening skills?
- How will you and the students record the evidence?

# What were the problems in implementation?

At the end of the first year of the key skills qualification, QCA announced:

'success has been mixed and many institutions plan to change their approach for the next year group. Reasons for the mixed success include:

- the time scale for implementation
- limited experience and expertise in some institutions
- the assessment regime
- the time involved in portfolio building and preparing for tests when students are studying an increased number of subjects
- the competence-based assessment and the language are unfamiliar to some because the units are written for a work context as well as for schools and colleges

Also, some teachers say that it is hard to motivate students who claim that HEIs have expressed little interest in Key Skills.'

(QCA, 2001b: 24)

Advice then follows to improve practice by assessing students' initial key skill level accurately rather than relying on GCSE grades and not entering them for the tests 'until they are at least half way through the programme' (QCA, 2001b: 25). A flexible approach to the qualification should be adopted as well as developing the three wider key skills, exploring workshops, tutorials, the Duke of Edinburgh Scheme and AS and VCE programmes for their delivery.

## What is the future of key skills?

Munday and Faraday (1999, 2001), in analysing the strategies that have led to the successful implementation of key skills in colleges, emphasize the future assessment and accreditation of key skills, the availability of additional funding and the key skills point score within the UCAS tariff as essential to their success. They identify a whole-college or -school approach and that the development and delivery of key skills need to be at the centre of policy and development of strategic plans and involve all members of staff.

The management and organization of roles, responsibilities and accountabilities of individuals and teams at all levels of key skills must be clear. Collaboration and partnership between schools and colleges and the employers and the higher education institutions for which they are preparing their students then needs further development. Allocation and development of appropriate resources including adequate funding, the use of the Internet and intranets and a well-developed central resource base are perceived as vital in the most successful case studies.

The development of staff to equip tutors with the ability to teach key skills, to share good practice and to mentor others ensures that the development is central to the college. Finally the inclusion of key skills in the self-assessment report, quality assurance processes and all development plans should be central to their development.

The future of key skills in the classroom will depend on not only the way in which they are assessed but the way in which students are helped to see the relevance of these skills in their future as employees and lifelong learners. QCA (2001a) lays emphasis on the process of preparation for 'employability' in which all six key skills have a crucial part to play. In a world of rapid change, students need to be able to adapt and it is the development of transferable skills rather than knowledge that will equip them for this.

'What will be important is the development of the critical skills (in all senses) to use information and to evaluate it. The education system must develop techniques for assessing people's abilities in using information, and in the personal skills that will be needed at much higher levels to cope successfully with a more complex world' (Bayliss, 1998).

## References

AQA (2001) *Key Skills Specification*, AQA, Guildford
Bayliss, V (1998) *Redefining Work*, RSA, London
Dearing, Sir Ron (1996) *Review of Qualifications for 16 to 19 Year Olds*, SCAA, London
DfEE (1998) *The Learning Age*, Stationery Office, London
Edexcel (2000) *The Key Skills User Guide*, Edexcel, London

Edexcel (2002) *Advanced Subsidiary and Advanced GCE in Drama and Theatre Studies*, Issue 3, Edexcel, London

Munday, F and Faraday, S (1999) *Key Skills: Strategies in action*, FEDA, London

Munday, F and Faraday, S (2001) *How Are You Managing? Key skills in colleges*, FEDA/DfEE, London

QCA (1998) *Qualifying for Success: Report on the consultation about the future of post-16 qualification*, QCA, London

QCA (2001a) *Key Skills for Developing Employability*, QCA, London

QCA (2001b) *Managing Curriculum 2000 for 16–19 Students*, QCA, London

# 4  Student guidance and support

## Lin Le Versha

In post-compulsory education it is the quality of teaching, guidance and support that determines whether students continue to attend their lessons and eventually complete the course successfully or whether they become another point in the retention statistics that all colleges and schools are trying to improve.

Since 1997 the government has made improving post-16 student retention a priority in an attempt to increase progress towards meeting the national learning targets in 2002. Retention was becoming a concern in 1993; the National Audit Office reported that 30 per cent of 16-plus students who started A level courses failed to complete them (OFSTED/Audit Commission, 1993). In 2000, 3.8 million students were studying 17,000 different qualifications in the 417 post-16/FE colleges in England, which is twice the number of students who are registered on undergraduate and postgraduate courses in higher education institutions. Progress towards the targets has been slow (see Table 4.1) and it is only by increasing participation and then retaining students on the courses on which they enrol through good teaching, guidance and support that further progress can be made.

## How do we retain our students?

Research from the Further Education Development Agency, the National Audit Office and the Economic Research Council (ERSC) Teaching and Learning research study suggests that students remain on courses if:

- they have chosen the right course;
- they are provided with an effective induction to their course;
- they are provided with financial or appropriate support based on their individual needs;
- they receive effective teaching that concentrates on their learning;
- they are able to measure their progress and achievement.

## Choosing the right course

The introduction of the National Curriculum in 1988 meant that students had only minor decisions to make about their programme of study at the age of 14. A choice between two

**Table 4.1** National learning targets for young people and adults

|  | *Position when Targets Were Launched in 1998* | *Position in Autumn 1999* | *Target for December 2002* |
|---|---|---|---|
| 19-year-olds with level 2 (five GCSEs at A*–C, an NVQ level 2, Intermediate GNVQ or equivalent) | 73.9% | 74.9% | 85% |
| 21-year-olds with level 3 (two A levels, an NVQ level 3, an Advanced GNVQ or equivalent) | 52.2% | 53.2% | 60% |
| Adults with level 3 | 45.1% | 46.2% | 50% |
| Adults with level 4 (NVQ level 4, a degree or a higher-level qualification) | 26.1% | 26.6% | 28% |
| Learning participation target – reduction in non-learners | 26% population not learning | data not yet available | 24% population not learning |

languages, the separate sciences or double science, and history or geography is often the extent of the decision making. At 16 students are then confronted with the vast array of subjects, styles of learning and qualifications as they explore AS, the Vocational Certificate of Education and a plethora of vocational courses. They must make decisions on the number of qualifications or the volume of study, the type and level of qualification, the nature of the assessment and then the level of key skills they will follow along with the possibilities for enrichment.

Colleges and schools produce prospectuses that provide summaries of the subject content and assessment methods (coursework or examination) but it is the detailed subject information, which 84 per cent of colleges provide to supplement the basic information, that can help students choose the most appropriate subjects and course. Information on these sheets might include:

- the content of the course;
- the level of entry qualification;
- the skills required for it;
- the time needed for study;
- the method(s) and timing of assessment;

- the individual support available;
- the additional cost of materials and field trips;
- the enrichment or extra-curricular activities;
- the progression routes or destinations of students on completion of the course.

## Task 4.1

- Analyse the skills or experience that would lead to successful completion of your course; then write a publicity leaflet for it using the list above.
- Think of three to five questions that you would ask a student considering your course to ascertain his/her previous experience, his/her suitability and the nature of any individual support that may be needed.

An initial interview is essential to provide information on the course for the student and for the interviewer to assess the suitability of the student for the course. In many schools and colleges this may be done centrally but it is in the classroom that an effective induction programme often makes the difference to retention rates at this stage.

# Induction

Induction is a process not an event. Even with familiar subjects, such as those studied as part of the National Curriculum, students need a carefully considered introduction to the course. During the first few weeks students need to be supported in making the transition from school to the more adult environment of the sixth form or a college and receive an induction into each subject.

Research by FEDA (Martinez, 1997; Martinez and Munday, 1998) and the Responsive College Unit (Aitken, 1999) suggests that students are at risk if they have been enrolled on the wrong course, experience poor induction, start a course late, have only achieved the minimum entrance requirements for admission to the course, need additional learning support or financial support, or have to combine their study with excessive part-time work. Through an effective college management information system (MIS) and individual tutorials during the first few weeks of a student course it is possible to identify and support those who are at risk, thus increasing the chances of retaining them on the course.

A student handbook makes an effective vehicle for an induction process. In it the students should be made aware of the specification and topics that they will be covering, the way in which the course will be taught and the expectations of them. The mode and timing of assessment for the subject is also an important element of the induction programme as it provides the student with an understanding of the demands of the course. Any equipment that the student is required to provide should be listed along with any additional expenditure anticipated during the course.

Study skills specific to the subject or appropriate to the level of the course are also usefully covered in induction. Sessions on note taking from discussions in the group, from tutor input and from texts can lead into ways of structuring essays or short answers. Information handling such as the use of an index in a book, the use of a search engine on the Internet or the way in which magazines, videos and books are catalogued in the library or resource centre will support the students in becoming confident, autonomous learners. It is in the first few weeks that the skills at the foundation of each course can be taught to all students and those who may require additional support identified.

The establishment of positive relationships within the classroom also helps to raise student self-esteem and confidence and, by making them feel part of the group, retain them on a course. 'Ice-breakers' are a useful means of developing these relationships between the students and for the tutor to get to know the group. Exercises such as pairing up students and each finding out the age, previous school, number of siblings, likes, dislikes and unusual interests of the other can lead to each student introducing his/her partner to the group. More disruptive activities include moving around the room to find as many students as possible with the same interests or experience – finding other students who own a cat, have a liking for a certain pop group or football team, or go ice skating. For the less extrovert students an introductory quiz where small groups work together can overcome the anxiety and inhibition of joining a new class and immediately involve all students.

For many students who settle well in the classroom it is the lunchtime or free period that causes the greatest concern. The long walk into the student refectory trying to look cool and confident yet unable to see a group of recognizable faces to join is the real nightmare of so many students. Within colleges and sixth forms social activities are often a part of the induction process and freshers' fairs, lunchtime activities, barbecues, discos and even barn dances have helped students to settle into their new environment and thus stay on their course.

## Task 4.2

- Write a list of contents for an induction handbook in your subject/course. How will it differ from other subjects? What makes your subject special?
- Using two columns, write a list of the skills necessary to study your subject in one column and then suggestions of how you might teach them in the second.
- Create an 'ice-breaker' to get students talking to each other in your particular subject.

## Additional support

Induction provides an opportunity to discover those students who may need additional support. Information on this may be provided for the tutor through the college or school MIS. Dyslexia, hearing or visual impairment, epilepsy and other serious conditions needing specific support will usually be identified at the initial interview when the level and type of support for the student will be agreed. Some students need specially adapted equipment, others are provided with facilitator support within the classroom while those with less severe learning difficulties may receive individual tutorial support from the learning support team. Some students may need subject-specific support for a short period while a particular topic is covered or during the course to help them to feel competent to write essays, structure project reports or construct a revision timetable.

In a class where students come from many different schools and backgrounds it is important not to assume knowledge or understanding but to establish the experience and competence of each student. This could be achieved by using a diagnostic test, which many colleges and schools administer during the first few weeks of a student's programme to ascertain his level in basic skills or to determine the level of the key skills courses he will follow.

A non-threatening task within the first few weeks of the course, incorporating the skills central to the subject, is a good way to identify the individual strengths and weaknesses of the students in the class. In business studies, for example, students need to have a grasp of statistics, be able to work out percentages and produce a graph. They should also be able to summarize a passage, select the salient points and construct a logical argument. These skills could be diagnosed by analysing brief case studies of commercial companies. This induction task would enable the students to experience the core of the subject and the tutor to become aware of the additional help individuals or groups of students may require.

## Task 4.3

Analyse the skills that students should possess to succeed in your subject and design an induction activity to diagnose their level of ability in each skill.

# Financial support and learning careers

In most colleges and schools there are student support services that offer advice on financial support, health care, counselling, study skills and assistance with travel costs. In 1993 the government provided access funds to colleges, initially to support post-19 students in further education, and then in 1999 the funding was increased to include 16- to 19-year-old students. Travel costs and educational maintenance allowances are also available for families on low incomes and students are given a weekly allowance dependent on their attendance in classes. Callender (1999) discovered that 23 per cent of students left study for financial reasons. Two-thirds of them received no information on the financial support available and half were unaware of the sources of support for which they might apply.

The financial support provided for students often enables them to cut down on the excessive part-time work that is now a feature in the lives of so many 16- to 19-year-old students. Research at the Institute of Education (Hodgson and Spours, 2000) and the University of Durham (Davies, 1999) found that over 80 per cent of 16- to 19-year-olds worked part time with the majority working between 10 and 15 hours a week. The research suggests that 10 hours' part-time work or less can have a positive effect on student life, supporting them in developing the wider key skills, but those who work above 15 hours are more likely to leave their course.

The Transforming Learning Cultures in Further Education project, as part of the ERSC study, 'aims to identify learning cultures in FE that are amenable to intervention and change' (ESRC Teaching and Learning Research Programme, 2001). As part of a four-year longitudinal study, across four universities and four FE colleges, Bloomer and Hodkinson (2000) have identified what they call 'learning careers' that have a profound effect on the attitude to study of 16- to 19-year-olds. Undertaking regular interviews with individual students and their tutors through the years of their post-16 courses, they identify critical moments when students' learning careers are transformed. The choice of the wrong subject, an illness, falling in love, moving out of the family home and growing awareness of the advantages of economic independence lead students to change their learning careers and to drop out of full-time study.

The tutor can do little to influence these dramatic, life-changing events, which inevitably adversely affect the retention statistics. The perceptive tutor, however, may sense the clues of radical change in a student's life. Individual tutorials are often the vehicle for students divulging their domestic upheavals and referral for financial or emotional support at a crucial moment may help a student to remain in study, if that is the appropriate course of action. The needs of the student and not the retention statistics should be at the centre of these discussions. For many students, intervention and support may be what they need but do not know how to obtain. For others, leaving study is the best path for them but the guidance offered as they leave may be a determining factor in their return to study later in their lives.

## Task 4.4

Draw a time line from birth to the present day showing the points when changes in your life affected your learning. Identify the type and timing of intervention that could have provided positive support and improved your learning.

# Teaching and learning

According to the National Audit Office (2001) the quality of teaching, class size and the degree of attention the tutor gives to individual students have a major impact on retention and achievement. Research from FEDA (Martinez, 2000) stresses the need for structured teaching with clear, explicit learning objectives for the programme as a whole and for individual teaching sessions, with a logical sequence of learning activities and assignments. Tutors would never dream of climbing into a car and driving off without knowing where they were going but many walk into a classroom having no clear, specific learning objective that they will achieve in the lesson!

Student-centred assessment should include structured feedback with instructions for improvement and focus on the individual learner. Individual learning is at the core of successful, effective teaching and the programme needs to have opportunities to differentiate to take account of the needs and skills of each learner. Individual review and action planning, linked with flexibility in the assignments set, offer each student a tailor-made path through the subject, and the opportunity to develop his/her own style of learning and to become an autonomous learner.

A flexible approach to learning taking account of individual needs and skills is perceived to be at the centre of successful teaching. Individual learning programmes, including review and action planning, help to motivate students, while differentiated activities help them to pick out a successful path through the course. Differentiated tasks or assignments, worksheets with extension or lower-level tasks and a choice of modules all supported by initial diagnosis and individual support will enable the learner to claim ownership of his/her learning.

The Hay McBer study on teacher effectiveness (2001) concluded that the professional characteristics of teachers, their teaching skills and the classroom climate that is created have an impact on an individual's progress and achievement. Nine dimensions of classroom climate were found to have a significant impact on student motivation and achievement:

- *clarity* – the extent to which students are clear about the aims and objectives of the lesson and their context;
- *environment* – the extent to which students feel that the classroom is a comfortable, well-organized environment;
- *fairness* – justice and equality within the classroom;
- *interest* – the level of stimulation and interest in the class;
- *order* – the structure, organization and discipline in the classroom;
- *participation* – the extent to which students feel that they can question and offer opinions in class and feel confident to work in groups;
- *safety* – the extent to which students feel safe from emotional or physical bullying;
- *standards* – students understand what is expected of them and they receive encouragement to improve;
- *support* – students are encouraged to try new things and learn from their mistakes.

It is the tutor's responsibility to create such a climate that is conducive to learning, and it is as relevant to the adult returning to education as to the 16-year-old who has just left Year 11. The stress on organization and order in which students feel safe to experiment and develop is relevant at all levels.

## Task 4.5

- Take a topic from your scheme of work and plan three ways in which you could provide differentiated activities for the most and least able in the group.
- Using the nine facets of classroom climate above, decide what you can do within your classroom to create a positive classroom climate.

# Assessing performance and measuring progress

Some form of target setting and review is necessary at the centre of an individual learning programme if learners are to measure their progress and take control of their learning. Most schools and colleges use some form of value-added score so they can measure the distance travelled between GCSEs and A levels. These systems can produce target minimum grades (TMGs) for students based on their individual GCSE results. These TMGs, when discussed with students, can improve motivation and enable the tutor to analyse those who are underachieving. Such systems are predicated on the ability of the tutor to understand what is expected of a student if s/he is to achieve a particular grade and the specific action a student might take to improve his/her performance.

Martinez (2001) and Coe (2000) stress that whatever target-setting system is used the targets that are set should be specific, challenging, achievable and measurable. They should also be owned by the learner, which is the philosophy at the core of the wider key skill, 'improving own learning and performance'. Target setting should also be a process, not an event. A number of actions should be identified that are sufficiently challenging to the student yet achievable. Managing the tension between the two demands means that the tutor should have detailed knowledge of both the student and the subject.

Individual action plans on which students record and review their targets are a good basis for target setting. A session on how to set targets using the acronym SMART is a good starting point for the group. Targets should be:

- **S**pecific;
- **M**easurable;
- **A**chievable;
- **R**elevant;
- **T**ime-bonded.

So, for example, a student studying *Northanger Abbey* by Jane Austen for A level English literature may decide that she would like to do some background reading so negotiates a target with her tutor: 'To read *Udolpho* by Mrs Radcliffe, to give me an idea of the contemporary novel Jane Austen was using as the source of her humour. I will provide a review of the novel on 20 December.'

It is, of course, vital to the system that the tutor records the date that has been negotiated for the completion of the target and checks that it has been completed. Target setting is being undertaken in many schools and colleges but it is the review and further development of the targets, the closing of the loop, that is not always undertaken and this emphasizes the need for detailed records to be kept.

If a tutor is to offer students differentiated material or approaches, along with individual targets that are reviewed at the time appropriate to the student, then careful, detailed records of individual progress and activities need to be established and maintained. Student profile sheets recording dates when tutorials were held, targets reviewed and grades achieved on assignments are essential accompaniments to attendance registers.

## Task 4.6

- Devise an appropriate target for yourself to follow in preparing some differentiated work for your students.
- Consider a topic in your subject that will take between four and eight weeks to teach. Now think of the milestones or points in the course of lessons where you would expect to be able to assess your students' progress. When would you set targets and what would they be?

- Write a list of the elements that are essential in an A-grade piece of work and a C-grade assignment in your subject. Then write a list of strategies that students should follow to move from C-level performance to A-grade work.
- What are the key words and concepts that students need to know to perform well in your subject? Write a list of them and consider strategies that students could use to acquire or develop them.

Our student is now enrolled on the right course, has received a well-structured induction programme and is enjoying a positive classroom climate, in which individual needs are met and progress is monitored. The student has received advice on the financial support available and tutorials have given confidence and raised self-esteem. According to the research your student should complete the course successfully – unless, of course, the student's love life means that s/he changes his/her learning career! Discussions on support and guidance, from the qualitative 'tea and tissues' school of thought to the quantitative target-setting regime, all have at their core the tutor working alongside the individual student to achieve results. So, at the foundation of all the benchmarks, retention and achievement statistics, we see that the secret to success lies in the personal relationship of those involved in the dynamic, individual process of learning – a secret that excellent teachers have always known!

# References

Aitken, G (1999) *20 Steps to Researching and Improving Student Retention*, Responsive College Unit, Preston, Lancs

Bloomer, M and Hodkinson, P (2000) Learning careers: continuity and change in young people's dispositions to learning, *British Educational Research Journal*, **26** (5), pp 583–97

Callender, C (1999) *The Hardship of Learning: Student's income and expenditure and their impact on participation in further education*, South Bank University, London

Coe, R (2000) Target setting and feedback: can they raise standards in schools?, Paper presented at BERA Conference 2000, University of Cardiff

Davies, P (1999) *Learning and Earning: The impact of paid employment on young people in full-time education*, FEDA, London

ESRC Teaching and Learning Research Programme (2001) Newsletter, **2**, April, University of Exeter

Hay McBer (2001) Teacher effectiveness and leadership: a framework for lifelong learning, *Secondary Leadership Paper*, **9**, National Association of Head Teachers, Haywards Heath

Hodgson, A and Spours, K (2000) *Earning and Learning: A local study of part-time paid work among 14–19 year olds*, Institute of Education, University of London

Martinez, P (1997) *Improving Student Retention: A guide to successful strategies*, FEDA Report, FEDA, London

Martinez, P (2000) *Raising Achievement: A guide to successful strategies*, FEDA, London

Martinez, P (2001) *Great Expectations: Setting targets for students*, Learning and Skills Development Agency, London

Martinez, P and Munday, F (1998) *9000 Voices: Student persistence and drop out in further education*, FEDA Report, **2** (7), FEDA, London

National Audit Office (2001) *Improving Student Performance*, NAO, London

OFSTED/Audit Commission (1993) *Unfinished Business: Full-time educational courses for 16–19 year olds*, HMSO, London

# 5 Learning styles: adoption and adaptation

Simon Lygo-Baker

> Young students embarking on a course of study in a college of further education are
> generally unaware of the nature and process of learning.
>
> (Curzon, 1990)

## Introduction

Learning is such a fundamental process that it is often in danger of being assumed and therefore taken for granted. In an ideal world how people learn could easily be defined and there would be an accepted method for recognizing when and where it has occurred. However, as with much of learning and teaching, it is not that simple. To compound these difficulties, variations in how people learn are often not acknowledged and teachers assume that, if they present information logically and produce enough notes and materials, all will learn effectively. If we follow this logic two people of roughly the same age and intellect and exposed to the same teaching environment could be expected to respond similarly to a lesson: but they do not. This suggests that people vary not only in their ability to learn but also in their style. So whilst individuals may share characteristics, the attitudes and behaviours that determine their preferred way of learning differ. These individual personal preferences can appear in isolation, whilst others are context-specific. If individuals are left to act independently, Cashdan and Lee (1971) found that they will tend towards these styles across a range of situations. Despite this, few can articulate their own learning style other than a vague notion of what they are comfortable with and how they learn more effectively. For teachers helping people become more effective learners, the case for acknowledging the importance of these styles should therefore be self-evident.

This chapter considers the development of learning styles and examines some established theories in relation to the development of styles and the impact this has upon learning strategies developed and encouraged in further education. After this the 'grey area' between child and adult is examined with reference to the self and the development of individual identity, to question how important age and identity formation are to the adoption and adaptation of learning styles. Meeting individual needs is then addressed by considering the use of new methodologies and technology. Finally the lessons that emerge from this are drawn into a series of conclusions.

## The development of learning styles

Whilst consideration has been given to how children develop their learning styles and more recently how adults then develop and adapt these, little has been investigated of the 'grey area' in between. Clearly individuals bring their own experiences to the learning process and during their education they will have encountered a variety of delivery methods that will have shaped how they learn. But what happens whilst an individual's identity is developing to the interpretation and development of this learning style? If we are born with a style, how does this develop and alter? For many, leaving school and entering further education come at a time of great transition in their lives: individuals are trying to make sense of their own make-up, how to react and interpret knowledge, and discovering the absence of stable elements upon which their learning has previously occurred, such as friends and teachers as well as learning resources and methods. For a teacher it is therefore important to recognize and build upon what has already been learnt but not to take too much for granted. It is important to place the learning style in context and note the large number of factors with which it interrelates. Learning and development are not merely ascribable to the process of growing up; they are dependent upon events and experiences that occur within an individual's environment (Gagne, 1977). Whilst all of the inputs are variables, it is the learning style that relates to the individual and can be seen as the filter that leads to the learning and development (see Figure 5.1).

The literature analysing the inputs to this model has grown, looking at learning related to age, anxiety, motivation and so on and trying to make a distinction between learning styles and learning strategies (Wintergerst, DeCapua and Itzen, 2001). The individual learning style is seen as an innate preference related to individuals' desired way of understanding the

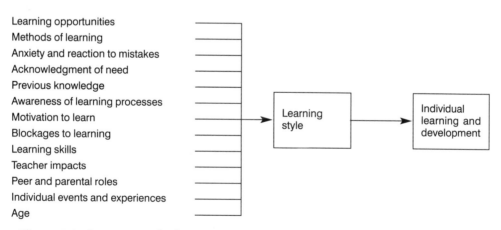

**Figure 5.1**   Inputs into the learning process (adapted from Honey and Mumford, 1992)

process of learning. For example, some individuals prefer to learn by watching action, whilst others prefer to learn by hearing information. Learning strategies are more difficult to define (Nisbet and Shucksmith, 1988). They are usually seen as a set of specific procedures or techniques that an individual uses to solve a problem. They can therefore be learnt, applied and selected by an individual, and can vary both within and between individuals. There is also a presumption that these strategies are associated with effective learning. As a consequence the role of the teacher can be seen to be key. Whilst styles may be innate, they and the associated strategies develop. The stimuli provided by the teacher towards the development of capabilities internal to the learner are therefore very important in assisting the learner's style, to recognize new points and develop strategies to meet the demands of different external situations. This has become even more pertinent to those working in further education today, as the development of new pathways into and through education for individuals, offering greater choice and flexibility, demands an even greater understanding of styles and strategies that individuals adopt and adapt. As patterns of progression develop, so do the motivations and experiences of the learners themselves (Smith and Bocock, 1999).

## Student learning styles

Whilst it is acknowledged that learning continues throughout life, theorists have attempted to understand and describe the processes involved. Kolb (1984) described learning as a four-stage process, a learning cycle consisting of concrete experience, observation and reflection, the formation of abstract concepts and generalizations, and the testing of the implications of these in new situations. Again these four stages are clearly impacted upon significantly by a range of key variables, such as age and experience, which begin to distort the process. We may therefore be able to adapt Kolb's model into a spiral that begins with the innate learning style and, as the individual grows older, the strategies increase related to this style to help incorporate the growing concrete experiences, and the ability to reflect and form new concepts and then test these (see Figure 5.2).

By the time that most enter further education they are moving up the spiral and beginning to develop their ability to reflect and utilize wider experiences. If we were able to isolate a correlation between the learning style and the strategies adopted, as a result of Kolb's work, it should enable us to understand student performance more fully and as a result improve learning. However, whilst the adoption of a particular strategy may be directly linked to a particular learning style, Warr and Downing (2000) have shown that it can also reflect that a student is more able, more motivated to learn or less anxious. The correlation is therefore not as straightforward. The spiral becomes further distorted according to Honey and Mumford (1992) when we acknowledge that most people have a preference for certain stages within the process. We are all familiar with people who appear very thoughtful but appear to do little, others who like to experiment but produce little concrete. These people are locked into the learning cycle at certain points. For example, Student A prefers to be continually experiencing tasks and quickly jumps to conclusions whilst Student B of similar age and ability likes to review situations and is less interested in first-hand experiences (see Figure 5.3).

Understanding how and why people have different preferences may help us to understand the different learning styles that people develop and the strategies that support these. The

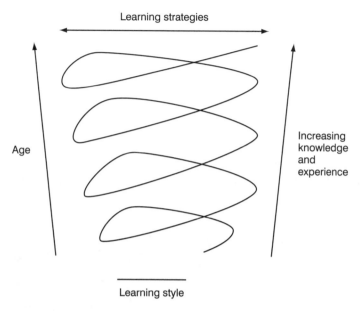

Learning style

1. Concrete experience
2. Observation and reflection
3. Formation of concepts
4. Testing in new situations

**Figure 5.2**   The development of learning strategies

**Figure 5.3**   Time in each stage of the learning cycle

learning style becomes associated with a set of strategies that are successful for the individual and the individual discontinues those that are not. Behaviour and patterns can therefore be seen to become habitual. As a result, Pask (1976) argued that students are likely to perform more effectively in certain subject areas and it may also explain career choices individuals make.

In an attempt to develop the correlation, Honey and Mumford (1992) took Kolb's learning process and grafted on four learning styles that they felt reflect a positioning closest to each stage (see Figure 5.4). These can be roughly described as follows:

- *Activists.* These are people who like to be challenged and fully involved in activity. They are open to new experiences and like to try out new ideas. They live very much for the moment and often act before they fully think through implications. They quickly lose interest, however, and move on to new areas once tasks become everyday or the norm.

- *Reflectors.* These are people who like to look at the broad picture and think at length about the issues involved. They tend to adopt a low profile and are thorough and cautious. They will not act on the spur of the moment, preferring to go through all the available information.
- *Theorists.* These are people who develop sound theories based on objective information. They tend to be perfectionists and do not like subjective judgements, preferring to analyse and synthesize information by taking a step-by-step approach to an identified problem.
- *Pragmatists.* These are people who are practical and like to try things out rather than become involved in lengthy discussions. They tend to avoid open-ended discussions and are quick to respond and take action. They tend to view problems and opportunities as challenges.

## Task 5.1

Given the descriptions above of the four stages, identify the characteristics that you display for these in your teaching.

|  | My Characteristics |
| --- | --- |
| Activist |  |
| Reflector |  |
| Theorist |  |
| Pragmatist |  |

We can see that when we define individuals in this way the responses to how these people learn most effectively will differ. The danger is that by adopting these labels we may typecast learners and forget that the learning experience is unique for everyone. The aim of identifying individual learning styles should be to develop individual potential and extend choice within the learning environment. If we recognize that individuals will

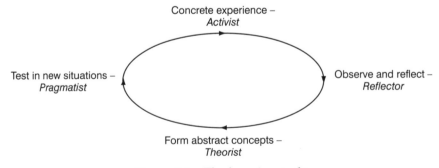

**Figure 5.4** The learning cycle

favour particular stages within the learning cycle (Figure 5.4), that may result in a distortion of the learning process. It becomes necessary to recognize that the teacher has a responsibility to assist the learner through all four stages. A teaching strategy adopted where a task is short and the reflection lengthy will suit a reflector more than an activist. The teaching strategies adopted therefore need to enable learners to participate in all four stages. When planning teaching it is therefore important to consider how each area of the learning cycle will be accommodated. Teachers also need to acknowledge their own style and how this distorts their own teaching style. If you view yourself as a pragmatist, can you see this in how you then present your teaching? Teachers need to devise teaching that moves the learning through all four stages. This requires teachers to consider all aspects of teaching to ensure that they are getting students involved in 'doing' (concrete response), 'thinking' (reflection and observation), 'concluding' (abstract concepts) and 'experimenting' (testing in new situations).

## Task 5.2

Write an assignment for your discipline and identify where and how it promotes the four stages.

*Assignment title or description:*

| Stage 1 | Stage 2 | Stage 3 | Stage 4 |
|---|---|---|---|
| | | | |
| | | | |
| | | | |
| | | | |
| | | | |
| | | | |

This all suggests that, as individual learners develop more consistent strategies that relate to their preferred style of learning, a pattern is emerging and that if this is recognized and understood it could be utilized by a teacher to develop more appropriate learning environments. As Prosser identified, 'learning strategies that students adopt play an important role in what students learn' (Richardson, Eysenck and Piper, 1987) and as these learners develop they become more likely to vary their implementation between tasks owing to their perceptions about teaching and assessment. As teachers, we need to acknowledge this and have greater discussion with the students about how their preferences are met or are engaged in by the teaching methods adopted and the assessment involved. How often do you sit down with the students and discuss this?

# Age and identity

It is important to remember that a human being is a unique and complicated patchwork of ever-changing personal attributes (Harre, 1998). An individual's experience of the world and his/her part within it has a point of singularity that is not shared by a group. The attributes, including our memories, taken together constitute a unique frame and one that is constantly evolving. This sense of identity, or self, is important and teachers need to use this to discover strengths and not make learners feel that they are starting from the beginning again. This is particularly key at the age when many are entering further education. According to Marcia (in Honess and Yardley, 1987) it is during the period of adolescence that our identity develops most, a period when it is generally held that the child becomes an adult in appearance and behaviour. A great deal of concentrated change is occurring but it is also seen as a period where learning can be very productive. Learning new skills, such as driving a car, is often thought to be easier at this age rather than later on in life.

A number of writers have highlighted that this is also the time when individuals are beginning effectively to interpret an understanding of their own learning style. Entwistle (1988) quotes Selmes and suggests that between the ages of 16 and 18 the defining features of a shift from surface to deeper learning strategies become more easily evident. Students are becoming more able at developing their previous learning to create new knowledge. Their learning style can no longer be explained as merely stylistic or part of a developmental phase. This is important because individuals are becoming increasingly effective at regulating their own internal processes (Gagne, 1977) and developing the ability to learn how to learn (Nisbet and Shucksmith, 1988). Their cognitive ability has developed to enable them to take in information, evaluate it and allocate meaning and values to both the old and the new. In doing this they are able to develop a unique style and exercise control over strategies that are adopted and then adapted to new situations that arise. They show signs of a growing interest and ability to create new knowledge and greater skill in combining information from different courses and taking theoretical ideas and relating them to everyday experiences that they have. Learning is becoming more internalized and no longer seen as an isolated set of tasks that have no relation to each other and that once completed can be forgotten. Although different individuals experience this change at different stages and with different emphasis, the shift is evident at this stage and needs to be recognized to enable appropriate teaching strategies to develop and encourage this further.

This transition period offers the teacher the opportunity to emphasize and enhance deeper learning strategies and help to consolidate this transition at a time when many have chosen a specialist subject area in which they have greater personal interest. The development of processes of reflection within the student appears to be represented in a shift from the mere reproduction of facts to recognition of the importance of personal meaning. Organizational principles that students apply to their learning are also shifting towards a more integrated approach, using old and new concepts together to develop new connections – a more holistic approach. This moves away from the surface approach characterized by a more atomistic concentration on details in isolation of other factors and issues. The student is becoming more aware of the pay-off involved and whilst we can identify a shift of strategies within the deep and surface dichotomy we need also to be aware of associated impacts of a shift from atomistic to holistic strategies (Marton, Hounsell and Entwistle, 1997). Whilst these shifts occur within students entering further education, their motivations can also vary from vocational to academic and from social to personal and a different mix of some or all to produce a grey area of potentially chaotic change.

## Task 5.3

Identify how a piece of work you have set encourages deep and holistic learning and surface and atomistic learning.

In further education, students should be given tasks that require them to develop more independent thinking and develop their own answers that they can justify. Tasks become more individually focused and not everyone within the same class undertakes the same activities. The reproduction of facts, following a standard set of procedures, will no longer always suffice. Students are beginning to be asked to interpret, predict and evaluate. This requires new strategies to cope and raises potential problems as a result, if the teacher has not built on what the student already knows. For instance, as Claxton (1990) argues, much of learning comes from mimicking. For those in a new environment, what have they to mimic? The learning strategies previously used cannot be relied upon and thus new ones need to be developed to plug the gaps that appear. These are then used to apply to more general use. The old safe peer group, in which previous strategies were used, is no longer available and the strategies required to be able to go beyond the surface learning approaches that characterized early learning are more complex. This is important because we considered earlier that a key role of the teacher was to move individual learners through each stage of the learning cycle. If we do not make learners feel comfortable with the learning environment, their likely response is to return and remain within the phase of the cycle they feel most at ease within, such as reflection.

This period is therefore likely to be one of great change, externally and internally, for students: they have a new set of classmates and a new set of teachers, and many are experiencing more freedom in their lives as they are treated as 'adults'. If their learning style is not accommodated within the learning environment this is likely to lead to conflict. This often leads to students presenting a greater challenge to both their peers and teachers. Some may express their opinions more forcefully as they discover a voice or voices they had not previously experienced; others will become more introverted and attend less regularly. This can therefore be identified as a period of uncertainty for learners who are questioning their own values and beliefs within a social setting and finding many of their previous stable supports have disappeared (Breakwell, 1986).

Writers such as Kolb and Honey and Mumford offer us a series of definitions to aid understanding of the learning process and how individuals' own preferences can be allied to generic learning styles. Recognition of these different styles offers teachers the opportunity to plan teaching more effectively to respond to these different styles. It also allows teachers to recognize their own style and therefore potential influence in the learning that results. Students entering further education do so facing a series of challenges and conflicts, some of which are internal and others external. Whilst individuals may become more aware of how they learn and are able to utilize different strategies more effectively at this age it is important for the teacher to recognize and consider the importance of age and identity, or self, upon this. To respond to the issues raised, much has been made of new methodologies, such as virtual learning environments.

## Learning styles and new methodologies

Learners arriving in further education colleges have left behind their old learning environments and now often find themselves faced with new learning methodologies, such as student-centred, where the emphasis of responsibility for learning is very much on learners themselves. They may also be presented with new learning technologies, such as interactive learning materials utilizing information learning technology (ILT). The role of the teacher is to assist learners to link their previous experiences and learning with the new, to enable the transition to be as painless and effective as possible (see Figure 5.5).

| Task | 5.4 |
|------|-----|

To assist the transition, how can you help learners to recognize good and bad learning experiences?

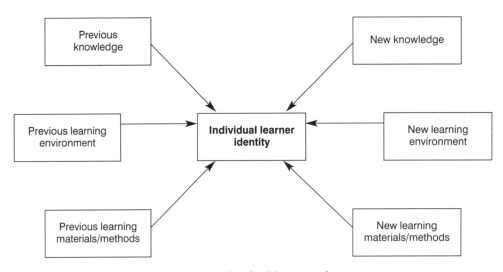

**Figure 5.5**   Individual learner identity

As a result of opportunities afforded by technology, learning can take place in a variety of settings. Teachers need to recognize the different settings and the impact they may have on both the teacher and the learner. There appear to be four identifiable options:

1.  *The student and teacher together*. This is the traditional learning environment, where the student and the teacher interact simultaneously. Traditional learning methodologies are likely to be employed. ILT is usually employed on the basis of teacher-driven activities.
2.  *The student and teacher together but at a different time*. Here ILT is crucial and there is a need to ensure that this is carefully thought through. However, it allows for more flexibility, allowing students to learn when it is most appropriate for them.
3.  *The student and teacher apart but at the same time*. This is again reliant on appropriate ILT and as a result can be very costly. However, colleges are increasingly using this option to enable students to participate who may otherwise not be able to access education, such as prisoners or those abroad.
4.  *The student and teacher apart and at a different time*. The costs of such virtual learning environments are extremely high but they have been shown to be effective and can suit learners. The Open University is a good example.

When considering the appropriate learning resources, teachers also need to acknowledge the importance that the senses have on learning styles. We can identify learners whose learning relates most effectively to auditory signals, words and sounds. Other learners respond better to visual signals and images. The final group relates more to feelings and taking action in order to learn. As a result you need to consider how your teaching strategies may affect the learning. Delivering a didactic session may mean that those who prefer the auditory style learn most. However, if the teacher also involves visual prompts and images then the second set of styles will also be incorporated and then by asking questions that make the students take some action or consider their views teachers may find that the needs of all the students have been met.

When selecting the right information and resources it is important to consider how this material supports learning at each stage of the learning cycle. If the students read a book and you ask them to take notes and answer a series of questions leading to a debate you are likely to help move them through the learning cycle as well as appealing to those who like to learn via visual means (reading the book), auditory learners (discussion and answering questions) and those who like to consider feelings (debate and questions).

## Task 5.5

How many different learning environments are there at your college/institution and how effective are these?

# Lessons

The context within which the above understanding is to be translated is important when considering the lessons we can learn from these debates. There has been growing interest in recent years in methods of improving student learning in the context of teaching and assessment. There is however a danger that much of this important debate will be clouded by new definitions and interpretations of what it means to be a professional. The emphasis appears to be shifting away from actual pedagogy and towards a predetermined product where the key is to be seen as competent and flexible. The danger for individual learning styles is that they cease to be taken account of for pedagogical improvement but for commercial reasons (Shain and Gleeson, 1999). For many in education, the way of making sense of this is to rework old practice when we actually need to be looking at new ideas. This has clear links to concerns raised earlier in generalizations being made over predictions of behaviour and related learning styles.

So what lessons can we learn? The work of renowned theorists such as Piaget into how children make sense of their environment has enabled practitioners to consider children as learners from a developmental standpoint. They lack a certain maturity in intellectual structure and are therefore incapable of taking in some information. Vygotsky crucially added that this lack of experience was accompanied by an inability to make appropriate connections. Learning strategies at this stage in life are therefore likely to be surface and atomistic. The role of the teacher becomes crucial at this point in working jointly to help construct meaning, and to examine what results can be achieved by the pupil and what potential the student has. The teacher therefore has a crucial part to play in cultivating a 'seventh' sense (Nisbet and Shucksmith, 1988). This role becomes increasingly important at the stage when students come into this 'grey area' because through school an expectation related to perceived ability has been added to by peers, parents and teachers. This stable support structure suddenly disappears. Whilst schools provide students with many skills and improve the range of strategies individuals utilize and feel comfortable with, students rarely enter further education with the ability to monitor situations, tasks and problems and respond accordingly. Their own styles are not mature enough and this needs to be acknowledged within the further education landscape where for students to succeed there is a need to utilize deeper and more holistic learning strategies. A learning style and the associated strategies are more complex than a chosen sequence or well-tried routine. They are difficult to define, often carried out unconsciously by individuals and vary in length and application. Knowing and understanding one's own learning is a complicated process and it follows that understanding other people's is even more difficult. The challenge for those teaching in further education is to enable these styles to develop appropriate and effective learning strategies.

This is made more challenging because within the classroom there are three key variables involved in a constant negotiation: the teacher, the learner and the task. As Galloway and Edwards (1992) reflect, it can be a confusing place. The teacher is there to assist by providing stimuli and assisting the selection of strategies to ensure the student moves through all stages of the learning cycle. To do this effectively the role goes beyond support and requires the teacher to understand the learning strategies adopted and presented and those being developed. This is clearly far from a simple task when the teacher is faced with a group of perhaps 30 individuals, all of whom have their own style and adopt different strategies to tasks requiring completion (Fox, 1993). The teacher must accept that knowing what one person will learn from a series of events may tell us very little about the likely outcome of similar events to someone else. Successful teaching involves bridging these gaps and filling the potential vacuum, ensuring that all stages of the learning cycle are completed. There are interactions taking place between the student and the teacher that transfer responsibility and assist in the development and implementation of strategies that are effective and also that the student is comfortable with. Howe (1998) argues that even then, unless we provide the opportunity to practise new strategies, they will be dropped in preference to previous ones. It is our responsibility to take this into account when developing teaching so that we move people through the learning cycle but also allow them to develop learning strategies within each area that they can utilize in the future.

If teachers are to improve the effectiveness of the learning process and therefore impact positively on the varied learning styles encountered, communication is crucial. This communication needs to have meaning for learners (be pertinent to their needs), be clear and coherent (in a style that can be interpreted by learners), and use images that put information into context, leading to further clarification that allows learners to synthesize and interpret information (Lockitt, 1997).

## Task 5.6

- For your own particular subject area identify the styles of learning that are encouraged and likely to lead to success in the subject.
- Reflect upon what you as a teacher need to do to understand the learning styles of your students and how to accommodate those who do not currently fit with either the subject learning style or your own.

# Conclusion

Learning styles impact on every aspect of our lives: how we gather information, how we use it and how we link it together are all determined by our preferred learning style. Despite this, many of us still fail to acknowledge how important they are and assume that knowledge comes with age. Understanding the importance and impact of learning styles may help to alleviate the disappointment many have with their learning. Understanding flexible learning styles combined with understanding efficient learning strategies is important and enabling this to happen with the support of information learning technologies where appropriate should help to produce a learning experience that allows for a variety of styles. Achieving this requires all those involved to be working together and communicating efficiently.

Whatever we learn from analysing the different styles and strategies that individuals adopt and then adapt we are warned by Warr and Downing (2000) that we need to consider these strategies in wider settings to see what effect other features may have upon them. This chapter has attempted to do this by looking at the importance and impact that identity has and the challenges faced by those in the grey area between child and adult. There appear to be significant changes occurring in this period within lives that affect the adaptation of adopted learning styles and strategies. The context within which this happens cannot be ignored if we are to be able to provide effective learning environments. Learning styles are clearly a very complex concept from which we still have much to learn (Sadler-Smith, 2001). This learning will enable us to gain a greater understanding of how students learn whilst within further education and how this prepares them for the future. Understanding the styles we promote through further education, the disciplines we teach and our own preferred style can develop this further. By considering how the students want to tackle a task and how they are able to, we may discover gaps that need further examination.

Improving our understanding of learning styles and the impact that these have upon a student's approach to learning can help us to understand the relationship between an individual learner and a task more effectively. To improve student learning a teacher needs to pay close attention to this relationship and that requires an improved understanding of learning styles and the associated strategies. A teacher needs to recognize that each learner is unique and use learning methodologies and technology that will allow for this, whilst at the same time ensuring that the learner experiences all stages of the learning cycle. Ultimately this requires us to consider how we understand our own style as well as how we interpret other people's and as a result to reflect on and improve our teaching.

# References

Breakwell, G (1986) *Coping with Threatened Identities*, Methuen, London

Cashdan, A and Lee, V (1971) *Learning Styles*, Open University Press, Bletchley

Claxton, G (1990) *Teaching to Learn*, Cassell Educational, London

Curzon, L (1990) *Teaching in Further Education*, Cassell Educational, London

Entwistle, N (1988) *Understanding Classroom Learning*, Hodder & Stoughton, London

Fox, M (1993) *Psychological Perspectives in Education*, Cassell Educational, London

Gagne, R (1977) *The Conditions of Learning*, Holt, Rinehart & Winston, London

Galloway, D and Edwards, A (1992) *Secondary School Teaching and Educational Psychology*, Longman, Harlow

Harre, R (1998) *The Singular Self*, Sage, London

Honess, T and Yardley, K (eds) (1987) *Self and Identity: Perspectives across the lifespan*, Routledge & Kegan Paul, London

Honey, P and Mumford, A (1992) *The Manual of Learning Styles*, Honey, Maidenhead

Howe, M (1998) *Principles of Abilities and Human Learning*, Psychology Press, Hove

Kolb, D (1984) *Experiential Learning*, Prentice Hall, London

Lockitt, W (1997) *Learning Styles: Into the future*, FEDA, Shaftesbury

Marton, F, Hounsell, D and Entwistle, N (1997) *The Experience of Learning*, Scottish Academic Press, Edinburgh

Nisbet, J and Shucksmith, J (1988) *Learning Strategies*, Routledge, London

Pask, G (1976) Styles and strategies of learning, *British Journal of Educational Psychology*, **46**, pp 128–48

Richardson, J, Eysenck, M and Piper, D (eds) (1987) *Student Learning*, SRHE/Open University Press, Milton Keynes

Sadler-Smith, E (2001) The relationship between learning style and cognitive style, *Personality and Individual Differences*, **30**, pp 609–16

Shain, F and Gleeson, D (1999) Under new management: changing conceptions of teacher professionalism and policy in the further education sector, *Journal of Education Policy*, **14** (4), pp 445–62

Smith, D and Bocock, J (1999) Participation and progression in mass higher education: policy and the FHE interface, *Journal of Education Policy*, **14** (3), pp 283–99

Warr, P and Downing, J (2000) Learning strategies, learning anxiety and knowledge acquisition, *British Journal of Psychology*, **91**, pp 311–33

Wintergerst, A, DeCapua, A and Itzen, R (2001) The construct validity of one learning styles instrument, *System*, **29**, pp 385–403

# 6  Changes post 16 = challenges post 18: considering the transition years

Rachel Macdonald Cragg

> The greatest hurdle they [students] face in higher education is the transition from school to university and recent research has shown that most students who drop out of university do so in their first year… without a successful first step into the world of higher education, a second step may never exist.
>
> (Cooke and Leckey, 1999: 157)

For many students the transition from further to higher education is an enormous leap. It occurs at a time when the student is developing as an individual, finding a new maturity in the adult world; it is often an unsettling and difficult social and academic transition. As the quotation above suggests, the experiences of this transition often lead to actions that have a profound effect on a student's future career opportunities and decisions.

This chapter investigates the extent to which the educational experiences in the post-16 and higher education sectors can be developed to provide greater support for the student and for those managing the transition by focusing on the contrast between the two learning environments and the pressures they share to widen participation and to retain students.

## The context of transition

In April 1995 Sir Ron Dearing was invited to 'consider and advise the Secretaries of State for Education and Employment for England and Wales on ways to strengthen, consolidate and improve the framework of 16–19 qualifications'. In addition he was asked if there was scope for measures to achieve greater coherence and breadth of study post 16 without compromising standards and to further strengthen qualifications.

Following in 1996, the National Committee for Enquiry into Higher Education was appointed to make recommendations on how the purposes, shape, structure, size and funding of higher education, including support for students, should develop to meet the needs of the United Kingdom over the following 20 years. Recognition here was that higher education embraces teaching, learning, scholarship and research. In July 1997 reports of the findings were published and are widely referred to as the Dearing Report of Higher Education.

These two enquiries have led to major changes within both the post-16 and HE sectors. The Curriculum 2000 qualifications framework is particularly important from the perspective of the higher education provider. Smith and Bocock (1999: 287) suggest that it has 'disturbed a deeply embedded notion... of progression as linear and vertical. Progression in this model fitted perfectly the historic focus of HE on admitting young people with A level qualifications'. Hence higher education has had to acknowledge a wider intake, both in terms of the widening participation agenda (of social and cultural factors) and in relation to academic background and qualifications.

Greenwood (2000) offers a useful summary of how the student experience is under-pinned by five aims and expectations as a result of the introduction of Curriculum 2000:

- *A notion of entitlement.* There is opportunity for the student to make choices from a scheme in which there is something for everyone.
- *Emphasis on breadth.* The curriculum encourages students to study more subjects at Advanced level. It is anticipated that this may prevent the specialization of the old A level (three subjects, sometimes clearly defined by university entrance criteria).
- *Mix of academic and vocational approaches.* This allows students to experience both approaches and prevents the need to make important decisions at 16 that may influence career opportunities.
- *Importance of key skills and enrichment.* This acknowledges and rewards the development of key skills such as application of number, communication and use of information technology. It establishes the ethos that the development of key skills is a continuous process rather than a qualification that, once achieved, can be forgotten.
- *Value placed on tutoring with support for students' learning.* The above aims all place responsibility for learning on the shoulders of the individual. The use of tutoring and support ensures that the individual is carefully guided at both an academic and a personal level.

These five points demonstrate that there has been a fundamental shift in the ethos of learning at Advanced level. Many of these changes are aimed at managing the transition from GCSE to Advanced level and allowing the individual to make career decisions based on experience as well as ability.

## Higher education's growing concerns about issues of student retention

Over recent years higher education has experienced the 'massification of an hitherto elite system' (Deem and Ozga, 2000: 156). Since the early 1990s there has been strong encour-agement, from the funding councils, for universities and colleges to expand student numbers. The greatest pressure has been the allocation of resources; funding is linked to the number of students studying a course, hence more students mean more money.

In addition to the issue of funding, colleges and universities are now assessed on student retention and satisfaction. The old and the new quality audits in higher education have a focus on the student experience and the institution's ability to attract students and to retain them.

A FEDA report (quoted by Spours, 1997) recognized that there is a gap between lecturer and student perceptions of reasons for withdrawal. Staff perceptions of reasons for student withdrawal were of external causes such as financial difficulties, problems with childcare arrangements, enrolment on unsuitable courses and previous learning experiences of the student. In contrast students quote that the 'college did not care' and expressed dissatisfaction with induction, quality of teaching and tutorial support. A clear dichotomy therefore exists; the basis of withdrawal seems clearly to link to student experience, particularly a requirement for adequate support.

The pressure to widen participation and to increase student numbers makes it more important than ever that these problems are solved. A greater understanding of the student experience in the transition from A level to degree study lies at the centre of this debate.

## The further and higher education (FHE) interface

Pressure to recruit and retain students is not isolated to the higher education context for it has been a major priority over the last five years in the post-16 sector. To assist both FE and HE to increase student numbers, to manage the students' progression to HE and to encourage participation in university programmes, many FE and HE providers have entered into a partnership in which the HE programme is delivered by the FE provider. This has usually only included the early stages of a degree programme and most commonly with vocational programmes such as business or construction studies.

This proves an interesting relationship. Higher education is acting as quality assurance and setting the curriculum for the FE provider. Often FE teachers are not trained in the delivery of higher education and hence continue to teach and to support students as they would in A level programmes. This is an interesting point and raises the question: should there be a difference in delivery styles between further and higher education? Is it the perception of 'difference' that is making the student transition more difficult?

# Understanding the transition

The changes discussed here demonstrate how the FE and HE sectors need to work closely together to manage the student transition. With the exception of returnees (who are often mature and in possession of a range of life skills), there is no other point within the education system where the transition to a new level lacks a natural handover or personal support system.

Amongst academic staff within HE there is considerable apprehension about the lack of students' motivation or maturity, their inability to write or perform basic mathematics and their non-attendance, and concerns that, in lectures, students either write everything that is said or nothing at all. These moans are no different than they were pre-Dearing but they do seem to be placed higher on the agenda. There is, however, a change in the tone of these complaints, which at least acknowledges that higher education has some responsibility to find strategies for dealing with these issues of student ability, aspiration and sense of self.

If these anxieties are explored it appears that an underlying issue is one of student support. Although the HE sector clearly has a 'depressing understanding of developments in the 16–19 curriculum' (Baty, 1997), it appears that the FE sector is in a position to offer more to support the transition process. Further education can reconsider its approach and consider how, in light of recent curriculum changes, students can be best prepared for the higher education experience.

## Task 6.1

Consider the types of challenges that the student may encounter as s/he progresses to higher education. Think back to your experience of going to university and try to remember the challenges you faced. One challenge may be coping with living away from home.

Use a table to record your reflections and decide whether these are issues that need to be considered in the post-16 sector, HE or outside of the education experience (see Table 6.1).

**Table 6.1** Challenges on progressing to higher education

|  | Responsibility | | |
| --- | --- | --- | --- |
|  | FE | HE | Outside |
| *Academic Challenges* |  |  |  |
| *Personal Challenges* Living away from home and coping with financial and domestic independence. |  |  | Personal issues but could be discussed in tutorial sessions before going to university. |

Look at the challenges you have identified and where you have allocated the responsibility for supporting them. Suggest what may be done to help the student to meet the challenge successfully (see Table 6.2).

**Table 6.2** Strategies to overcome challenges

| Challenge | Strategy to Overcome It |
|---|---|
| Financial independence. | Post-16 providers to include 'managing your finances' in the tutorial programme in Year 13. Invite student welfare officer from local university to talk to students about the support that is available for them at university. |

## Student ability

'Without scrutinising the specifications our admissions tutors cannot determine… whether the new A levels will still deliver the subject-specific grounding required for successful progression to my first-year undergraduate degrees' (comment from university assistant registrar, *THES*, 22 October 1999).

The comment above is a useful indication of the higher education sector's response when trying to understand the new qualifications framework. The emphasis seems to lie on what the curriculum can deliver to help academics rather than concentrating on the knowledge, skills and experiences a student will bring to degree-level study. There appears to be some suggestion that the student will not find it easy to progress to an undergraduate degree because the prerequisites, as defined by the old curriculum (pre-Curriculum 2000), have not been achieved. In reality the issue is whether the lecturer knows the content of the new qualifications and the modes of assessment and can understand the ability of the student from the grade achieved. Most degree programmes are sufficiently broad in their first year to take account of a wide range of prior learning. Indeed research (Spours, 1997) suggests that, rather than subject-specific knowledge, the greatest underlying concern is a lack of basic key skills to underpin the content: those such as literacy, numeracy, communication and IT.

Two issues emerge here: 1) the development of key skills as integral to the Advanced level curriculum; and 2) specific issues of Vocational Advanced-level study in relation to both delivery and transferability to the higher education context.

Key skills have been viewed as crucial to the student experience of Curriculum 2000 (Greenwood, 2000). UCAS (2001: 13) clarifies that 'the Government is committed to key skills… and is encouraging the incorporation of key skills in all post-16 programmes'. The intention is that students should be encouraged to attain key skills qualifications in areas in which they hold no prior award. This may encourage Advanced-level students to develop skills that may be of more importance to their progression to higher education or the workplace such as the three 'soft' skills – improving own learning and performance, problem solving and working with others. Students may also continue to develop these skills to a higher level whilst at university or college. This ensures that prospective employers should be able to gauge what can and cannot be expected of the candidate.

To this end, key skills have been integrated into the sixth form programme. Many tutors and students of AS and A levels are concerned that there is too much content and assessment required by Curriculum 2000 without the additional burden of skills-based assessment. Indeed this burden appears to deprive students of the opportunity to develop themselves via extra-curricular activities such as sports or drama. Informed by the views of students and teachers, Revell (2001) informs us that students no longer have study time at college, have considerable homework pressures and hence are under pressure to drop elements of their social life (which themselves develop personal skills). At some schools there are direct reports of community involvement and award-bearing curriculum enhancement programmes being dropped because of the need to deliver key skills programmes.

The involvement in extra-curricular activities has always been an element of the UCAS application procedure. Many higher education institutions have been interested in how the student has developed beyond the academic programme as it has been recognized as a gauge of the personality and attitude of the individual. There are fears that the present strategy is encouraging the system to become more qualification-led, one that is orientated towards activities that can be accredited and institution-led rather than optional and individually based.

There is, however, an academic rationale for including key skills in the academic curriculum, which was referred to earlier. There is clearly a departure from the rather outdated expectation that, once achieved at a satisfactory level, a key skill should be seen as successfully completed. For example, the achievement of O level or GCSE mathematics is no longer viewed as sufficient in itself but as a platform from which a set of knowledge and abilities can be continually improved and honed. In most cases skills are embedded within the curriculum and developed in relation to the discipline outcomes. The key skills framework facilitates a developmental approach and provides a benchmark from which skills development can be mapped.

The expectation of attainment of key skills at levels 2 and 3 on entry to HE and 4 and 5 on graduation enables HE and potential employers to understand what can be expected of the individual. It is therefore clear that both higher and further education need to have some basis on which they can demonstrate achievement to ensure that the participant can progress with ease from one sector to the next. For this approach to work effectively, university admissions policy would need to stipulate the required level of skills attainment, provide credit for any qualification achieved and work from this foundation in the delivery of the undergraduate programme.

Issues of student ability during transition to higher education appear to be more contentious for those who choose a vocational route, particularly those who progress to non-vocational degree programmes. Wolff and Sutcliffe (1999: 17) have found that those who entered HE by the vocational route had 'little or no previous experience of "traditional" approaches to teaching, learning and assessment'. Indeed, in an exploration of progression to mass higher education, Smith and Bocock (1999) recognize that the weaker students are often encouraged to follow the vocational route. For example, for these students the 'poor' result of prior experience of the traditional assessment route means that unseen, written, essay-style and end-of-year/end-of-term exams are associated with failure. Once these individuals progress to HE and are faced with a repetition of this bad experience there may be issues of confidence and perception that need to be understood.

Curriculum 2000 attempts to overcome the stigma attached to vocational qualifications by highlighting the comparability of level and standard. Indeed teachers of the VCE have reported a need to move towards more traditional teaching methods, representing a perceived loss of vocational content and a definite 'academic shift' (www.lsda.org.uk/curriculum2000/centrefeedback.asp, 2001).

It is essential that post-16 tutors offer detailed guidance and support to students whose programme is designed around Double and Single Award VCEs when they apply to higher education. The structure, delivery and modes of assessment that have proved successful with these students at A level may be found in many degree courses. The students need to have detailed profiles describing their knowledge, skills and experience and match these against the courses offered by universities. Again it is liaison between the two sectors, particularly in local syndicates, that has led to successful progression routes and transition to higher education.

## Student aspiration

The Dearing recommendations for the 16–19 curriculum and the review of 16–19 qualifications recommended that 'individuals have greater choice and flexibility in constructing their learning pathways and that self-management of learning should become a vital competence' (Butterfield, as noted in Smith and Bocock, 1999: 291).

## Task 6.2

A senior common room discussion:

*Dr Typical:* Did you know, I have just been teaching urban regeneration to the second years. I am sure they don't know how to read! I ask them what they know about urban policy from the 80s until the present day – I think the short answer is 'nothing'. Do you think they ever listen to the news or read the paper?

*Prof Worrying:* Don't worry, it's the same in my class – I sometimes wonder why they are here at all. Indeed, why do I write extensive book lists? I am sure they are only looked at by me and during QAA.

*Dr Typical:* Oh, I know. The last batch of essays I marked had hardly any reference to the key texts.

*Prof Worrying:* That's not strictly true. The last essay that Shirley wrote was excellent. The range of reading was very impressive. Unlike the others, she didn't just regurgitate my lecture; she really thought about the issues.

*Dr Typical:* It was the same with her comparative planning essay. I am amazed how she does it – her attendance is appalling! The thing is, the rest of them aren't bright enough to perform without attending the sessions. This afternoon only half of them had chosen to turn up – the rest were no doubt too engaged stacking shelves at Sainsbury's.

*Prof Worrying:* If they can't act responsibly now, when will they? What do you prefer, tea or coffee?

The fictional conversation raises a number of important issues associated with student aspiration and tutors' frustration. List the skills or activities that the tutors perceive as essential to successful study in their subject and then suggest strategies that the tutor might employ to develop the skill or activity in the session (see Table 6.3).

**Table 6.3**  Strategies to develop skills

| Skill/Activity | Strategy |
| --- | --- |
| Reading newspapers. | Provide a selection of newspapers and ask students to find evidence from them to use in an essay. |

In the transition from A level to degree study, students have to acquire a vast range of new study skills such as how to acknowledge references, how to make use of book lists and how to take notes from formal lectures. Imagine that you are responsible for planning a study skills Web site to support students in their first year of undergraduate study. Write a list of the skills you would include on the site and underline those you consider essential to success.

As in the Typical and Worrying conversation above, student commitment is often linked to issues of part-time employment. Students in both FE and HE tend to have some form of part-time employment. Hodgson and Spours (1999: 5) have found that the 1998 Labour Force Survey assessment that just over 50 per cent of 17-year-olds are in both education and employment is conservative and suggest that this figure could be as high as 65 or 75 per cent. This work is often shop or bar work, but sometimes it is related to future career prospects. The reason for taking employment is more usually to gain additional financial independence and to fund higher education and/or the pattern of conspicuous consumption (cars, computers, mobile phones and fashion). Indeed, by the time the student reaches higher education, he or she is likely to require a part-time job for financial survival.

The job is an important element of personal development. The routine of attending work and managing finances is a key skill for the future. It is something that has often been acknowledged by the higher education application process and is certainly recognized by potential employers. It is imperative therefore that this function remains but the issue here is balance between paid employment and study.

Students work to gain money and experience. They study to gain the qualification that will take them to higher-skilled employment and pay. The process of working, however, may jeopardize the very thing that they are working to pay for – their qualification. For this reason educationalists sometimes recommend that the student makes a decision between work and study, as there is not time to make a full commitment to both. The activities that get lost in this overcommitment are often self-directed study time and the opportunity to develop a personal interest and enthusiasm in the subject.

The Butterfield quotation at the outset of this section suggests that Curriculum 2000 is intended to allow the individual to manage his or her own learning pathway. In reality the burden of assessment and the choice of options at all levels may incite confusion. Choice may actually result in less-focused individuals who are not ready to embark on a specific course of study. Hence within HE there may need to be the opportunity for transfer between degree programmes as individuals settle into their studies.

Within FE there are attempts to overcome some of this confusion. In the QCA review of July 2001, the 'importance of giving information to students that clearly co-ordinates workloads, maps combinations and identifies assessment requirements' www.lsda.org.uk/curriculum2000/centrefeedback.asp, 2001) was recognized. Students have been made aware of the demands of their learning programme and as a consequence have taken more control over it. The same transparent approach could be explored in higher education to ease the transition to degree study.

Teaching and learning strategies similarly present difficulties for students. During this time of transition to HE there are issues associated with the experience once in higher education. Smith and Bocock (1999: 293) write: 'Lack of familiarity with the educational world, lack of educational confidence... the absence of adequate guidance and signposting into and through the system... comprise a formidable barrier to successful progression.'

Here the authors are reporting findings of a survey of participation and progression in higher education. It is suggested that some of the issues of student progression are partly related to issues of commitment by the individual while others are related to insecurities created by the perceptions of a different system with its own rules and regulations. It appears that, if higher education is keen to encourage progression and retain students, it must address the economies of mass teaching to generalist groups, as this may only serve to lower commitment from the weaker students and further isolate them in their learning.

Many higher education first year programmes are quite general in content and as such act as a foundation to later study. One consequence of this is a programme that may lack the focus anticipated by the participants, one with little or no specialization, one that is taught to large groups of people from different parent courses. Hence the weaker or less secure participants may fail to see the benefit of the content and opt out. This non-attendance and lack of background reading results in 'lost' students being unable to regain their position academically or status as individuals and eventually leads to them leaving higher education.

The issue of academic content is just one example. The development of the skill of learning how to learn is another. What makes this different is its skills-based nature. A need to learn the process of learning straddles the FE–HE interface. By developing teaching and learning strategies that overlap both sectors, students are far more likely to demonstrate development and engagement.

## Sense of self

'The new undergraduate identifies "independent learning", "self-discipline" and "self-reliance" as basic goals of their university education. Yet many are unsure about how to achieve those goals, and often find that they are expected to somehow "know" how to be independent and self-reliant' (Pargetter *et al*, quoted in Taylor, 2000: 108).

Progression to higher education often represents the dawn of a new maturity in which the individual is introduced to new challenges and responsibilities. Some are ready to take on board this maturity; others find it extremely difficult to manage and it is here that student support is essential.

Within the A level experience it has been acknowledged that the tutor has become 'pivotal to the 16–19 experience'. This individual has the role of managing the student's programme of study, demands on workload and key skills development (www.lsda.org.uk/curriculum2000/centrefeedback.asp, 2001). Within FE there is thus a forum for discussion about progression to HE and support for personal and academic issues. These sessions could be used to support a range of issues to develop students in their progression and as a way of encouraging the potential HE participant to assess his or her maturity, personal development plans and interests.

In a number of ways the tutor is therefore adopting the role of a life coach with concerns for students' academic and personal development. Some universities have developed this approach and have provided tutorial support in skills-based units or courses in which students demonstrate their attainment of key skills, which have been practised and developed via the taught element of the programme.

Running through this difficult territory is a strong vein that needs to be broken. There is a feeling within some sectors of HE that students must have the maturity to work independently and to take control of their own learning before they enter the arena. However, the contradictory view is that students can only develop at their own pace and that this is different for each individual. Some students will therefore have the required maturity; others will not. Similarly each student is coping with different personal and domestic challenges, for example some students will have moved away from home and be learning a new way of life, while other students won't. Both FE and HE need to consider their responsibilities in understanding and supporting students to cope with these situations.

## Task 6.3

This task encourages you to consider how you can support students through the transition to HE.

Look at the profiles shown in Tables 6.4 and 6.5 of two 18-year-old students. Consider the challenges each might face in higher education. How could a sixth form tutor help them before they leave A level study and how could an HE tutor support them once they are at university?

Table 6.4 James Rider

| School | Rural sixth form in a school 15 miles from home – he walks two miles to the bus and then, following a 20-minute journey, takes a train and has a further half-mile walk to the school. |
| --- | --- |
| Home | Farmhouse on a working farm where he lives with his parents and grandparents. He is an only child. |
| GCSEs | 1 A*, 8 grade As and 1 grade B. |
| A levels | English literature, grade B.<br>Music, grade B.<br>German, grade C.<br>Maths AS, grade D. |

**Table 6.4** continued

| | |
|---|---|
| Interests | Mountain biking.<br>Piano – has passed Grade VIII examination. |
| Employment | Earns money from working on the farm. |
| Travel | Has been skiing with the school to France in Year 11. |
| Personal relationships | Has a long-term girlfriend his age who lives in the village and who left school at 16 to work in the post office. |
| University | Has chosen a university in a large city four hours' train journey away from home where he will study a joint English and German degree. |

**Table 6.5** Dan Ware

| | |
|---|---|
| School | FE college in city centre. |
| Home | Flat in tower block a short walk from college. |
| GCSEs | 1 grade A, 3 grade Bs and 4 grade Cs. |
| A levels | Double Award leisure and recreation, grades C, C.<br>PE, grade C. |
| Interests | Football – participating in local league and supporting local team each Saturday in the premiership.<br>Has completed bronze Duke of Edinburgh award at college.<br>Representative on student council and organizes social and sports events at college. |
| Employment | Works Tuesday evening, Wednesday evening and Sunday in supermarket chain – 16 hours in total. |
| Travel | Has been on holiday with his friends to Majorca and Greece for the last two years, using money he has saved from his job. |
| Personal relationships | No long-term girlfriend but a large group of mates who spend free time together watching sport and going to clubs. |
| University | Has chosen a campus university nine miles from a city where he will study sports management. |

# Conclusions – managing the transition

The curriculum reforms for 16- to 19-year-olds were implemented with the intention of consolidating and streamlining the learning experience. This should make the transition between levels more transparent. A clear perceptual divide exists between FE and HE, mainly because HE is associated with the physical move to a university or college away from home and a loss of the support of school friends. In many respects there is also an imaginary boundary around HE, a sector that has a history of elitism. The widening participation agenda is clearly challenging this notion and creating a welcome discussion of some of the issues associated with this.

The discussion above highlights the complexity of the relationship between post-16 and HE sectors. To ease the transition between the two sectors for the student we need to consider the attitude of admissions tutors, the development of key skills, the academic and personal support systems required for individual students and the need to be explicit about the level of commitment that is necessary for successful study in HE.

There is a fine balance of blame in which sectoral divides have previously allowed responsibility to be pushed to 'the other'. The current climate and culture of education does not fit this approach. Led by government initiatives, there is an opportunity for FE and HE to work together to build a community, and to listen to and work with the other sector and hence support the students at the centre of the process to achieve their aspirations and potential. Figure 6.1 offers a summary of possible responses by each of the sectors. Responsibility for creating successful transition for students clearly lies with both sectors and, although

**RESPONSE BY SECTOR**

| ISSUES OF TRANSITION | FURTHER EDUCATION | HIGHER EDUCATION |
|---|---|---|
| STUDENT ABILITY<br>• Key skills<br>• Equity between vocational and 'academic' courses | • Key skills are integral to C2000.<br>• Counsel students in their preferred study regime. Relate the A level experience to that expected in HE. | • Recognize the value of key skills awards.<br>• Require clear criteria for entry to HE, including an understanding of skills ability and previous study experiences. |
| STUDENT ASPIRATION<br>• Time management<br>• The challenge of paid work<br>• Level of commitment<br>• Learning how to learn | • Recognize the role of paid work and acknowledge how the skills achieved here can be incorporated into Advanced-level study.<br>• Carefully manage work programmes to ensure that participants are not unduly challenged by the burden of over-assessment. | • Encourage participation and engagement by demonstrating the value and role of material covered, particularly at level one.<br>• Reassess the relationship between economies of scale and retention. |
| SENSE OF SELF<br>• Maturity<br>• Self-discipline | • The personal or academic tutor is pivotal to the student experience.<br>• Recognize the value of appraisal and link this to the development of workplace skills. | • Continue to offer support for academic and personal development, but wean student over later years to facilitate independence and maturity and progression to the workplace.<br>• Recognize the value of appraisal and link this to the development of workplace skills. |

**Figure 6.1**  Managing the transition

communication between the two is not always easy, there is scope for the common issue of transition to be taken on board and worked at by both post-16 and higher education.

# References

Baty, P (1997) 16–19 curriculum is 'misunderstood', *Times Higher Education Supplement*, 8 August

Cooke, A and Leckey, J (1999) Do expectations meet reality? A survey of changes in first-year student opinion, *Journal of Further and Higher Education*, **23**, pp 157–71

Deem, R and Ozga, J T (2000) Transforming post-compulsory education? Femocrats at work in the academy, *Women's Studies International Forum*, **23**, pp 153–66

Greenwood, M (2000) Delivering Curriculum 2000: the reformulated A/AS levels, *College Research*, **3** (3), Summer, p 28

Hodgson, A and Spours, K (1999) *Planning for the New 16–19 Qualifications Era: An Institute of Education and Essex LEA research and development project*, Institute of Education, London

Revell, P (2001) Generation exhausted, *Guardian*, 20 March

Smith, D and Bocock, J (1999) Participation and progression in mass higher education: policy and the FHE interface, *Journal of Educational Policy*, **14** (3), pp 283–99

Spours, K (1997) Issues of student retention: an initial study of staff perceptions, *Research in Post-Compulsory Education*, **2** (2), pp 109–19

Taylor, P G (2000) Changing expectations: preparing students for flexible learning, *International Journal for Academic Development*, **5** (2), pp 107–15

UCAS (2001) *Changes to Post-16 Qualifications: A briefing for higher education on changes to the post-16 curriculum in England, Wales and Northern Ireland*, UCAS, Cheltenham

Wolff, P and Sutcliffe, N (1999) GNVQ time bomb and NVQ depth charge, *New Academic*, Spring, pp 17–18

# Part 2

# Teaching for learning

# 7 Managing students' behaviour in the classroom

Lin Le Versha

*Brian: (Front of Curtain)* That's enough! (*Pause. Almost at once, louder*) I said enough! Another word and you'll be here until five o'clock. Nothing to me is it? I've got all the time in the world. (*Moves across without taking his eyes off them.*) I didn't even get to the end of the corridor before there was such a din all the other teachers started opening their doors as much as to say what the hell's going on there? SOMEBODY'S TALKING NOW! (*Pause, stares again like someone facing a mad dog.*) Who was that? You? You, Mister Man?… I did not *accuse* you, I *asked* you. Someone in the back row? (*Stares dumbly for a few seconds. Relaxes, moves a few steps. Shrugs.*) You're the losers, not me. Who's that? (*Turns on them again.*) Right – hands on heads! Come on, that includes you, put that comb away. Eyes front and sit up. All of you, sit up!

(Extract from Nichols, 1967)

Surely this dramatic monologue could never be delivered in a post-16 classroom? Not to students over the age of 16, in the 'post-compulsory' stage of their education, who are highly motivated, committed and enthusiastic in the study of their chosen programme and who present little of the challenging behaviour evident in secondary schoolchildren?

We must remember that only a summer holiday separates the schoolchild of Year 11 from the serious student in Year 12, and tutors in school sixth forms and colleges assume that, with no intervention whatsoever, those students have been magically transmogrified into independent, autonomous learners.

The reality is, of course, very different. Students may have rid themselves of the irritations of sitting in a classroom being forced to follow a subject prescribed by the National Curriculum but they have not yet acquired the skills that lie at the foundation of independent learning and their behaviour, particularly as inclusive learning and widening participation are embraced, may be as challenging as that in the secondary school classroom.

## Managing challenging behaviour

This is one of the areas that beginning teachers or newly qualified teachers (NQTs) ask to concentrate on most of all when starting work with new groups. Research from the school sector can provide some useful frameworks for approaching the issue. Rogers (1997) emphasizes that language is the primary tool in claiming control in the classroom and advocates a balancing act that could be presented as shown in Figure 7.1.

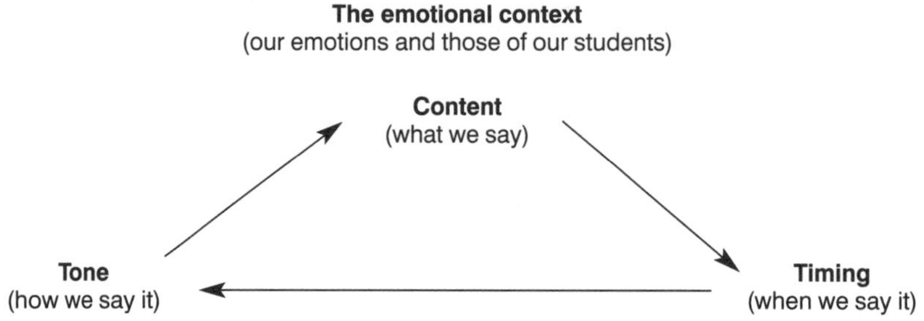

**Figure 7.1**   Language in claiming control in the classroom

Too often we see ourselves as the central and sole influence in the classroom, like a pebble dropped in a pool creating ripples that affect all in the classroom. Indeed this is one image used by Kounin (1970) of interaction in the classroom. We must, however, be aware of the group dynamics and the nature of the two-way relationships that exist between the tutor and each student in the room and the complex relationships between the students themselves.

We mistakenly take full responsibility for the students' behaviour; indeed we are accountable for it, and often react aggressively, leading to escalation instead of analysing the dynamics of the interrelationships in the group so that we can find a way to change them. We must be aware of our own emotional state as well as that of our students and consider carefully the way in which we communicate with the group of individuals before us.

Robertson (1989) expresses the view that it is the degree of our confidence in the classroom that has the greatest influence on the behaviour of our students. A confident teacher communicates to students that s/he has high expectations of them and develops the self-fulfilling prophecy that is so successful in so many groups. However confident the teacher, s/he must be aware that each group has its own identity and indeed a life that is relatively autonomous of his/her control or facilitation.

## Task  7.1

Make two lists of situations or circumstances that could have a positive and a negative effect on your performance as a teacher and decide whether they arise from factors inside the classroom or are generated outside (see Table 7.1).

**Table 7.1** Effects on your performance as a teacher

|  | Internal | External |
|---|---|---|
| *Positive*<br>Lessons with the group are timetabled mid-morning, which means that punctuality should not be a problem. |  | Yes. |
| *Negative*<br>Students crowd at the back of the room, making it difficult for you to set up group work or to communicate effectively with them. | Yes. |  |

Make a list of situations that could adversely affect a 16- to 19-year-old student's attitude to a particular lesson. Decide which of them you could change and which you are unable to affect (see Table 7.2).

**Table 7.2** Whether you can change situations that adversely affect lessons

| Situations that Adversely Affect Lessons | Change Them? |
|---|---|
| Three weeks of art exams take different students from your lessons each Wednesday. | Yes.<br>Negotiate with the art department to have all those students during their art lessons the week following their exam to catch up with the work they missed. |
| You are timetabled in a small room with a large group so learning activities are limited. | No.<br>Despite investigations you are unable to make a swap as all rooms are timetabled during that period. *But* you can ask your head of department to introduce a rota so that all tutors share the problem. |

Now make a list of the situations or experiences that could have a negative effect on the entire group and do not originate from your behaviour or the activities in your lesson.

Rogers (1997: 16) develops a model for classroom management based on prevention, support, consequences and corrective behaviour and presents this as a means to developing the motivated learner in a stable learning environment (see Figure 7.2).

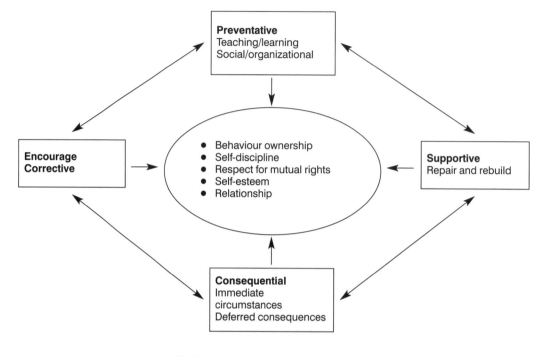

**Figure 7.2**  Model for classroom management (from Rogers, 1997)

## Prevention

In producing strategies for behaviour management that can be developed from this model we should start by considering prevention. The following can help to avoid time wasting and irritating confrontation:

- *Before the lesson*:
    - careful lesson planning;
    - appropriate organization of the furniture in the classroom;
    - ensuring that any technological aid actually works;
    - planned differentiation.
- *During the lesson*:
    - positive, purposeful start to the lesson;
    - the establishment of clear, fair, positive rules that are agreed with the group;
    - explicit and understood consequences for infringing rules or routines;
    - the development of routines;
    - awareness of group dynamics;
    - well-ordered finish to the lesson.

In many classrooms these expectations are implied rather than explicitly stated and this can lead to class management problems if the expectations are not understood by all. With some groups, such as those in tutorial sessions or following personal, social education programmes, it is worth while to develop a 'bill of rights and responsibilities' at the beginning of the sessions. The group can then agree, for example, that all will be given a hearing, sarcasm or put-downs will not be used and, although different views may not be accepted by all, the right of others to hold them will be respected.

In spending time negotiating such an explicit set of values the group will be able to explore the boundaries of acceptable behaviour and to take responsibility for it themselves. This does not mean that teachers can abdicate their responsibility but allows the students to assume responsibility for their own behaviour rather than relying solely on teachers to assume a policing or refereeing role.

## Task 7.2

Look at the two bills of rights below and discuss their relative strengths and weaknesses with a partner. Which will be the most effective in encouraging the class to take responsibility for its own actions? Are there non-negotiable rules or guidelines that you would include?

- *Bill of rights and responsibilities 1*
  We agree that:
  - All students in the class have the right to be heard.
  - Even though we may disagree with others' views, they have the right to be heard.
  - All ideas are acceptable.
  - The teacher is not always right.
  - Everyone must speak in every lesson.
  - Sarcastic comments are not allowed.
- *Bill of rights and responsibilities 2*
  We agree that:
  - All points of view are acceptable.
  - If someone is speaking everyone else listens.
  - There should be 100 per cent attention from everybody in the group all lesson.
  - Those who don't want to speak shouldn't be forced to.
  - In any disagreement the teacher should decide who is right.

In pairs consider the rights and responsibilities of any group learning together and produce your own 'bill of rights'.

If it is not appropriate for such a formal process to be undertaken, consider strategies for making your expectations explicit and accepted by your teaching groups.

Think of lessons that have resulted in less-than-perfect behaviour or outcomes. Using the grid (Table 7.3) analyse what went wrong, why it went wrong and what you could have done to prevent it.

**Table 7.3** Analysing outcomes

| Issue | Reason | Prevention |
|---|---|---|
| Students chatting. | Unable to find correct place on videotape. | Set up videotape before lesson and leave in correct place. |

## Correction

At times it is necessary to correct students' behaviour. This should be done with the least disruption to the session, taking account of the impact of language shown above. One of the first researchers into classroom management was Kounin who, in 1970, was stimulated to write his book after he had reprimanded a student for reading a newspaper in his class and was amazed by the 'ripple effect' of how the entire group was affected by this single exchange.

He coined the word 'with-it-ness' to describe the tutor who is aware of the subtle growth of disrupting behaviour and is able to intervene before it becomes an enormous issue. We all welcome the opportunity to be distracted from our work with the unexpected treat of watching a dramatic confrontation in which the beleaguered tutor is outsmarted by the wit of one of our peers.

When correcting behaviour:

- Consider what you say, and when and how you say it.
- Avoid sarcasm – it is an easy weapon to draw but a difficult one from which to re-establish the harmony in a classroom.
- Judge the seriousness of the offence and match the reprimand to it.
- Use a non-verbal cue to make your point.
- Avoid eye contact with the student who constantly seeks your attention.
- Maintain eye contact with a student to deter him/her from disruptive activity.
- Change your position during your input – you might stand behind students to improve their concentration or at the back of the room.
- Avoid aggressive hand gestures such as finger pointing.
- Use assertive eye contact and a gesture, such as pointing to a mobile phone, to convey the message that it should be put away.

On some occasions a simple reminder of the rules may be all that is needed: 'Please check that your mobile phones are switched off – this work is too important to be disturbed by phones.' Simple choices, and casual or direct questions can deflect serious confrontation, for example: 'James, would you like to put that phone away or' (smiling) 'shall I add it to my collection?' or 'James, in your essay you made an excellent point about the foreign policy of Henry VII; could you share it with the group?' or 'James, when did Henry VII come to the throne?'

Managing and correcting the behaviour of 16-plus students is a fine balance of achieving your goal while letting them avoid embarrassment or losing face in front of their friends. At all times you should preserve respect, and using a student's first name will help to do this. Never invade a student's personal space, grab personal property or touch a student unless it is a case of preserving health and safety.

When correcting behaviour, use a respectful but assertive tone of voice, avoiding aggression and emotion. Instead of taking on a student in front of his/her friends, it is often more effective to tackle the issue with the student after the lesson or even later in the day when time has been given to cool off. Many students find it difficult to take reprimands, or indeed praise, in front of a class. When discussing the incident it is important to separate the student from the behaviour and to be honest about your emotions. The student has seen that s/he has made you angry (indeed that may have been the main aim) so do not be afraid to admit it: 'James, your insistence on playing with your mobile phone throughout my lessons is making me extremely angry. I feel that your behaviour is rude and shows a lack of respect to me and to your group. This college has a "no mobiles in lesson" rule, which is written in the student diary and on the wall in every classroom. So I would be grateful if you would switch off your mobile phone when you come to my class and leave it in your bag rather than on the desk. How would you have felt if in our tutorial last week I kept checking my mobile for text messages instead of listening to you?'

It is at this point that many students will not defend behaviour that they know is unacceptable but they will try to divert the conversation away from their misdemeanour by bringing up a secondary issue such as: 'Mr Jones always lets us have our mobiles switched on in his lesson.' Do not be tempted to discuss the relative merits of Mr Jones's policy to mobile phones compared with yours or even whether in Mr Jones's lesson a mobile phone will not disturb the flow. Stick to the issue in your lesson and the solution that you and the student find acceptable.

Secondary issues take up a great deal of time in the dialogue of the classroom and successfully create a diversion from the task in hand, as this exchange with subtext illustrates:

*Teacher*: James, please put that mobile phone away.
(*How many times does that boy need telling?*)

*James*: But it's switched off, look.
(*How sad is she? Just finding an excuse to nag at someone – she's always picking on me.*)

*Teacher*: No phones on desks – you know that.
(*Why does he have to score points like this? He is always seeking attention.*)

*James*: But other teachers let me keep it on the desk without going on at me.
(*You are a failure compared with others who can keep control even when we use mobile phones.*)

*Teacher*: And which teachers are they then?
(*What do they think of me? Am I making a fuss? Should I let them?*)

The teacher is now trapped in a discussion of secondary issues, which will waste more time and give the student a larger platform from which to perform to the absorbed class. Making an explicit request for all phones to be turned off and put away at the beginning of the session or ignoring the phone until it provokes attention could have been wiser choices here.

## Task 7.3

Consider a classroom you have encountered, for example with a student who talks to her neighbour every time you address the group. Consider what you might say, when you might say it and the tone you might use, and note these in the three columns below (Table 7.4), moving from the least intrusive to the most interventionist.

**Table 7.4**  Content, timing and tone

| Content | Timing | Tone |
| --- | --- | --- |
| OK, everyone, look at this example on the board, please. | Wait for students to finish chatting. | Quiet and apologetic. |
| Right, everyone, pens down and look at the board – now, please. | Cutting across students chatting. | Assertive, stressing particular words. |
| Right, the next person to interrupt me will stand outside the principal's office for the rest of the day! | In one of the few silences between chats. | Shouting angrily. |

Consider the same process for an incident you have experienced in a classroom. It is useful to have a graded list of responses worked out so that you may deliver them in a controlled fashion rather than leaping to the disciplinary tactics typical of an oppressive regime immediately!

## Consequences

In post-16 education we are preparing students for independent study in higher education or for successful careers in the workplace. Employers have codes of conduct and grievance procedures that are strictly adhered to and schools and colleges have a responsibility to prepare students for that world.

Persistent absence or failure to complete work in employment would lead to specified warnings and then dismissal. In college or school sixth forms, students need to realize that if they break the rules certain consequences will follow. Individual circumstances may be taken into consideration but consequences should be well publicized and followed. Student codes of conduct, disciplinary procedures and appeals procedures are usually published in college charters, student diaries or handbooks so that transparency and their wide publication will lead to acceptance and understanding of the consequences of breaking the rules.

Students should:

- take responsibility for their behaviour and understand the consequences of their actions;
- know the rights and values behind the rules that exist for the good of the community and that create a feeling of mutual respect.

Rules should:

- preserve the dignity and rights of individuals;
- incorporate expectations of human rights;
- lead to a secure and safe educational environment.

Infringement of rules should:

- be treated fairly;
- be treated consistently;
- lead to well-publicized consequences.

Expectations in the classroom must be made clear or the 'actions lead to consequences' sequence will be muddled and difficult to enforce. Research shows (Doyle, 1986) that teachers introduce rules and procedures in the first days with a group. The most effective teachers integrated them into their classroom routines, while the less effective had vague rules and in the second and third weeks of teaching the students no longer adhered to them. Rogers (1991) noted that teachers who have 'unclear expectations' and 'poorly enforced rules' look passive and they are easily threatened by their students. Whatever the level of formality, one thing is always true – if we don't say what we expect then we get what we deserve!

## Task 7.4

Think of the problems you have with your classes or have observed in those of others. Perhaps the issues may be concerned with behaviour, punctuality or completion of work by the deadline set. Consider the consequences you would impose. How reasonable are they? (See Table 7.5.)

**Table 7.5**  Problems, consequences and reasonableness

| Problem | Your Reaction and Consequences for the Student | Reasonableness |
| --- | --- | --- |
| One student insists on chatting whenever you turn to the whiteboard. | Move the student to a new seat away from friends, which will make the student feel isolated and embarrassed. | Entirely reasonable, as the student was distracting others and slowing the pace of the lesson. |

## Support

After carrying through the consequences it is vital to re-establish a working relationship with the student once again. As in family behaviour, it is important to close the door on that particular incident and to start afresh without constant carping back and reference to it. Offer individual support to the student through a tutorial or simply reinforce good behaviour or a contribution to a lesson.

If the student persistently repeats the unacceptable behaviour, then ask for support from higher authorities in the school or college. A formal contract or plan may be negotiated with the student, which may include:

- handing in work on the deadline set;
- catching up with missing assignments according to an agreed schedule;
- setting short-term targets tied to realistic dates;
- involving parents if the student is in danger of being asked to leave school or college;
- making the consequences of not meeting the targets explicit.

If the conditions in the negotiated contract are not met, it is essential that the stated consequences are carried out.

This action is usually at the end of a series of misdemeanours and following several warnings. In the classroom, support is provided on a daily basis and in a less formal fashion. Teachers of younger children are often advised to 'spot them doing something right', as children respond to positive encouragement. Students in the 16- to 19-year-old age group are no different and they too appreciate recognition of their efforts. Too often we readily reprimand students for doing wrong and fail to congratulate them when they are working well. Positive reinforcement of the group and the individual in the lesson will lead to the development of high standards and increase motivation. Assignments returned to students swiftly with positive comments on how to improve performance will lead to students completing their work on time.

## Task 7.5

- Draw a seating plan for each of your groups and at the end of each lesson tick the names of students whom you have complimented or reinforced. Try to find something positive to say to each student each week.
- Consider your attitude and approach to classroom control. Using the list of student behaviour (Table 7.6), decide what you will do about it. Will you ignore it or make an issue of it? How will you take it on and what will you do as a consequence? Discuss this with another tutor and compare reactions.

**Table 7.6**  Student behaviour

| Student Behaviour | Action |
|---|---|
| Arrives late to lesson | |
| Always arrives late on Monday morning | |
| Never brings books or equipment | |
| Mumbles to friend when you are talking | |
| Falls asleep during lesson | |
| Refuses to follow instruction | |
| Text messaging below desk | |
| Interrupts you constantly | |
| Makes clever comments constantly | |
| Fails to hand in work on deadline | |
| Distracts other students who are working | |
| Swears constantly | |

## Classroom management checklist

- *Before the lesson*:
  - Is the organization of the room suited to the activity?
  - Is the classroom a learning environment with appropriate posters or student work displayed?
  - Is group work possible in the room?
  - Does your lesson have a clear, explicit learning objective?
- *During the lesson*:
  - Have you shared the learning objective with the students?
  - Do students understand what they should be doing or are they confused?
  - Are you aware of the atmosphere in the classroom and the body language of students?
  - Are they bored, attentive, holding private conversations?
  - Is poor punctuality or failure to hand in work challenged?
  - Who is in control, you or the students? Does this change at various stages in the lesson?
  - Are routines clear to everyone?

- How do students address the tutor and other students? Do they show respect?
- Is there a feeling of purposeful activity in the lesson?
- Are students using their time effectively?
- Are students encouraged to work collaboratively?
- Are all students challenged intellectually?
- Is questioning used constructively to manage the class?
- Do individual students sabotage the lesson through 'red herrings'?
- Are timings given for activities such as individual or group work?
- Are questions structured in a way that encourage students to listen to each other?
- Does the feedback include all students in the class?
- Is the lesson ended promptly and appropriately?
- Has the learning objective been achieved?

# References

Doyle, W (1986) Classroom organisation and management, in *Handbook of Research on Teaching*, ed M C Whitlock, 3rd edn, Macmillan, New York

Kounin, J (1970) *Discipline and Group Management in Classrooms*, Holt, Rinehart & Winston, New York

Nichols, P (1967) *A Day in the Death of Joe Egg*, Faber & Faber, London

Robertson, J (1989) *Effective Classroom Control*, 2nd edn, Hodder & Stoughton, London

Rogers, B (1991) *Dealing with Procrastination*, Topic 2, Issue 6, National Foundation for Educational Research, Slough

Rogers, B (1997) *The Language of Discipline*, 2nd edn, Northcote House, Plymouth

# 8 Planning lessons to reach all your students

Lin Le Versha

Teachers and teaching teams need to be effective in interpreting curriculum requirements in order to devise learning outcomes, programmes of study and assessment
strategies as well as adopting appropriate teaching and learning strategies.

(FENTO, 2001)

Imagine getting into your car one morning, starting the engine and just driving. The questions that follow are where? why? what for? Whenever we set off on any journey from the
long trek of a holiday to a short hop to the shops we make preparations and plan it. To ensure
that our students achieve their programme aims, we need to plan how they are to do it. We
need to plan exactly what we want them to learn and the activities they will undertake to
achieve that understanding. We also need to distinguish between our activity as tutors and
their participation as students. We have the examination specification, we know which
topics, books or areas we have to cover but how do we plan for students to cover the specification and achieve the learning necessary for them to pass their examinations?

How do we move from the examination specification…

## The AQA specification

Candidates should examine:

1. different explanations of crime, deviance, social order and social control;
2. the relationship between deviance, power and social control;
3. different explanations of the social distribution of crime and deviance by age, social class, ethnicity, gender and locality;
4. the social construction of, and societal reactions to, crime and deviance, including the role of the mass media;
5. the sociological issues arising from the study of suicide.

… to the scheme of work (Figure 8.1)…

**SOCIOLOGY DEPARTMENT SCHEME OF WORK**

| COURSE: SOCIOLOGY | MODULE/S: CRIME AND DEVIANCE | |
|---|---|---|
| LEVEL: A LEVEL (YEAR TWO) | BOARD: AQA | CODE |

| WEEK & TUTOR (Generic) | ROUTE THROUGH THE SPECIFICATION BY TOPIC or UNIT | LEARNING AND TEACHING ACTIVITIES (Highlighting Differentiation) | ASSIGNMENTS (Key Skills and Subject-Specific) | Educational Resources Used Type and Location |
|---|---|---|---|---|
| Wk 9–10 | Marxist theories - a description and evaluation: • traditional Marxism • neo-Marxism • corporate crime | • Tutor presentation of the theories • Small group work and mini-presentations • S Hall video on mugging • Group brainstorm and evaluation | SS: Complete activities in booklet (first half by week 10) SS: Complete activities in booklet (second half by week 11) | Marxist theory booklet S Hall video on mugging (OU) |

**Figure 8.1** Scheme of work

... to the individual lesson plan (Figure 8.2)?

**SOCIOLOGY DEPARTMENT LESSON PLAN**

| Unit | Crime and Deviance |
|------|--------------------|

| Date | 01/02/2002 |
|------|------------|

| Topics | **Theories of crime and deviance:** *Marxist approaches* **Study skills:** *Essay themes* **Synoptic linking to education section** |
|--------|---|

| Class | 6; SOB; A5 |
|-------|------------|

| Aims | 1. Consolidate student understanding of Marxist approaches. 2. Develop essay planning skills applying core studies. 3. Create awareness of strategies for approaching synoptic questions. |
|------|---|
| Objectives | Ensure that students: <br> • can recall, describe and evaluate Marxist approaches to crime and deviance (Aim 1); <br> • are familiar with some of the language, themes and range of A level questions (Aim 2); <br> • can apply appropriate research studies and perspectives to selected A level crime and deviance questions (Aim 2); <br> • are familiar with some of the major links between crime and deviance section and education using selected key concepts (Aim 3). |

| Sequence | Activities | | Resources |
|----------|-----------|---|-----------|
| | **Teacher** | **Student** | |
| **1** <br> 10 mins | Highlight aims and objectives of session. | Individual/pair work on worksheet. | Whiteboard. |
| 10 mins | Review previous session through management of student responses to summary activities. | Whole group debrief. | Theories template worksheet in Marxist booklet. |
| | **Directed questioning/allocation of evaluation tasks.** | **Level of difficulty of questions and tasks allocated.** | |
| **2** <br> 10 mins | Set the context for the activities (non-synoptic questions). | Individually grade questions in terms of difficulty. | Past question sheets. |
| 10 mins | Collate group's responses and negotiate selection of question(s) for analysis. | Apply allocated core study to the selected question using question template. | Whiteboard, question template. |
| | **Directed questioning/allocation of evaluation tasks.** | **Level of difficulty of questions and core studies allocated.** <br> **Additional exam questions and/or additional materials (if appropriate).** | |
| **3** <br> 10 mins | (Re)introduce idea of synoptic questions and linking sections. | Brainstorm potential concepts. | Whiteboard. |
| 10 mins | Focus on selected concepts: allocate pairs and tasks. | Pairs to complete knowledge application exercises. | Synoptic question template. |
| | **Directed questioning/allocation of evaluation tasks.** | **Level of difficulty of questions and concepts allocated.** | |

**Bold** = differentiation strategy

**Figure 8.2**   Lesson plan

'ion specification will provide an outline of the content of a course and its
.ssessment. Tutors, as part of a team or subject department, will be expected to
.oute to the development of a scheme of work and to undertake individual lesson
.anning themselves.

The scheme of work may be structured according to a prescribed format produced by the college or school. In it the sequence of delivering the specification will be evident and each area to be taught will be broken down into content, method, resources, time-scale and assessment. The lesson plan may also be structured according to a prescribed format but it should include the context of the session, the learning objective(s), a brief summary of the activities that will be undertaken, the resources that are to be used and any follow-up work or assessment that will be made.

# Planning the lesson

Clark and Yinger (1987) provide three reasons for planning lessons. Tutors need to walk into the classroom with confidence so planning meets their immediate personal needs; secondly, planning is a means of organizing the time and activity in the classroom; and finally, it is a way to prompt tutors and to provide a framework during the lesson. The content of the plan depends on the tutor's relationship with the class and the topic to be taught.

Minton (1991, quoted in Armitage *et al*, 1999: 77) produced a planning framework that uses control as its organizing concept, while Forsyth, Joliffe and Stevens (1999) explored the way in which a desired activity determines the methodology and the resources to be used. Following their thinking the tutor could consider the framework in Table 8.1 as a way of approaching planning.

In exploring the variety of appropriate learning activities expected in the FENTO standards the tutor has many from which to choose including:

- lead lectures;
- short presentations;
- class discussions or question-and-answer sessions;
- seminars;
- group work;
- brainstorming;
- problem-solving teams;
- research groups;
- role plays;
- visits and field trips;
- individual tutorials;
- individual research.

The selection of the appropriate activity will depend on the relationship with the class, the confidence of the tutor and the learning objective, taking into account the learning styles of the students and the desired outcome and method of assessment.

**Table 8.1** Framework as a way of approaching planning

| Level of Control | Activity | Methodology | Resources |
|---|---|---|---|
| Tutor has strong control. | Providing instruction, information giving, introducing a topic, demonstrating a process. | Whole-class teaching.<br><br>Students work individually.<br><br>Students respond to directed closed questions. | OHP.<br><br>Handouts.<br><br>Workbooks.<br><br>PowerPoint presentation.<br><br>Whiteboard.<br><br>Practical equipment. |
| Tutor has less control. | Explore an issue, share an experience. | Discussion with closed and open questions leading to debate.<br><br>Share an audio or visual presentation.<br><br>Watch a video.<br><br>Study a text.<br><br>Seminar or tutorial. | Prompt sheets with questions for individual or pair work.<br><br>Posters.<br><br>Slides.<br><br>Video.<br><br>Texts. |
| Shared control. | Work through examples, provide direct experience. | Small group work.<br><br>Practical work.<br><br>Simulation, games or role play.<br><br>Resource-based learning.<br><br>Visits. | Practical equipment.<br><br>Worksheets or agendas for discussion.<br><br>Access to computers and learning resources. |
| Student control. | Learners apply their learning through research, distance learning and real-life experience. | Assignments.<br><br>Research projects.<br><br>Workshops.<br><br>Work experience. | Briefing sheets.<br><br>Notes.<br><br>Diaries.<br><br>Logbooks.<br><br>Planning sheets. |

## Task 8.1

Consider a topic that you intend to teach. Construct a grid like the one in Table 8.1 to show how you will teach it, the level of control you anticipate, the activities you will undertake and the resources you will need. An example is given in Table 8.2.

**Table 8.2**  Topic: Effects of planning regulations on a locality

| Level of Control | Activity | Methodology | Resources |
|---|---|---|---|
| Strong. | Tutor input on regulations. | Whole-class teaching. | Interactive whiteboard and PowerPoint presentation. |
| Shared. | Role-play interest groups to explore a local planning application. | Small groups of three or four students. | Worksheets defining task and outcomes. Role descriptions. OHP slides for groups to prepare for presentations. |

# Learning objectives

There are two types of learning objectives, those that aim to change behaviour and those that aim to develop cognition (Cohen and Manion, 1989). In developing behavioural objectives the tutor needs to specify who is to perform the behaviour, and give a clear description of that behaviour, the conditions under which the behaviour is to be performed and the standard for success or failure. These objectives are appropriate when teaching students skills that can be demonstrated easily and provide clear, achievable and measurable targets.

For example, in a PE lesson the tutor may have one of the following as the objective for a lesson: to learn the rules of badminton and to demonstrate their use in scoring a game; to demonstrate three ball-passing skills in basketball. In drama the objectives might be: to write, rehearse and perform a dramatic monologue; to develop and use a Liverpudlian accent in a performance of an extract from Willy Russell's *Educating Rita*.

Cognitive objectives are more flexible and are linked to broader learning experiences. They are used when developing learning and understanding. For example, in English literature such learning objectives might be: to develop an understanding of the effect of different types of imagery in *Othello*; to understand the theme of appearance and reality in *A Room with a View* by E M Forster.

Business studies tutors might plan for their students: to research three theories of motivation and to understand their impact on organizational management; to appreciate the influence of ethics in decision making in a company.

A learning objective is a 'clear statement of instructional intent written in any form as long as it clarifies the intent' (Forsyth, Joliffe and Stevens, 1999). They add that the objective should say something about the learner, be concerned with ends rather than means and define what the learner should be able to do and to what level. The need for sharp, clear learning objectives is an obvious starting point for all lesson plans if the tutor is to be able to evaluate how successful the lesson was in achieving the learning objectives set.

Learning objectives should be explicit and shared with students. They need to know the destination of the journey you are taking together. Jenson (1996) states that the visual reinforcement of key learning points through posters or key words placed at or above eye level improves long-term recall by 90 per cent. In one school all tutors are expected to write their learning objective(s) on the top left-hand side of the whiteboard. When students look up at the board they automatically look at the top left of the board so they are reminded of the objective for the lesson. It also reminds the tutor to keep on track! At the end of the lesson the tutor asks the students if the objectives have been met as a way of evaluating success. Those who feel that they have achieved the desired level of understanding share it with other students thus reinforcing and synthesizing the learning.

Smith (1996, 1998) in his work on accelerated learning emphasizes the notion of connecting the learning for students. The learning objectives need to be put into context so that students understand how a particular lesson relates to the previous session and where it fits into the overall scheme of work. They must be aware of the relevance of this short-term objective to the long term and understand the benefit of the lesson to them. He also emphasizes that the outcomes should be specified at this stage in language that all the students will understand and that differentiation should be evident.

## Task 8.2

For the topic you have planned above, write the learning objectives for two or three lessons, specifying the learning outcomes and the way in which you will explain them to your students. You might find it helpful to consider sentences that begin 'At the end of this lesson you should be able to...'

## Checklist on learning objectives

- *Before the lesson*:
  - Will your objective develop the students' behaviour or their understanding?
  - Is the learning objective clear?
  - Can its outcomes be evaluated or measured?
  - Do you have the necessary resources to achieve your objectives?

- *During the lesson*:
  - Is the learning objective shared with the students?
  - Is the objective put into context?
  - Does the learning objective build on their prior knowledge and understanding?
  - Do students understand what they are doing?
  - Do they know why they are doing it?
  - How does the objective fit into the bigger picture?
  - Have you planned sufficient time to achieve the objective?
  - How far is the objective achieved?
  - Who evaluates it, you or the students?
  - How will this evaluation affect your next lesson?

# Differentiation

In the 16–19 classroom the students will be self-selected on programmes of study that will provide progression to further education, higher education or employment. For most level 3 Advanced programmes they will be accepted on to the course only after achieving the entry requirements at Intermediate level. This should mean that the range of ability before the tutor is much narrower than that in a mixed-ability group in a Year 9 class in a comprehensive school, for example. The students will still differ in ability, motivation and commitment. There will be students with different preferred learning styles in the room and those requiring additional support for specific learning needs or difficulties. It is at the lesson-planning stage that these individual differences should be taken into account and provision made for them.

Differentiation plays a role in improving achievement and motivation in individual students according to Pollard and Triggs (1997), and the work of Martinez (1997, 2000) shows that if student motivation is improved or maintained then retention and achievement rates increase.

When we plan for differentiation in the classroom we are attempting to meet the individual needs of each student while providing a challenging learning experience for all students in the class. Many pro formas for planning lessons issued by colleges and schools include an assumption that differentiation is part of the plan and provide a section for it.

Examples of differentiation observed in lessons might include:

- accepting different responses to questions from students of different abilities;
- asking students different types of questions;
- using different vocabulary;
- allowing students to take different times to complete a task;
- using different materials for different students;
- expecting students to complete different amounts of work;
- giving students different levels of support;

- using different criteria to assess students' success in achieving the task;
- giving all students the same task but accepting different outcomes from them.

The most common forms of differentiation are by task and outcome. The former is evident in the classroom in the interaction between tutor and student while the latter is part of the assessment process once the task has been completed. The process of differentiation assumes that the tutor has some way of analysing student ability in the subject. Data on GCSE performance, value-added scores and special needs such as dyslexia are all available and can be used to provide information on the previous performance of students. Some subject departments administer diagnostic tests so that support may be given to individuals who need it – for example, a business studies student may be happy with the numerical demands of the subject but less confident in structuring an essay. This information may provide the tutor with an immediate strategy when it comes to differentiation in class but must be handled sensitively as 16- to 19-year-olds are not enthusiastic about being identified as different to their peers.

*Differentiation by outcome* has the advantage that students are not made aware of being treated differently in any way in the lesson. They all have the same opportunity to attempt the task and avoid being labelled. If working in groups or in pairs, students support one another in completion of the task. Tutors do not have to provide a range of materials or tasks, or make unsound judgements on student abilities that, when made explicit, could become self-fulfilling prophecies. The tasks, however, tend to be more open-ended and, as they are carefully designed to accommodate all levels of ability starting with the weakest student, the more able students may find the task insufficiently demanding.

*Differentiation by task* is advantageous for the brightest students as they can be challenged and stimulated to achieve, while those at the other end of the ability range are also motivated by a task at which they can succeed. As mentioned above, this form of differentiation has the problem of labelling students and leads to fixed expectations of student performance once they have been established.

In VCE the coursework is differentiated in the design stage. Students can choose whether to follow the assignment brief to the level that *they* wish, selecting E, C or A criteria.

## So how could you approach differentiation in the classroom?

Worksheets can be produced with sections that increase in difficulty so the more able student covers more ground and moves on to more difficult subject matter and tasks or extension material. All students can be given the opportunity to finish this in private study time so that all have equal opportunities.

When covering different topics or different areas of the syllabus students who appear to be high achievers in one area may need additional support in another. Carefully structured workbooks could offer a solution here. They could include sections that all students must cover as a basic requirement and then a variety of different activities, covering a range of learning styles, as optional sections that could be pursued by those who wish to develop their knowledge and understanding further.

Offering students the opportunity to volunteer for particular areas of research will often lead to students 'self-differentiating', with the more able students choosing the more challenging abstract area while the less able select the more factual.

Grouping students according to understanding is an obvious strategy with peer tutoring as a feature. One way of evaluating a session is to ask students to write down areas or topics that they could explain to others and those on which they would appreciate further explanation. Pairing students who can 'teach' a topic to those who need it explained again not only enables 'student teachers' to synthesize their knowledge and understanding but offers 'students' the possibility of having the areas taught in their own language rather than that of the class tutor, thus improving their understanding.

## Task 8.3

- Think of a topic and write a list of differentiated questions that you might ask five students in your class – ranging from the student who is having problems in the area to the most confident. Pay particular attention to the vocabulary you use.
- Design a worksheet that incorporates the opportunity for differentiation in your lesson.
- Plan a lesson that covers a variety of activities to suit different learning styles in your class – consider those who prefer to reflect on their learning, those who are active learners and those who prefer drawing or speaking to writing, for example.

---

## Differentiation checklist

- *Before the lesson*:
  - How aware are you of the different ability levels in the class?
  - Do you know which students are receiving individual support from study skills or learning support units?
- *During the lesson*:
  - Are more able students challenged and extended?
  - Is questioning appropriately directed?
  - How do you react to different types of student response?
  - Do all students feel valued in the class?
  - Is support available for students experiencing difficulty?

---

## *Differentiation for boys*

The introduction of Curriculum 2000 has continued to stimulate the debate in the media on the improvement in girls' performance compared with that of boys (*TES*, 23 August 2002). Sukhnandan (1999) points out that it is the dramatic increase in the achievement of girls that accounts for the difference in attainment. There is a growing body of research of this trend in schools, which suggests that there are strong local effects underlying educational performance and suggests the following action:

- *At institutional level*:
  - Open the debate with parents, governors, students and tutors.
  - Monitor trends of achievement and performance in the school or college and by subject.
  - Look for evidence of prejudicial beliefs in policies and practices.
  - Challenge stereotypical thinking ('boys are more difficult', 'girls work harder').
  - Explore and develop boys' and girls' different approaches to learning.

## Task 8.4

Consider your own school or college experience. Were boys and girls treated differently? Were you aware of different policies or practices that encouraged this difference? In your experience did boys and girls exhibit different learning styles?

- *In the classroom*:
  Evidence from case studies on performance (Arnot *et al*, 1998; Black and William, 1998) and from the practical experience of tutors suggests that there are strategies that can be employed in the classroom to support underachievers, especially boys:
  - Offer clear targets for each lesson that are shared with students.
  - Explain the purpose of the session and what is in it for them.
  - Make outcomes clear.
  - Give information in bite-size chunks.
  - Organize tasks in small, logical steps.
  - Include a variety of activities in the lesson.
  - Make tasks time-bonded and measurable.
  - Give five steps for all activities: five solutions and then select one, five paragraphs, five points.
  - Challenge students by the task rather than completion of the task ('I bet you can't find five reasons for the change in foreign policy').
  - Provide opportunities for active work, group work and practical work.
  - Offer more discussion and role-play.
  - Mix boys and girls together in group work.
  - Devise tasks that incorporate different styles of writing.
  - Give praise and criticism in private, not in front of the group.
  - Respond positively to changes in behaviour or performance.
  - Provide plenty of positive feedback with specific advice on how to improve work.
  - Set assignments that are clear, with suggestions for length, format and style.
  - Set short deadlines for assignments.
  - Break up large pieces of coursework into sections so that you are able to check on progress and offer support.
  - Provide models or frameworks for writing or assignments.
  - Show students previous examples of good assignments.

- Mark and return assignments quickly.
- Provide concrete advice on how to improve a piece of work.

## Task 8.5

Using the list above look at one of your lesson plans and consider the adaptations you might make to improve the learning of boys in your group.

Those in schools and colleges where efforts have been made to develop strategies to improve boys' learning claim that all they have done is to develop good practice. Indeed it is evident that strategies that encourage boys to learn are exactly the same approaches that improve girls' performance. The solution appears to be in planning lessons for the students in front of you – such an obvious point that it seems absurd! Yet the tutors who incorporate a variety of activities to appeal to the individual learning styles of their students, provide opportunities for differentiation and have clear objectives certainly seem to be successful.

# References

Armitage, A *et al* (1999) *Teaching and Training in Post-Compulsory Education*, Open University Press, Buckingham

Arnot, M *et al* (1998) *Recent Research on Gender and Educational Performance*, OFSTED Reviews of Research Series, Stationery Office, Norwich

Black, P and William, D (1998) *Inside the Black Box*, King's College School of Education, London

Clark, C M and Yinger, R J (1987) Teacher planning, in *Exploring Teachers' Thinking*, ed J Calderhead, Cassell, London

Cohen, L and Manion, L (1989) *Research Methods in Education*, Routledge, London

FENTO (2001) *Standards for Teaching and Supporting Learning in England and Wales*, www.fento.ac.uk

Forsyth, I, Joliffe, A and Stevens, D (1999) *Preparing a Course*, 2nd edn, Kogan Page, London

Jenson, E (1996) *Completing the Puzzle: A brain-based approach to learning*, Turning Point, San Diego, CA

Martinez, P (1997) *Improving Student Retention: A guide to successful strategies*, FEDA, London

Martinez, P (2000) *Raising Achievement: A guide to successful strategies*, FEDA, London

Minton, D (1991) *Teaching Skills in Further and Adult Education*, City & Guilds/Macmillan, Basingstoke

Pollard, A and Triggs, P (1997) *Reflective Teaching in Secondary Education*, Cassell, London

Smith, A (1996) *Accelerated Learning in the Classroom*, Network Education Press, Stafford

Smith, A (1998) *Accelerated Learning in Practice*, Network Educational Press, Stafford

Sukhnandan, L (1999) *An Investigation into Gender Differences in Achievement, Phase 1*, NFER, Slough

# 9 Using questions and group work effectively

Lin Le Versha

## Questions

Socrates understood the value of sharp questioning in developing learning and higher-level thought and a large part of many lessons will be spent on 'Q and A'. Strategic use of questions in the classroom can provide the best examples of learning and play a vital part in classroom management. Poorly used, however, they can result in dull lessons, where a few students dominate in a teacher-led quiz.

Questions increase motivation and the development of concepts if they are intriguing and thought-provoking, and require a student to reflect. Robertson (1989) pointed out, however, that they can create problems in classroom management if they require lengthy answers and allow other students to drift away from the interchange between the tutor and an individual student. It is quite a balancing act to give attention to an individual while keeping control of the rest of the group.

Cullen (1998) emphasizes that questions play a major role in developing what he calls 'communicative' student–teacher interaction, which leads to learning. It is the development of purposeful, challenging questions that are at the centre of this process. Tabberer (1995), however, notes that only 2 per cent of the time in the classroom is spent on challenging questions. It would seem then that consideration of questioning techniques as a means to develop learning is essential.

### Directed questions

Good and Brophy (1997) explore the way in which some students will monopolize small group discussion just as they dominate whole-class activities, while Good's Model of Student Passivity (1993) highlights the role of the tutor in reinforcing this through poor questioning techniques. Teachers direct fewer questions at less able students and, when they do, they wait for much less time for a response from them than they do from the brighter students. Link this to Jacobs's research (1999), which indicated that tutors allow only 0.7 second for students to answer questions addressed directly to them, and we see that students whatever their ability have to be remarkably quick off the mark if they are to respond to directed questions before the tutor moves on.

When asking questions of passive students, tutors also provide the answers rather than waiting for a response and they show a tendency to criticize failure readily while withholding praise. As these students rely primarily on tutors to structure their learning and behaviour, it is essential that tutors should employ questions appropriately to involve these students in the learning process.

The use of directed questions that are differentiated according to student ability is one strategy to ensure that all are included in the lesson and the learning experience. This questioning is usually directed to individual students but it may also be directed to a sub-group in the class. For example, if a particular group of students has not been participating then the question may be asked of 'that group by the window' or 'girls'. Such approaches ensure that all students feel included in the lesson and the learning experience.

## Task 9.1

Ask someone to observe a lesson and using a plan of the class (as shown in Figure 9.1) ask him/her to mark each time you direct a question to a particular student. Analysis of the diagrams after the lesson will enable you to reflect on whom you include and whom you ignore. Do you show a preference for males or females, or address one side or area of the room? Do your questions encourage a few students who you assume know the answers to dominate the lesson while the less able are passive?

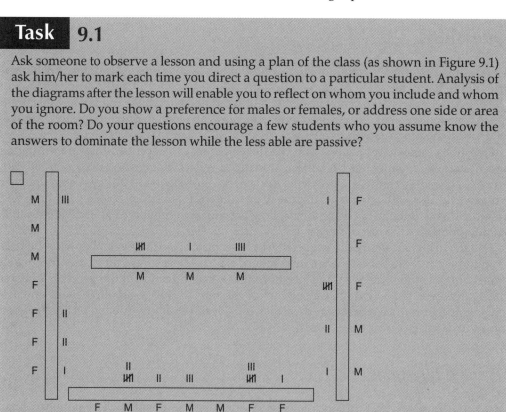

Figure 9.1  Class plan

## Open and closed questions

At the most basic level, questions can be categorized into open and closed questions. A closed question is usually factual and has only one answer so gives the student no room for expressing a personal view or opinion:

- Who killed Hamlet's father?
- What is the map reference for Ipswich?
- Did Henry VIII execute Katherine Parr?

Such questions can increase the pace of a lesson, provide a swift recap at the beginning of the lesson or involve a student who is drifting off or distracting others.

Open questions are the questions that can lead to higher-level thought, that require reflection, personal comment and analysis. They are also by their nature unpredictable so you must be able to respond to the answer your question provokes:

- What were Hamlet's feelings about his father's death?
- Having seen the video on the developments in Ipswich, what do you think of them?
- Do you think Henry VIII was a cruel king?

Such questions, for which there is no right answer, can create the foundation for debates, explore cause and effect, and allow students to think creatively, leap into speculation and produce hypotheses. They are, however, time-consuming and difficult to evaluate so many teachers avoid them.

## Questions to avoid

Beware the use of the 'false' open question. 'What is the poet saying about love here?' provokes a response that the student feels is valid. If the tutor replies, 'Yes, but don't you think…?' or 'Anyone else?', then the real question the tutor is asking is 'What do I think that the poet is saying about love?' or 'Please will you read my mind?' Students recognize this type of question and will become passive, leaving the response to the student who appears to be on the same wavelength as the teacher.

Questions that appear to bully or nag the students can produce resentment or lack of interest. The desperate tone of 'Oh, come on, you all know the answer to this' or 'Now add a little more' do not provoke thought but emphasize the problems the tutor has in stimulating a discussion or getting the group to remember something the tutor thinks s/he has taught them.

The use of questions asking students to guess may also be considered a waste of time by students. They know that they do not know the answer as you have not given them the information. Although they may be used occasionally to start discussion, guessing questions should be avoided.

## A range of questions

Frameworks for evaluating or using questions in class have been developed by Brown and Edmonson (1984), Good (1993) and Pollard and Triggs (1997), who suggest that if a framework is understood then more effective learning follows. To check on learning, to provoke discussion and to challenge students, an appropriate question may be considered from the list in Table 9.1. Directed questions that are differentiated will involve all students.

As questions play such a central role in the learning process it is a good idea to incorporate them into your lesson planning. Short, factual questions to test knowledge may be followed by more demanding, challenging questions that will provoke students to higher-level thinking and discussion. To ensure that you elicit the response you want it is important to frame the questions appropriately, and time spent producing a list of them is an excellent investment.

## Task 9.2

Consider a topic that you teach. Write a list of questions that could test knowledge, check on learning and challenge your students. Answer the questions yourself and see if they really elicit the response you want.

**Table 9.1** Appropriate questions

| Closed/ Specific | Asking for a particular answer. | When was the first atomic bomb deployed? |
|---|---|---|
| | To recap or check learning. | What is an atomic bomb? |
| | To develop understanding and to make links with previous learning. | How does an atom bomb work? Who invented it? What effects does it have on the environment? |
| | To place the topic in a context and promote discussion of cause and effect. | What led up to the bomb being dropped? What happened as a result? |
| Open/ Challenging | To push students beyond the facts. | Can the use of an atomic bomb ever be justified? Could you justify its use in a 'just' war? |
| | To consider attitudes and to construct arguments to support a point of view. | You live in the USA: how would you support its use? As a Japanese student, how would you argue against its use? |
| | To challenge students to think analytically and creatively. | What alternative strategies can you think of that might have led to victory for the USA? |

## Questions checklist

- *Before the lesson*:
  - Have you planned the questions you will ask and their purpose?
  - Have you considered to whom you will address particular questions and the vocabulary you will use?
- *During the lesson*:
  - Are open and closed questions used appropriately?
  - Are questions clear and do they address only one issue?
  - Are questions addressed to the class or directed to individuals or sub-groups within the class?
  - Do the same students always answer and dominate the lesson?
  - Are students addressed personally?
  - Are questions differentiated? Are easier questions asked of the less able?
  - Do you wait for students to answer or do you answer your own questions?
  - Do you ask supplementary questions to challenge students?
  - Do you respect the answers and opinions that students give?
  - How do you respond to incorrect, irrelevant or negative contributions?

# Group work

What I hear, I cannot remember
What I see, I do remember
What I do, I understand.
(Chinese proverb)

It is often in small groups that the opportunity is provided for the higher-level, challenging questions to be explored and learning to take place. It offers students the opportunity for active learning and involves all students, even the most passive or shy. Group work can become a means of developing peer tutoring and enables students to share different views of the area of learning. Within a group, students can evaluate their learning, synthesize their knowledge and explore the area creatively. They are also able to develop their key skills of communication and working with others. This point is emphasized by Petty (1998: 193) who argues that 'research, especially from the USA, shows that well managed group work greatly increases attention to task and develops subject specific as well as vital communication skills'. He goes on to argue that poorly managed group work that does not incorporate effective monitoring and demanding feedback may go off task and become dominated by particular students while permitting others to become passengers.

It is the development of higher-order cognitive skills that provide the 'buzz' for so many A level tutors along with the excitement and enthusiasm of students who begin to make intellectual sense of the subject for themselves. It is the personal ownership of learning that is typical of the high-achieving A level student and it depends on the development of individual learning.

Research with A level English literature students by Le Versha (1990) suggested that developing the student's individual understanding and making it explicit, through the use of heuristics, led to higher standards of written work incorporating well-developed arguments and sophisticated analysis. Her work, based on the personal construct theory of Kelly (1955, 1966), built on the notion that we all construct personal views of the world, the subject or the topic. We can change our construct and we can share our construct with others.

It is through discussion that we can become aware of others' constructs and either strengthen or adapt our own. Tutor-dominated sessions, where the tutor's construct of the play, the theory or the attitude dominates the lesson, may well equip students to answer A level questions competently, as they reproduce the tutor's carefully considered construct, but do little to challenge students intellectually or encourage them to take intellectual ownership of the subject. A lesson where the tutor dominates may be represented as in Figure 9.2.

- 1 The tutor introduces the topic and the main points that should be developed.
  A The student, with his/her own construct of the topic listens to see how the tutor's views fit in with his/her own.
- 2 The tutor continues to explain his/her construct emphasizing the points that the students should remember.
  B The student realizes that his/her construct is 'wrong' so adapts it and begins to accept that of the tutor.
- 3 The tutor continues to expound his/her view.
  C The student adapts his/her construct so that it is in line with that of the tutor.

Research on conformity may not be known by all A level students but many are certainly aware of the feeling of cognitive dissonance evoked by holding different views to those of the authority figure in the classroom. Within a small group with carefully structured activities, students have the opportunity to describe their construct, to develop or even adapt it, but they are more likely to disagree and stick with their view in a group of their peers than they are in a didactic session dominated by the tutor.

Bligh (1998) surveyed research evidence on different forms of teaching and concluded that discussion was more effective than a didactic approach for stimulating thought, for personal and social adjustment and for changes of attitude. Luker (in Brown and Atkins, 1988) explores student and tutor likes and dislikes about group work. Students like having

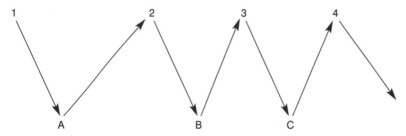

**Figure 9.2** Tutor-dominated lesson

influence over what is discussed, finding out others' ideas and the way group work helps them to develop their analytical skills so that they arrive at solutions. Tutors like the informal atmosphere, getting to know the student individually and the way in which students are able to grasp an idea for the first time, but dislike getting the discussion going, the potential loss of authority and the need to keep quiet and let the students speak. Brown and Atkins (1988) concur with this and report research that the time tutors spend talking in student–tutor discussion is 64 per cent but could be as high as 86 per cent!

Figure 9.3 shows that the highest rate of retention is linked to active learning. Discussions, practical sessions and the process of teaching others are all means of reinforcing learning. Too often our lessons push students to the top of the triangle where they remain passively. Didactic teaching has a crucial part to play in developing students' learning but it needs to be supported by other activities if students are to retain the knowledge and understanding we have worked so hard to teach them.

It is the development of metacognition or higher-level learning, which can be developed through group work, that Biggs (1999: 52) found exciting: 'such learning is an integral part of a well-run group. Group learning gives students practice in thinking and explaining; it exposes them to multiple viewpoints, which helps them to make connections among concepts and ideas; it provides opportunities for "scaffolding" (students supporting each other's learning); it often results in students teaching each other.'

Group work requires careful planning and management if it is to support learning and all students are to be involved in the process. Discussion of some well-known research into the way management teams function may be of help in supporting planning for the 16–19 classroom. The work of Belbin (1981) and Tuckman (1965) is the basis of many management courses to develop an awareness of the ways in which groups function. When groups are

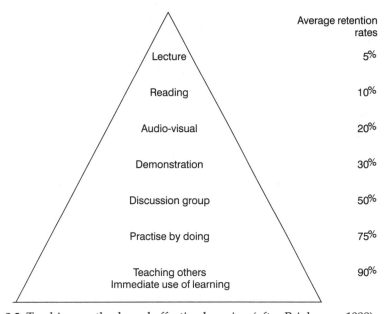

**Figure 9.3** Teaching methods and effective learning (after Brighouse, 1989)

set to work in a classroom the strategies to manage them in their learning are similar to those employed by managers in the workplace.

## Working in teams

Belbin explored the role people play when they are part of a team and the characteristics that make up the best teams. He immediately discovered the Apollo syndrome: that the brightest group does not always prove to be the best. He describes eight roles that are needed for the fully effective team. Obviously it is not always possible to produce the 'dream team' but Belbin noted that too many of the same roles in a group create a lack of balance while too few of his roles mean that the job may not get completed.

Groups of eight are often not desirable in the classroom, so in smaller groups each person will perform more than one role. The tutor needs to be aware of the make-up of groups and the roles that students play in them. If they are not given roles, do students always play the same roles in group work? Do they play different roles in different groups? What is the effect on the group of changing the role a student plays?

Having taken into account the roles students play the tutor needs to understand the organic development of groups. Tuckman's work traces the stages of development of groups in four stages:

- *forming*: a group of individuals define their task and their role in the process;
- *storming*: a conflict stage where purpose, leadership and other norms are challenged, often leading to a more realistic approach to the task;
- *norming*: the group develops a way of working together and roles are accepted;
- *performing*: only at this stage will the group be productive.

This process of maturity lasts for different periods of time depending on the group's commitment to the objectives. In some cases the first three periods appear to take no time at all and the group functions effectively immediately. Sometimes the storming process is not explicit and leads to disruptive behaviour on apparently unrelated issues that subvert the performance stage.

## Task 9.3

Consider groups in which you have been a member and apply Belbin's and Tuckman's theories to the experience. What was your role? Did you play more than one? Did you play different roles in different groups? How long did the group take to go through the first three stages and actually produce a result?

## Setting up groups

In the classroom, understanding of these issues can make managing group work more profitable. Ascribing roles or leaving them to be developed by the groups is an important decision and depends on the routines established in the classroom. Are students used to working in groups? Do they always work in the same groups? Are the groups organized by the students or the tutor?

- *Roles.* Roles that are easy to allocate and will be readily understood by the group are:
  - chairperson;
  - secretary;
  - timekeeper.

  Additional members of the team could be nominated to provide feedback following group work or this could be part of the role descriptions above.
- *Space.* In setting up groups it is important to ensure that the space is appropriate. Groups of three or four students sitting in a row are not likely to interact and the students at the end will be excluded. Move students and furniture so that they work around a table or they are in a circle.
- *Self-selecting.* Self-selecting groups based on friendship or their seating in the room will exploit well-established relationships and roles so may lead to more efficient use of time. They may also lead to distracting conversations and the formation of cliques.
- *Tutor selection.* Allocating numbers 1–4 or four roles from a novel, historical situation or chemical reaction to students around the class and then grouping the 1s, 2s, 3s and 4s together or the roles will ensure a social mix, which may also mean that groups are mixed ability and mixed gender.
- *Organic development.* Groups can also be developed organically. Individual thoughts on a topic are noted down and then shared with a neighbour. This pair then joins another pair to develop a group that produces the 'best' solution to a problem.
- *Expert groups.* Ask groups of four or five to explore specific questions, with each student taking responsibility for one of them. After the set time reorganize the groups so that all the students responsible for question 1 join up, those with the response to question 2 and so on. This way extensive interaction leads to detailed and deep discussion on particular topics and produces a consensus of the best views for the group.
- *Similarities or differences.* Predetermined groups based upon the tutor's observation of the roles students play in class, particularly mixing the introvert and extrovert elements, are also useful in achieving different outcomes. In a geography lesson, grouping students from similar areas of the locality provides an informed, detailed discussion of local geography, while music students who study different instruments may benefit from working together on composition techniques.

## Ideas for group work

- *Discussion groups.* The most common use of group work is to take a topic, issue or text being discussed and to produce a set of answers to specific questions with all groups following the same task or the allocation of a particular question for each group.
- *Experts.* Groups may be given completely different topics or subjects and they will work over a longer period to become 'experts'. Their work can then be part of a presentation to the class or a set of notes for the rest of the class, or the students can be a brains trust responding to questions by the class.

- *Setting assignments.* Having researched an area a group might be asked to produce the title of an assignment or a list of questions that a second group will answer using the research notes provided by the first group.
- *Other sides of the argument.* Groups could be asked to analyse the same situation from opposing viewpoints, to look at the points for and against a particular strategy, to undertake a SWOT analysis and explore the strengths, weaknesses, opportunities and threats of a situation or to brainstorm a problem creatively.
- *Visualizers.* Students with a preference for a visual approach to their learning might produce a poster, a storyboard or a brain map. These could lead to presentations or exciting wall displays.
- *Pyramids.* Packs of cards on which are written relevant words or ideas can be put into sequence or order of priority or constructed into a pyramid with the top idea at the apex and the less important forming the base.
- *Sorting.* Lists of ideas or words can be sorted into piles and the rationale as well as the composition of each pile explained, or they can be paired, again with the explanation, providing the opportunity to make the creative thinking explicit.
- *Jigsaws.* Missing words can be put into a poem or a piece of prose and a 'jigsaw' of lines of a poem, speeches from *Hansard* or even the sequence of setting up a spreadsheet can test students' understanding of text in a way that the finished article provided on a handout cannot.
- *Circus.* Groups can undertake a single task or follow a logical sequence of activities. They can all do the same task or, as in science practical lessons or PE, there may be several activities arranged around the room and the groups progress from one to another in the 'circus'.
- *Brainstorming.* Group work could be used to encourage creative thought with 'brainstorming' rules where no suggestion can be mocked or rejected, or with the blank sheet of paper where students, at the start of a topic, provide their solution to a problem.
- *Examiners.* Following individual work or the return of marked assignments, students could mark each other's work or discuss the points in the assignments that attracted the highest marks.
- *Hot-seating.* Hot-seating has been a technique used in drama to support a student in developing and maintaining a character. A student sits on the hot seat and the group ask questions, which the student must answer in character. This approach can be explored in many other subjects, such as in history where the student is a historical character or a political movement, in geography where the student is a country at the G7 conference or even in science where the properties of an element could be put on the hot seat!

Whatever the strategy that is used for organizing the groups the instructions that are given to them must be clear and the outcomes well defined within explicit time limits. As part of the 'forming' process, groups will spend time understanding, redefining and arguing about their task. Written instructions or a pro forma describing several stages to the task given to each member of the group or to the chairperson will provide a focus for the discussion and move groups on quickly. While this process is going on, it is worth while to visit each group to ask if they understand the task or would like any further explanation or help.

Observation from the edge of the class will then provide time for the groups to go through the 'norming' and 'storming' phases with appropriate intervention should either stage appear to be an end in itself!

Moving towards groups and offering suggestions, even playing one of the roles, is a useful ploy to keep the group on task. For example, if students are not participating, take over the role of chairperson and direct questions to all students or ask each to give their views for one minute with no interruption from the others.

Time limits should be set at the beginning of the session and reminders given to promote a sense of urgency and purposeful activity.

## Feedback

The nature of feedback from groups is determined by the way in which the groups are established and the task allocated to them:

- A nominated reporter may provide an oral account of the group discussion.
- Each member of the group may make a contribution in a group presentation.
- A PowerPoint presentation or OHP slides may be the tangible outcome.

Providing variety in methods of feedback is important if the class is not to become bored by the repetitive nature of many lesson structures where 'tutor talks; we discuss; then we report back'.

Maintaining the attention of a group of 20 students while their peers provide feedback following group work can be difficult unless they are asked to become active listeners:

- Ask for feedback from the groups in an apparently random order so students do not drift off task while they wait for their turn.
- Providing a pro forma for the listeners to complete using the information or views presented by their colleagues provides a motivation to listen.
- Ascribing roles to the audience is another way of involving them and developing the argument further. In a geography lesson, for example, when students are presenting cases for and against the development of a particular site, the remainder of the class could be planning officers who must note three positive points and three negative points from each proposal. This could then provide the basis for an independent assignment or a further discussion on the way in which different angles of vision produce different constructions of reality.

---

## Checklist for group work

- *Before the lesson*:
  - Is the room layout appropriate?
  - Are the room size and structure appropriate for the activity?
  - Is the task clear?
  - Have you prepared appropriate pro formas?
  - Have you worked out the timing for the lesson?

---

- Have you worked out the routines or ground rules for the groups?
- Have you prepared additional work for the group that finishes first?
- Will feedback involve all students in active listening?
- *During the lesson*:
  - Do the students know one another?
  - Is the group the right size: large enough for development of ideas but small enough to allow the involvement of all?
  - Are ground rules set? Are the groups following them?
  - Are all students on task?
  - Are all students involved?
  - Is there mutual support within the groups?
  - Do students respect the views of others and engage in high-level debate?
  - Do all students understand the task and the standard required in the outcome?
  - Are students who are ascribed roles undertaking them satisfactorily?
  - If students are working outside the classroom are they working purposefully and safely?
  - Are the groups keeping to time?
  - Are all students involved in listening to feedback?
  - Is sufficient time left for feedback from all groups?
  - Is there sufficient time to pull all the points together and to consider what has been learnt?
  - Is the feedback given in the most appropriate way?

# References

Belbin, R M (1981) *Management Teams*, Heinemann, London

Biggs, J (1999) *Teaching for Quality Learning in Higher Education*, Society for Research into Higher Education/Open University Press, Buckingham

Bligh, D (1998) *What's the Use of Lectures?*, Intellect Books, Bristol

Brighouse, T (1989) Conference presentation, Birmingham LEA

Brown, G and Atkins, M (1988) *Effective Teaching in Higher Education*, Routledge, London

Brown, G A and Edmonson, R (1984) Asking questions, in *Classroom Skills*, ed E C Wragg, Croom Helm, London

Cullen, R (1998) Teacher talk and the classroom context, *English Language Teaching Journal*, **52** (3), pp 179–87

Good, T L (1993) Teacher expectations, in *International Encyclopaedia of Education*, ed L Anderson, 2nd edn, Pergamon, Oxford

Good, T L and Brophy, J E (1997) *Looking in Classrooms*, 7th edn, Longman, Harlow

Jacobs, M (1999) *Swift to Hear*, 2nd edn, SPCK, London

Kelly, G (1955) *The Psychology of Personal Constructs*, Vols I and II, Norton, New York

Kelly, G (1966) A brief introduction to personal construct theory, in *Perspectives in Personal Construct Theory*, ed D Bannister, Academic Press, London

Le Versha, L (1990) Whose text? A case study of the use of heuristics in exploring reading theory in A level English literature, Unpublished MSc dissertation, University of Surrey

Petty, G (1998) *Teaching Today*, 2nd edn, Stanley Thornes, Cheltenham

Pollard, A and Triggs, P (1997) *Reflective Teaching in Secondary Education*, Cassell, London

Robertson, J (1989) *Effective Classroom Control*, 2nd edn, Hodder & Stoughton, London

Tabberer, R (1995) The only way is up, *Education*, **185** (23), p 15

Tuckman, B W (1965) Developmental sequence in small groups, *Psychological Bulletin*, **63**, pp 389–99

# 10 Managing coursework and assessment

Lin Le Versha

## Coursework

The introduction of Curriculum 2000 has led to the production of coursework in most subjects. In 1987 school teachers had a similar experience with the move from O levels to GCSE, so faced many of the issues of managing coursework at that time. Students, although experienced with GCSE coursework, still experience problems with structuring, planning and meeting deadlines for completing their coursework. Through careful planning and monitoring the tutor can alleviate many of the problems associated with its production and assessment.

### *Planning*

Students need the exact requirements of the coursework they are to produce with the assessment criteria that are to be used. Handouts with the specific objectives, the length of the assignment required and the criteria for assessing it should be the starting point. A list of dates with exact requirements at this stage will provide a way of managing the work and break it down into bite-sized chunks.

Examples of coursework completed the previous year could be shown at this stage, particularly if they illustrate a range of levels of achievement and different approaches and ways of presenting the topic. If you are unable to obtain previous assignments, examination boards publish sample material that will serve the same purpose. Look at their Web site or the materials they send to the head of department. Group discussions on the way in which each example meets the assessment criteria are useful and, by role-playing an examiner and seeing where the marks can be awarded, students are able to understand how their own work will be assessed.

If the examination board does not prescribe the title and structure of the coursework, the student could spend an initial period devising a question to answer so that the assignment is given a focus. As coursework is differentiation by outcome it is essential that at this stage the tutor should evaluate each title or outline in the light of the student's ability. Can the less able student successfully answer the question asked and can the most able achieve the top marks through this particular investigation?

## Monitoring

A list of 'milestones' should be given to students and it should be insisted that all are met. A leisure and tourism tutor produced the information shown in Figure 10.1 for his students.

At the first stage of the work students should be made aware of the range of information, material and research that should be undertaken. Booklists, lists of Web sites, picture libraries and places to visit are useful to stimulate activity. A realistic plan from students showing the structure, the methodology and the style of their coursework will make a good first milestone and enable the tutor to offer guidance and support.

The collection of data and the personal research undertaken will differ according to the subject. Lessons on the appropriate methodology and the collection and evaluation of data will be essential during this initial period if students are to make the most of the limited time available.

Insist that students hand in each section as agreed on the plan, even if the sections are not complete or polished. At this stage you can still intervene and help students to become realistic in meeting their goals. Some students become so overwhelmed by the size of the task and the quest for perfection that they produce nothing as the task is so daunting.

'Coursework clinics' for students needing help and advice can be advertised on the classroom wall along with the deadlines. One-to-one tutorials following your assessment of progress at each section will be vital in reinforcing a student's achievement and encouraging the less productive.

A monitoring chart could be constructed for each student, plotting progress and setting the next targets. The chart shown in Table 10.1 has been used for design and technology projects where the student fills in each week's work as it is achieved and sets targets for the next. In the workshop the tutor has time to check on each student's progress every week.

## Final assessment

Experienced tutors stick to deadlines and always publish a final deadline that is well ahead of that of the examination board. With careful monitoring all students should meet their final deadline but there are always a few who become overwhelmed and find that their organizational skills do not match their ambitions. Even at 16–19, students can be urged to finish their coursework during or after lessons with tutor supervision and support. Even at this stage, parents' support may be sought to encourage reluctant students to bring in their work for assessment.

In the final stages, presentation of the work is a priority. A title page, contents and bibliography are essential. Clear, well-labelled diagrams, numbered pages with an index, and accurate spelling and punctuation are small but vital ways of ensuring that your students

## UNIT 20: POPULAR ENTERTAINMENT (7374)

In this unit we will be examining the popular entertainment industry and finding out what form it takes, the size and structure of the industry, how it is funded, who its customers are, what employment opportunities exist within it, why it has developed in recent years and how it will develop in future years.

This is a very diverse and interesting component of the leisure and recreation industry and one that deserves to be examined in depth. For this report you are required to complete the following tasks.

### E1. The Main Components
In this section write a **description** of the different 'components' of the popular entertainment industry. For each component you must include **examples** of local, regional and national facilities and provision.
**Deadline: 14 November**

### E2. Sources of Funding
For this section you must **identify** and then **describe** how the entertainment industry is funded. You must clearly reference (describe) the involvement of the public, private and voluntary sectors in this provision. Again provide examples of the different providers at local, regional and national level.
**Deadline: 21 November**

### E3. The Growth of the Industry
In this section you must **research** and then **describe** the growth and development of the entertainment industry over recent years. You will need to provide data to support this section.
**Deadline: 28 November**

### E4/C4/A3. The Future
Here you must make a **valid prediction** on the future development of the industry. You will need to **state** why you have made these predictions and then **justify** them. Also **evaluate** any barriers that might or do exist to the development of this industry and **offer** alternative strategies to minimize these barriers.
**Deadline: 5 December**

### E5/C3. The Customer
**Describe** and **evaluate** how the different providers meet customers' needs and also how they are attracted (marketed) to the sector.
**Deadline: 10 December**

### E6. Employment
**Identify** and **describe** the current employment opportunities within the industry, detailing a typical career structure for two areas in particular and then **explain** how the industry is influenced by the changing nature of the leisure and recreation industry.
**Deadline: 15 December**

### C1/C2/A1/A2. Your Researching and Writing Skills
For these four criteria you will need to demonstrate your abilities in researching from a variety of sources (bibliography) and then in excellent writing skills when you present this work. You need to not only write clearly and accurately but also demonstrate that you have understood and applied your understanding into this work.

In this unit we will be undertaking a day trip to London and visiting a variety of popular entertainment facilities. This will enable you to experience the industry first-hand, gather research material and help you to appreciate this fascinating component. While on the visit we will also be examining Unit 15: Business Systems in Leisure and Recreation. This unit will be sat in the January examinations period.

This is a fun unit and one in which you can all gain a very high grade, providing you put the effort into it. Also, it is a small unit and we can complete this work in a short period of time.

### E1. Describe the Main Components

| Component | Done |
| --- | --- |
| Mass entertainment (rock concerts, football matches, going to the cinema or theatre) | |
| Home-based entertainment (computer games, personal computers, Internet and television) | |
| Retail entertainment (shopping in out-of-town and purpose-built retail complexes) | |
| Hospitality entertainment (theme restaurants, bars and nightclubs) | |
| Theme parks | |
| Experience entertainment (virtual reality, farmyards, interactive museums) | |
| Seasonal entertainment (Christmas, Easter, summer and winter) | |
| Local, regional and national examples | |

**E2. Funding**

| Component | Done |
|---|---|
| Public (taxation) | |
| Private (shareholders) | |
| Voluntary (subscriptions, grants and donations) | |
| PPP | |
| Lottery grants | |
| Local, regional and national examples | |

**E3. Growth**

| Component | Done |
|---|---|
| An increase in disposable income | |
| Increase in accessibility of activities and venues | |
| Influence of marketing and promotion | |
| Changing fashion and trends | |
| Attractiveness and appeal of venues and activities | |
| The rapid development of new technology | |

**E4. The Future**

| Component | Done |
|---|---|
| Further advances in technology (virtual entertainment, cinema, Internet) | |
| Constantly changing fashions and trends (customer choice) | |
| Rising cost of mass entertainment provision (football matches) | |
| Increasing availability and accessibility of popular entertainment (purpose-built out-of-town shopping malls) | |

**E5. The Customer**

| Component | Done |
|---|---|
| Individuals | |
| Groups | |
| People of different ages | |
| People of different cultures | |
| Non-English-speaking customers | |
| People with specific needs | |
| Business customers | |

**E6. Employment**

| Component | Done |
|---|---|
| Part-time | |
| Full-time | |
| Permanent | |
| Seasonal | |
| Contracted | |
| Junior | |
| Supervisory | |
| Managerial | |
| Career structures | |

The tables above are designed to help you structure your report and to make sure you have included everything. Once you have completed a section tick it so you know exactly where you are. The examples in brackets are just a few areas; there are others that you come across and will need to include.

**Figure 10.1**   Information for leisure and tourism students

**Table 10.1** Monitoring chart

| Week 1. 7/10/02 | Week 2. 14/10/02 | Week 3. 21/10/02 | Week 4. 28/10/02 |
|---|---|---|---|
| Project outline | Research | Research completed | Design brief |
| Done. | Visit made. | Done. | Not completed. |
| Need to visit design centre on Saturday and collect info on materials | Collect more info on materials | Produce initial sketches of three designs | Redo sketches by 4/11 |
| **Week 5. 4/11/02** | **Week 6. 11/11/02** | **Week 7. 18/11/02** | **Week 8. 25/11/02** |
| Evaluate initial ideas | 2D/3D modelling | Produce plans | Making |
| Done. | Done. | Problems with CAD. | Plans need finishing. |
| Ready for modelling | Plans to be drawn on paper and CAD | Book tutorial for help from JOF | Will spend Tuesday afternoon catching up in workshop |
| **Week 9. 2/12/02** | **Week 10. 9/12/02** | **Week 11. 16/12/02** | **Week 12. 6/01/03** |
| Making | Making | Making | Making |
| Problems with joints. Spend two additional lessons in workshop | Making progress. Take photos of process | Good progress. Up to date with planning | Problems with polishing. Need to strip and start again |
| **Week 13. 13/01/03** | **Week 14. 20/01/03** | **Week 15. 27/01/03** | **Week 16. 3/02/03** |
| Photos | External testing | Evaluation against spec. | Hand in for assessment |
| Completed and photos taken | Absent – flu. Need to do testing and evaluation next week | All completed. Print out all material. Present in folder. Paginate. Index | Done!!!!! |

achieve the marks they deserve. Work that is presented using IT is easier to read and makes a better impression on the examiner but students should be careful not to produce pages of Internet-based information or masses of clever bar charts, pie charts and graphs as page fillers all presenting the same information.

A 'dress rehearsal' assessment will provide the student with the opportunity to improve presentation or clarify and improve a section of the work. It will also provide you with an initial opportunity to check that the work can be judged according to the marking criteria and to nudge borderline students to have a second look at a specific area.

Moderation of coursework between teaching groups is now a routine activity in schools and colleges. It is useful to discuss students' coursework with another tutor throughout the process to ensure that your assessment is in line with the marking criteria and the standards set by others.

## Task 10.1

Consider the coursework element in your subject. Produce a planning sheet for students and a monitoring sheet for the process relevant to your subject.

---

### Checklist for coursework

- *Before setting it*:
  - Is it appropriate?
  - What guidance has been given?
  - Is it challenging?
  - Have you supplied assessment criteria?
  - Have you provided deadlines?
  - Have you identified milestones for monitoring?
- *During its production*:
  - Have you ensured that each student has developed a realistic question or title?
  - Have you discussed sources of information with each student?
  - Have you advised on appropriate data collection?
  - Do all students understand how to present and set out their work?
  - Have you publicized the dates of milestones so you can monitor progress?
  - Have you arranged tutorials with all students to discuss their first draft?
  - Have you left yourself enough time to mark each piece of work and for departmental moderation?

---

## Assessment

Assessment is derived from the Latin *assidere* (to sit beside) and *ad sedere* (to sit down beside). The friendly, supportive tone in the origins of 'assessment', which suggests a joint activity between student and tutor, is a long way from the reality our students now experience in the plethora of formal assessments they face, from baseline assessment, through the National Curriculum and Curriculum 2000 to their university degrees or qualifications in the workplace.

The debate on the burden of external assessment of students has raged in the media as those who have been tested at the Key Stages of the National Curriculum have now completed the assessment cycle and emerged from the assessment in Curriculum 2000. A student who took four subjects at AS and three at A2 will have been assessed for 12 modules by written or practical examination or coursework at the end of Year 12 and nine at the end of Year 13. Key skills examinations and resitting modules would, of course, be additional.

It is a vital part of your role to prepare your students for their final assessment through a variety of assessment techniques.

## *Why assess?*

The first reason to assess your students is *diagnostic* assessment. You will want to discover what your students know and understand when they start your course, whether they have learning difficulties that will require support or whether they will need small group tutorials on particular issues. Many departments will issue an initial assignment that will provide information on the students' prior learning and their particular strengths. In most colleges, students will be assessed for basic skills. Those with specific learning difficulties will probably have had them assessed before Year 12 so the purpose of this initial diagnosis is not to select students – their Year 11 assessments should do that – but to give you an idea of how your teaching can support the learning of each student in your group.

The following initial assessments are given to students at enrolment and they are asked to bring the completed assignments to their first lesson a week later. The assignments give the students a taste of the type of work they will be doing in the subject and provide the tutors with a piece of work to assess the level of skills of their students. Obviously this is a blunt instrument and it is meant to provide material for initial discussions rather than an accurate measure of their ability.

# Induction assignment for drama

Write a review of a play that you have seen at the theatre in the last two years:

- Introduce the play with comments on its style and the themes of it. (1 paragraph)
- What style of staging is used? Describe the set and say what is visually effective. (1 or 2 paragraphs) Include a plan of the set.
- What impact do other elements have – lighting? sound? costume? (1 or 2 paragraphs)
- Comment on the performance of up to three roles, saying what impression is created and how each actor creates it. (3 paragraphs)
- Does it work as a play? (concluding paragraph)

You will need to bring your review to your first drama lesson.

# Law diary

Throughout the year we will be following news items of legal interest. As well as making your studies more interesting, this is an important way of helping you to develop good writing skills and the ability to analyse and summarize information. This work is done in a law diary. For this you will need either a separate ring-file or an A4 notebook. Your law diary will be checked regularly.

The main sources of information for the law diary are the news and features in newspapers – in particular *The Times*, the *Daily Telegraph*, the *Guardian* and the *Independent*.

To start your law diary, find a news item from a newspaper that seems to have some legal relevance – for example, an account of a legal trial or a report on the sentencing of someone who has been convicted of an offence. Then:

- Read the article carefully (probably more than once).
- Cut out the article and stick it in your law diary.
- Highlight the most important points in the article.
- Write in your law diary a summary of the article and say what you think of it.

You will be engaged primarily in *formative* assessment of your students as part of your constant collection of data on what students have learnt and the way in which they have learnt it. You will want to know how they have processed new concepts you have taught and whether they can connect their learning. This form of assessment can be a dynamic learning tool as long as it is an integral part of the learning process and not an end in itself. Review and feedback are essential elements of this form of assessment.

The third purpose of assessing students is *summative* assessment. It is usually graded and certified and leads to transfer between the various levels in education, for example between Intermediate and Advanced level, or between education and work. The results of the assessment are also public so this form of assessment is used to make schools and colleges accountable and open to scrutiny.

## Task 10.2

- Using the two examples of diagnostic assessment above, evaluate what each would reveal about a student. What strengths and weaknesses would be evident? Is one more effective than the other? Why? How would you use the assessments in a follow-up lesson?
- In your subject what skills, knowledge or understanding would you like to assess at the start of the course? Design an assignment to do it.
- Consider your most recent assessment. Was it diagnostic, formative or summative? Was it effective in supporting or summarizing your learning? Discuss your experience with a partner.
- How does it feel to be assessed? Provide three examples as in Table 10.2, analysing the type of assessment, your feelings towards it and the way in which it assessed your learning.

**Table 10.2**  Feelings on assessment

| Assessment | Feelings | Assessed Learning? |
|---|---|---|
| Driving test – summative. | Nervous, angry when I was in a situation I couldn't control – cut up on hill start – felt his choice of minor faults was trivial. | His aggression meant that I did not perform as well as I had in the lessons – I failed first time but learnt from the test to move the mirror slightly out of alignment so he could see me using it and to practise with someone sitting beside me only giving directions. |

## How to assess?

A variety of assessment including portfolios, coursework and modular assessment has, according to Black (1998: 101), 'enriched the approaches to testing by breaking away from the dominance of the single terminal test and by promoting a widening of the range of pupils' characteristics that can be assessed and tested'. Black applauds the variety of summative assessments that are now available to us but it is in our classrooms that this range of approaches can provide us with information to develop our teaching and to extend our students' learning.

*Essays* explore individual students' understanding of complex issues and demand that they should develop an argument or display their reasoning but marking or grading is not as reliable as objective testing. Types of essays include:

- quotes or statements followed by 'Discuss';
- a topic or area to describe, explain or compare and contrast;
- essays beginning with 'Analyse' or 'Evaluate';
- 'Imagine you are…' – empathizing with a person or situation;
- a scaffolding essay suggesting how the student should structure the argument;
- interpretation of pictures or data.

*Practical assessments* require students to exhibit a skill, perform a task or display a level of competency. Students with more active learning styles prefer this mode of assessment but, as it usually takes a long period of time to assess the whole group as individuals or part of a team, some form of recording such as audiotaping or video will enable standardization to be undertaken in areas such as:

- orals – students make presentations or respond to questions based on a project or on their knowledge and understanding;
- performance – practical work in a laboratory, or a drama or music studio, observed and graded;
- presentation by individual students or a group.

*Project work or coursework* is the result of extended, individual work in which feedback during the process can play a major part. Students may be assessed individually or as part of a group. It is usually assessed and moderated without the student present and it can include:

- exhibition of student work;
- sketch books, logbooks or diaries analysing and evaluating the learning process;
- long essays, videos, models and artefacts.

*Objective tests* provide the most reliable way of assessment. A student's knowledge is tested but little opportunity for constructive feedback is provided. Such tests may be:

- multiple choice;
- right or wrong, true or false;
- short answers;
- filling in the space;
- matching two lists.

In selecting a form of assessment the following should be borne in mind. The assessment should be:

- *Valid.* It should assess what the students can do or exhibit their learning and understanding.
- *Transparent.* The task should be clear and understood by all students. The briefing notes or session should include the purpose of the assessment, the criteria against which it will be assessed and the deadline(s) that should be met.
- *Fair.* All students in the group should be able to complete it regardless of their experience or ability. It may be differentiated by outcome or within its structure but this should be clear in the directions for its completion.
- *Challenging.* The students should not only have their existing knowledge and understanding tested but they should be challenged by the assignment to develop their thinking further and to explore new ground.
- *Summative or formative?* It should be clear whether the piece of work is intended to develop student learning as a part of the study of a topic or whether it is testing the achievement of the student at the end of the topic.

## Types of assessment

Your assignment has been set, your students have completed it and now all you need to do is assess it. There are three main approaches to assessment well described by researchers (Freeman and Lewis, 1998; Black, 1998): norm-referenced, criterion-referenced and ipsative assessment.

*Norm-referenced* assessment is similar to a race. In a race all those who compete are compared against each other with all the competitors put into a rank order. The statistical model of the bell-shaped curve is usually produced when this method of assessing assignments is used (see Figure 10.2).

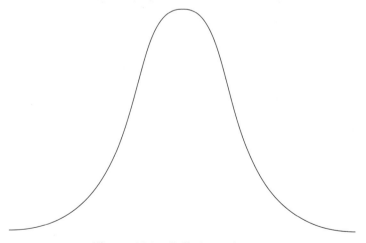

**Figure 10.2**   Bell-shaped curve

There are few students who achieve the top marks or grades, with a similar number who achieve the lowest grades and the majority bunching together in the middle.

*Criterion-referenced* assessment involves measuring the performance of a student against standards that are predetermined and are transparent, explicit and known by the student and tutor. AS, A2 and VCE examinations are based upon this method with published criteria for achievement of each grade. This means that when students produce their coursework they are able to write it with the criteria alongside and consider what they must do to achieve an A grade, a B grade and so on. The students' learning is then linked directly with the assessment. They see what will earn them the greatest credit so they learn it, and where the greatest number of marks may be obtained so they concentrate on that section and include more material in it.

In terms of the race image, an athlete who is going to compete in the 100-metre dash has a very different training regime from one who is going to run a marathon. In the same way, students knowing the nature of the 'race' they are entering are able to prepare for it accordingly. It is essential that the criteria are shared with students so that they can perform to the best of their ability.

Criterion-referenced assessment allows the tutor to give detailed, formative feedback, which is usually acted upon, as students can see the point of the suggestions and the way in which it will improve their performance. Statistically this method is not based on a normal distribution as students achieve the grade the standard of their work determines so they could all pass with high A, B and C grades as their final grade does not depend on how well they do in comparison with others. An example of the assessment criteria that are provided by the examination boards (see Figure 10.3) shows exactly how a piece of coursework will be assessed against the criteria.

*Ipsative assessment* shows how well a student has performed against his/her previous efforts. As athletes, for example, may only be interested in timing their races against a clock rather than against others so students may be interested in achieving marks, grades or targets set specifically for them. Achieving 80 per cent in one test and 85 per cent in the next will plot the development of the student and bear no relation to others in the group. This type of assessment is based upon careful tutoring and target setting and helps the student to become self-critical and motivated.

## Assessing the learning process

All the examples above describe ways of assessing a finished product or assignment. Formative assessment with constructive feedback is essential if students are to improve their learning. Rather than waiting for the final piece there are many ways to assess the process:

- *Short sections of assignments.* Instead of waiting until the final piece of coursework thuds on to your desk, get students to submit it in sections, which you can read and on which you can provide feedback for improvement. This way you can ensure that they are actually working on it and help them to organize their time and what may initially appear to be a mammoth task by breaking it down into small pieces.
- *Notes.* Ask students to hand in their notes for you to see. You can assess whether they have included the right information, comment on the way in which they have made

# VCE in Travel and Tourism

## Unit recording sheet – Unit 1: Investigating Travel and Tourism

OCR★
RECOGNISING ACHIEVEMENT

| Candidate name | |
| Centre name | |
| Portfolio reference | |

| Candidate number | |
| Centre number | |
| Specification code(s) | 7775/7795 |

| Date to hand work in by | |
| Date work submitted by student | |
| Unit code | 7470 |

**Evidence:** findings of an investigation into the UK travel and tourism industry covering: reasons for the rapid development of the industry since the end of the Second World War: its scale and significance to the UK economy: its structure and key features: commercial and non-commercial organisations and how they interact. Findings of an investigation into employment opportunities in the travel and tourism industry that involves: outlining the range of employment opportunities: identifying one job that interests you, with a description of the personal and technical skills required to do the job: producing your own CV.

### To achieve a grade E you must show you can:

| | | A | B |
|---|---|---|---|
| E1 | clearly explain, giving suitable examples, the post-war developments that have supported the growth of the industry | | |
| E2 | describe fully the scale of the UK industry and its economic significance, quoting relevant data accurately | | |
| E3 | summarise the current structure and key components of the UK travel and tourism industry, giving suitable examples | | |
| E4 | summarise the range of commercial and non-commercial organisations in the industry, giving suitable examples | | |
| E5 | summarise the range of employment opportunities available within the travel and tourism industry and describe in detail one job that best matches your aspirations, skills and abilities | | |
| E6 | produce a CV appropriate for seeking employment in your chosen job | | |

### To achieve a grade C you must also show you can:

| | | A | B |
|---|---|---|---|
| C1 | give a logical and well-structured analysis of the industry that effectively summarises key information and data | | |
| C2 | use appropriate language and terms associated with travel and tourism | | |
| C3 | evaluate the key features of commercial and non-commercial organisations to illustrate differences in their funding and their business objectives | | |
| C4 | collect and use additional information to evaluate critically why your chosen job best matches your personal circumstances. | | |

### To achieve a grade A you must also show you can:

| | | A | B |
|---|---|---|---|
| A1 | display a thorough understanding of the reasons for the rapid growth of the industry and the factors that will affect its development in the future | | |
| A2 | use a comprehensive range of information sources and show how you have cross-checked the reliability of each source | | |
| A3 | analyse critically information and data to draw valid conclusions about the scale and structure of the industry. | | |

**Column A:** Location of evidence. **Column B:** Tutor initial.

I certify that to the best of my knowledge and belief this is the candidate's own unaided work.

Assessor name _____  Assessor signature _____  Date _____

| Overall grade | |
| Points score | |
| Standardised points | |

URS461/Rev Sept 00

7470/URS

**Figure 10.3** Assessment criteria

their notes and ensure that their notes will be useful for revision. Again it also ensures that there are some notes in their files!

- *Student files*. Tutors are often amazed that some students pass any examinations when they look at the state of their files of notes and handouts. A regular 'file check', where you make sure that they have the right notes and handouts in the right place can provide students with a regular reminder that success in study is often based on effective organization.
- *Annotated texts*. For subjects such as English, students are able to take their set texts into the examination room with them. Following discussion of the way in which to annotate the text using coloured pens and symbols, the annotated text could be given in for assessment so that the extent of the annotations can be assessed.
- *Diaries and logs*. In many subjects diaries or logs may be used to ensure that students in economics or law, for example, are reading up-to-date information on their subject from newspapers and journals. Articles are stuck in and commented upon by students. In art, media studies and drama, similar logs record the creative process as students describe their research and the development of their ideas, and evaluate their final product. In some subjects these logs are assessed as part of the examination; in others it is a way of developing the creative understanding of the student. Regular assessment of progress in these logs will ensure that students are spending time in research and thought, provide them with status and enable you to intervene when students need encouragement or support.
- *Draft plans and assignments*. Too often we give students an essay title and walk away. They may have little idea how to complete the assignment, how much they should produce or what they should include. Scaffolding or sample plans will help them face the blank sheet of paper and if you assess their initial plans and draft then you can provide feedback at a very early stage and have a positive effect on their learning.
- *Reviews*. Short reviews of plays, films, television programmes and documentaries, CDs, books or a series of articles will provide breadth to a student course and ensure that students are exploring a variety of stimulating sources.

## Feedback

Giving appropriate feedback on an assignment is essential if students are to learn and improve their performance. It is natural to look at the final mark or grade and ignore the painstaking notes that you have provided in the margins and at the end of their work. A tutorial with the student going over the points made will reinforce them and answer questions that the student may have. Paired discussions where students read the work and comments and pick out the most important three points for their partner are a fruitful exercise with students who know each other well. Whatever your strategy for digesting the feedback, the way in which you produce the feedback is vital if it is to inform learning:

- *Relevant*. First of all it must be relevant to the assessment criteria and to the student. Link the comments to the explicit criteria and make them personally relevant to the student's performance and the effort made.
- *Evaluative*. The comments should encourage students to evaluate their own work and provide them with a vocabulary and a willingness to become self-evaluative, thus

engaging them in their own learning. You could ask students to assess their own work against the assessment criteria before handing it to you for your assessment.

- *Question*. The use of questions will open a dialogue between you and students and show them that there is not always a final or indeed right answer to a question. The questions can be discussed in the tutorial or in group discussion.
- *Next time*. The feedback you provide should encourage students to take action, to improve that area of their work, to pursue a new line of research or thought or to produce the assignment in a different way. It is only through your comments that they can develop their approach to the assignments and their learning. They should be able to formulate an action plan of two or three clear actions that they will take before handing in the next assignment. It may be useful for them to produce this plan so that you can see whether your comments have really been as clear as you intended.

## Feedback sheets

An alternative to 'bleeding' all over a student's work is to use a feedback form. This will have the effect of structuring your thinking as you assess the work, and enable you to formulate a clear action plan with the student. The sociology essay skills sheet shown in Figure 10.4 uses questions for the tutor to answer and gives evidence to the student of the way in which the essay has been assessed. This means that the student can immediately see the thin areas or holes and concentrate on those in a second draft or the next essay. The second part is completed by the student so that the dialogue between tutor and student has a sharp focus and the student learns to become self-evaluative. For some essays, the student will complete the entire sheet with the tutor adding comments.

This type of marking sheet does take time to complete but it does have a direct effect on improving student performance and demands that the tutor should consider exactly why a piece of work has been assessed to meet a certain standard or grade. It may, therefore, be better for tutors to give students fewer essays that are properly assessed, interspersed with shorter, process tasks, than to give a large number of essays that are returned to the student with cursory comments and a grade.

Another approach, used by a VCE tutor, is to give the students A4 feedback sheets (see Figure 10.5) following the first draft of their coursework. This is completed by the students following discussion with the tutor. The students fill in what they need to do, in their own language, and they make the decision for themselves on how they wish to develop their work. The tutor ensures that students are on the right track and records the date that tutor and student have agreed for the work to be handed in.

## *Timing*

The timing of assignments and the length of time it takes the tutor to assess them are also important in improving learning and motivation. Assignments should be relevant and obviously related to the topic or area of study, and the purpose of them should be transparent and shared with students. Deadlines should be clear, well publicized and adhered to by all students. Procedures for negotiations of an extension of the deadline should be made clear

## STUDENT ESSAY SKILLS - SOCIOLOGY

| Name: Charlie Burgess | Set: B3 |
|---|---|

| Title: Evaluate the impact of two sociologists on the development of research methodology. |
|---|
| |

| THE INTRODUCTION | | EVIDENCE |
|---|---|---|
| Does your essay address the question immediately? | Yes/No<br>Yes | Good opening sentence followed by summary of main points in essay. You could have used the quote in line 3 as a dramatic introductory sentence. |
| Does your essay show an understanding of the different parts of the question that need to be covered? | Yes/No<br>Yes | Good summary of the central issues and contribution of each sociologist.Make sure your quotes are clear; they tend to disappear into the text. |
| 3. Does your essay define problematic key areas? | Yes/No<br>No | Charlie, you need to add one or two sentences here ** (see essay). More evaluation needed here *** (p 4 essay). |

| THE MAIN BODY | | EVIDENCE |
|---|---|---|
| 1. Content<br>(a) Are enough studies and/or illustrations mentioned? | Yes/No<br>No | You need to include more examples from both - on pages 4 and 6. Try to find 3 more examples for each. |
| (b) Are enough theories and theoretical debates included? | Yes/No<br>No | Here again provide more detail and analysis of the central contribution of their work. You have the idea but do not go into sufficient detail. Have you looked at pp 235-269 in the text? |
| 2. Relevance<br>(a) Are the studies/ illustrations mentioned in a relevant context? | Yes/No<br>Yes | Well done here. You provide a solid context and apply the studies you have used very well indeed |
| (b) Have the theories been used to answer the questions set? | Yes/No<br>Yes | The theories you have used are effective and you write in fluent style - just include more!!! |
| 3. Line of Argument<br>(a) Does the discussion follow a logical sequence? | Yes/No<br>Yes | Well planned and logical - just rather short. |
| (b) Are points developed to an adequate depth? | Yes/No<br>? | You need more of them - add 4 more to get to next grade boundary. |
| 4. Evaluation<br>Are the theories/ evidence critically evaluated? | Yes/No<br>Yes | Impressive use of critical vocabulary, and comparison between the two is good. |

| THE CONCLUSION | | EVIDENCE |
|---|---|---|
| Does the conclusion attempt to evaluate the relative importance of conflicting claims? | Yes/No<br>Yes | Sharp points made that follow from the central argument in your essay. At last you have cracked the conclusion. Well done! |
| Is the conclusion justified (given the points raised in the main body)? | Yes/No<br>Yes | You get there in the end! |

**ASSESSMENT ELEMENTS**

1. I HAVE DEMONSTRATED KNOWLEDGE AND UNDERSTANDING IN THIS ESSAY BY
*Researching work of sociologists from different decades and showing how they fit into social context. I have used quotations and references correctly and used them to support my argument.*
*I now need to return to the texts and provide more detailed information on both to add after paragraph 5.*

2. I HAVE DEMONSTRATED SKILLS OF INTERPRETATION AND APPLICATION IN THIS ESSAY BY
*I have applied the theories accurately and provided a range of relevant applications.*
*I need to look at two more theories from each.*

3. I HAVE DEMONSTRATED EVALUATION SKILLS IN THIS ESSAY BY
*Showing the different impact each had and using my judgement to say which I felt was the most relevant.*

**Figure 10.4**  Essay skills sheet

**Additional Work Required**

**Name:** *Emma Richardson*  **Date:** *15th December*

**Unit Title:** *Unit 20*  **Date work required:** *19th January*

**Assessor:** *RJG*

**Please write below what you have to achieve. Remember to reference each section clearly. Please hand in this sheet with your work on the required date.**

*E1. I need to reprint the table with corrections.*

*E3. I need to include more examples of developments in new technology.*

**Student signature:** *E. R. Richardson*  **Date:** *15th December*

**Assessor signature:** RJ Gresham  **Date:** 15th December

**Figure 10.5**  Feedback sheet

and followed. Students of 16–19 years have a strong sense of what is fair and if they have made great efforts to meet a deadline only to hear their tutor say 'OK, bring it in sometime next week' to a student who has failed to organize their work then they are quite right in expressing their indignation!

Similarly if a student has been given a deadline to produce an assignment then we should be committed to return a marked assignment at the stated time. College charters usually incorporate a comment such as: 'An assignment handed in on time should be marked and returned to the student within 10 working days. The tutor will announce the time-scale for marking longer pieces of coursework when it is completed and this commitment will be adhered to.'

Student surveys within subjects or across the college will test whether this standard is met, as the prompt return of work is essential if students are to be motivated and to learn from the experience of completing the assignment.

## Recording

Whatever the method of assessment, the results of student performance should be systematically and meticulously recorded. These results may be used as evidence to report on students' progress, to predict their performance in examinations or to provide information for individual support or for disciplinary procedures.

---

### Checklist for assessment

- *Before administering the assessment*:
  - Is the assessment appropriate?
  - Does it come at the right point in the course?
  - Is it summative or formative?
  - How will the outcome affect your teaching?
  - If it is diagnostic, what does it diagnose?
  - What is the expected end product?
  - How long will it take you to complete the assessment?
  - How will it be assessed: norm-referenced, criterion-referenced or ipsative?
- *During the assessment process*:
  - Have you shared the purpose of the assessment with your students?
  - Do they understand the criteria you will use to assess them?
  - How will you assess absent students?
  - Do students have sufficient time to complete it to the desired standard?
  - Are students aware of the significance of the assessment? What will happen if they fail?
  - Is feedback positive?
  - Does it provide a plan of action?
  - Is the work marked and handed back promptly?

---

Managing coursework and assessment has taken on greater importance in Curriculum 2000. The range of assessment methods and the inclusion of coursework in many more subjects mean that post-16 tutors are able to play a much greater role in the examination experience of their students. Tutors are able to guide students to select activities appropriate to their ability and in line with their strengths. Tutors are able to support students through the process of learning to a much greater extent than they were able to in preparing for the end-of-course examinations of the previous A level system.

Departments have set up a dialogue about the management of learning and assessment as they have offered their students the opportunity of having the process of their learning assessed as well as its outcomes in the final examinations. For many tutors, who may have taught the same syllabus as they followed themselves as sixth formers, the introduction of Curriculum 2000 has been a wonderful opportunity to examine their practice and to develop it, and any initiative that encourages teachers to talk about ways of improving learning must be good!

# References

Black, P (1998) *Testing – Friend or Foe? Theory and practice of assessment and testing*, Falmer Press, London

Freeman, R and Lewis, R (1998) *Planning and Implementing Assessment*, Kogan Page, London

# 11 Dealing with individual needs within the classroom

Jeanne Holloway

My principal weakness was a poor memory for words and texts.

(Albert Einstein)

If we are to teach students and not just subjects then it is apparent that every student has a special need. We all have individual needs or styles of learning and these also determine the teaching style of teachers, which will inevitably have an influence on students' learning. As teachers we must create opportunities for all students to have access to learning whatever their cultural and social background, gender, physical or mental health challenges, specific learning difficulties or past learning experiences.

The move to inclusive learning (Tomlinson, 1996) places responsibility for individual learning needs in the hands of all teachers, not just those with special responsibility for learning support. It also emphasizes the importance of the learning environment and building support for the individual into the teaching methodology and the resources we use.

Central to the thinking of the Tomlinson Report is the view that:

> put simply we want to avoid a viewpoint which locates the difficulty or deficit with the student and focus instead on the capacity of the educational institution to understand and respond to the individual learner's requirement. This means that we must move away from labelling the student and towards creating an appropriate educational environment; concentrate on understanding better how people learn so that they can better be helped to learn; and see people with disabilities and/or learning difficulties first and foremost as learners.

As a result of inclusive learning, inspection has as its focus learning and the effectiveness of the learning process. Learning support will no longer be inspected as part of the territory of the learning support tutors but it will be observed in all classrooms. Inspectors will observe the experiences of individual students, the range of provision and the support for them, as well as course content. They will report on how well teaching and training meet both individuals' needs and course and programme requirements. They will evaluate and report on the extent to which learners, irrespective of their age, gender, race, ethnicity, learning difficulty or disability, acquire knowledge and skills.

Inspectors will explore how information on the individual needs of students is used in lessons, materials and providing effective additional support. The tutor then becomes a facilitator of learning – a resource for learning rather than solely a 'chalk and talk' educator who has all the answers. We need to help students to manage their own learning through learning how to learn.

The Disability Discrimination Act 1995 demands that disabled people should have the same opportunities as non-disabled people within education and this includes post-16 education. The Act makes it unlawful for a responsible body to discriminate against a disabled person. 'A disabled person' is someone who has a physical or mental impairment and this includes sensory impairments and also hidden impairments (for example, mental illness or mental health problems, learning difficulties, dyslexia and conditions such as diabetes or epilepsy). It is our responsibility to ensure that all students, including those with disabilities, have equal access to learning. If you look at the statistics of students in higher education with disabilities, you will appreciate how much provision for them in further education is needed.

## Skills needs within the classroom

The inspection focus includes 'whether students have enough time to practise and develop their skills'. Both teachers and learners need to get out of the **SACK** by approaching learning with these questions in mind:

- What **S**kills are needed?
- What **A**ttitudes are to be developed?
- What **C**oncepts are to be understood?
- What **K**nowledge is to be gained?

### How do I become 'skills aware'?

It is important to know what strengths and weaknesses all students bring to the learning situation with regard to the skills that are essential for effective learning in your subject. For those with disabilities, however, a skills deficit, either as a result of the disability or simply as a result of a lack of skills awareness, could be considered to place the student at a substantial disadvantage. It is important to anticipate some possible needs with regard to skills. For example, we may reasonably anticipate that there will be a diversity of reading speeds within a class. We may further reasonably anticipate that those with sight impairment, epilepsy and dyslexia will be amongst the group of students with a slower reading speed. We must ensure that we do not treat those with disabilities less favourably, so what can we do? First of all it is important for the teacher to be aware of the skills demanded by the tasks that are set.

## Task 11.1

Consider a lesson you have set students in one of your classes. For the areas below, indicate the current level of your skill in each:

                                                                    Low         High

Understanding how students learn
Using a variety of teaching styles
Teaching skills alongside knowledge
Awareness of skills demanded by task you set
Checking that learning is taking place
Awareness of the diversity of skills needs within the class
Addressing learning style preferences
Broadening learning styles
Addressing support needs in materials
Recognizing when additional support is required
Anticipating possible skills needs within the classroom

We will return to this checklist at the end of the chapter.

Write down a task that you have recently set for your students. Brainstorm for just two minutes the skills that would be demanded by that task.

It is important to be aware of the skill demands of the task you set. Some students may have the knowledge but not the skills to undertake a task. It is only by being aware of the skills students need to complete a task that we can help them to access learning effectively.

If a student does not hand in a piece of coursework, how do you check if it is due to a lack of skills? The student may wish to undertake the task but not know how to:

- understand concepts such as 'describe', 'outline', 'justify', 'evaluate';
- make useful notes;
- incorporate notes into the assignment;
- plan and time-budget;
- break down the task into manageable parts;
- find relevant information;
- understand the required writing genre;
- understand technical terms used;
- understand what the task requires.

You could use the above list as a student checklist and ask your students to rate on a one-to-five scale how confident they feel with each aspect of the task you have set. You may think of some more ideas and extend the list. You will then have a whole-class view with regard to adapting your teaching and learning strategies. One teacher, for example, used this idea and found that many students did not understand the concepts or the technical vocabulary so he set up some lunchtime workshops on 'language' to address this need.

What we want to see is the learner in pursuit of knowledge and not knowledge in pursuit of the learner.

(George Bernard Shaw)

Now, look back at your brainstorm of skills above; compare it with this history teacher's 'skills brainstorm':

> Selecting, rejecting, surveying, searching, categorizing, sequencing, modelling, summarizing, comparison, analysis, identification of main ideas and supporting details, recognition of main ideas, recognition of cause-and-effect relationships, interpretation of directions, following sequences of events, critical comprehension through recognition of author's intent and attitude, bias and use of propaganda, appreciating ideas and emotions, interpreting pictorial materials, judging diction, tone and style. Affective comprehension through recognizing one's own intellectual and emotional response to the reading, recognition of the significance of headings, subheadings and summary paragraphs. Reading between and beyond the lines with regard to predication, inference of detail and cause and effect. Effective and efficient note making, selective copying, note organization through the use of selected, appropriate headings and subheadings, editing, drafting, proofreading, planning, time budgeting. Appropriate writing skills – grammar, punctuation, spelling skills, the skills of skimming, scanning and selective, intensive reading.

Phew!

As you can see there is a multitude of skill demands for all students yet those with defined disabilities and disorders may experience greater difficulty than others in acquiring necessary skills. Thinking about skill demands helps us to adapt our teaching and learning strategies in order to accommodate the needs of all students. There is a place in all subjects for skills teaching specific to that subject.

## How do we raise student awareness that learning concerns developing skills as well as learning facts?

The following ideas can encourage whole-class involvement in thinking about learning. As a classroom task:

1. Prepare a list of the skills that are essential for effective learning in your subject area.
2. Undertake a whole-class brainstorm with regard to skills.
3. Ask the class to call out the skills needed in your subject area.
4. Write them on the board.
5. Compare the brainstorm with your list.
6. How 'skills aware' are the students? Do you need to have 'skills awareness' workshops in which you show students how to, for example: make notes, organize facts, justify points, write a persuasive essay, critically analyse?

Use *your* list of essential skills as a student questionnaire and ask the students to rate on a one-to-five scale how confident they feel they are with regard to these skills. This can help you prioritize whole-class skills needs. For example, one history class teacher at a sixth form college found that 92 per cent of the A level history students did not feel confident with using the library or with research writing. The librarian organized some library-skills-based lessons for the students, and the teacher provided workshops that involved looking at writing frameworks and the use of language in an 'ideal' piece of research.

You may also help your students to link the skills needed in your subject to others by the following activity:

1. Divide the class into five groups.
2. Give each group a sheet of A3 paper and ask them to write down skills needed from one of their other subject areas in large print.
3. Pin the sheets up around the room.
4. Discuss the skills. Are there skills common to two or more subjects? How easy was it to think about skills?
5. Did the students have difficulty with distinguishing between knowledge and skills? Are they aware that some skills are transferable across the subject boundaries?
6. How diverse are the perceived skills needs?
7. Discuss how the students might transfer the skills from one subject to another.

The development of student skills can be supported by skill-based marking of assessments. Look at a recent set of assignments you have marked and ask yourself these questions:

- How many of the comments are related to study-skills-based needs?
- Having identified skill deficits, how are the students going to develop and practise those skills?
- Do some students have far greater skills needs than the others?
- Do they have an identified special need?
- Is there a need for referral for additional support?

In one set of marking a teacher had written 'a need for essay structure' on six different assignments. By providing a small group lunchtime workshop on essay structure the students were able to learn about essay structure for that subject.

Another teacher identified a small group of students who needed to learn how to read and make notes rather than try to trust everything to memory. She practised this skill with the small group of students within the classroom at a time when the remainder of the class broke into groups in order to discuss, research a topic or watch an extract from a video.

## How can I assess the diversity of needs within the classroom with regard to the basic skills needed for effective learning?

These simple, whole-class assessments are intended to alert you to the diversity of needs within the classroom as a whole. They will provide useful information with regard to teaching and planning. They may also reveal students who need to be referred to the learning support coordinator for additional support as many may have masked difficulties through the use of technology.

The procedure is to give the whole class some or all of the following basic assessment tasks, depending on how much information you already have with regard to skills needs. For example, if you do not ask students to copy from the board, do not assess this. The tasks do not have to be undertaken in one session; they could be a warm-up part of lessons. The students should be put at ease by being told that the assessments are to help you in teaching and planning future lessons. All students should take part, even those already diagnosed as having a specific learning difficulty, as this will enable you to have a broad view of the students' reading and writing speeds, ability to copy from the board and put thoughts on paper as well as on their handwriting abilities.

By appraising each of the assessment tasks undertaken you will be aware of the diversity of basic skills needs within the class.

The tasks involved are:

- copying from the board;
- making notes from a page of text;
- taking notes from a lecture;
- reading a piece of set text for one minute and underlining the place that they have read to by the end of the minute;
- a spelling test of subject-related words essential for effective learning;
- a piece of free writing to assess quality of handwriting, use of vocabulary, spelling and awareness of grammar.

## Copying from the board

Ask students to copy notes from the board for five minutes. The notes should be typical of those that you might present in the normal lesson. Take all student notes in for assessment after the set time:

- How effective are their copying skills?
- Did all students manage to copy the notes?
- How useful would their attempt be when needing the copying for homework or revision?

Teacher tips:

- To make the copying task easier, use clear lower-case print.
- Use different coloured pens every three or four lines to make location easier.
- Number points.
- Draw frames around specific points.
- Underline key points.
- Have handouts available for those who may need them to supplement their efforts as they are developing the skill of copying.

Question: is the copying really necessary? Could a handout have provided a basis for discussing the information rather than a copying activity?

## Making notes from a page of text

Give students a page of text from which you would normally expect them to make notes on key points. Allow 10 minutes. Take the notes in. If students are not making effective notes from a page of text, they are often just copying out the information that is already presented.

Teacher tips:

- Give them a set of 'ideal' notes to look at and with which to compare their own attempt.
- Assess who needs to be told how to take notes, when to take notes and why it is important to take notes.
- The type of note taking will depend on the subject, the student preference and knowledge with regard to how they take notes.
- Show students how to highlight specific key points. Have they noted main points?
- Show them how to recognize and number significant points.
- Show them how to make a spider diagram and flow chart.
- Tell them to use different-coloured pens. For example, students could be encouraged to write 'cause' issues in one colour and 'effect' issues in another.

## Taking notes from a lecture

Tell the students that you will be giving a 10-minute lecture-type lesson to begin the session and that you would like them to make notes of key points for revision purposes. Take the notes in for assessment.

Teacher tips:

- Assess how effective the notes would be in a week, a month or a year's time.
- Discuss this with the students.
- Give the notes back a few weeks later. Ask them to assess the effectiveness of their notes at this later date. Discuss what they need to do to improve these skills.

## Reading a piece of set text

By looking at how much of the text each student has read in a given time you can become aware of the diverse range of reading speeds there are in any one class. This enables you to allow time for all to finish reading.

Give each student a piece of text that you would normally hand out for classroom reading and discussion. Tell the students that you want them to read it through from the beginning in a set time (five minutes). At the end of the given time ask them to draw a bold line indicating where they have reached. Take in the papers to assess the diversity of reading speeds within the whole class. To check understanding, ask the students to note the main points with regard to what they have read on a different sheet of paper or have a class discussion.

Assess the different reading speeds. How many students did not read more than one paragraph? How many completed the reading?

Teacher tips:

- Students often have to be directly taught how to read for study purposes. Tell them how to use flexible reading strategies by:
  - first reading the headings and subheadings;
  - then reading the first sentence followed by reading the summary;
  - skimming and scanning the text to get the gist and then intensively reading the key concepts.

- If the brain is prepared for the content in this way the reading speed and comprehension will increase. Tell the students to read with highlighter in hand as a rule rather than an exception.
- Practise skimming and scanning for specific words in order to develop flexible reading strategies rather than a rote, mechanical approach that gives equal emphasis to each word.

## A spelling test of subject words that are essential for effective study in your subject area

Select 15 to 20 words essential for effective learning in your subject area.

Tips for teachers:

- Have essential words on a wall chart.
- Encourage students to write the words that have been spelt incorrectly on a Post-it so that it can be transferred from folder to folder and on to the side of the computer screen where necessary as a constant visual reminder.
- Retest errors – make spelling important to the students.
- Suggest mnemonics for essential words in order to aid memory. For example, a business studies teacher taught the word 'accommodation' with the mnemonic 'a cold caravan or **m**agnificent **m**ansion' as it was the two c's and two m's that caused the most problems.

If there are more than 5 per cent spelling errors or if spelling errors are so bizarre that they would mar meaning then you should refer the student to the learning support department.

## A timed piece of free writing

This can take just five minutes if prior to the task there has been discussion and time to think about what the student will write about. A free writing task can reveal:

- difficulties with spelling;
- use of vocabulary;
- speed of writing;
- ability to collect thoughts together and get ideas on paper.

With the use of the word processor we may often be unaware of individual difficulties unless we assess some writing by hand. All students will have to write their examinations by hand even though their coursework may be word-processed.

- Does the student have difficulty getting ideas on to paper?
- Does the percentage of spelling errors indicate a need for referral or advice to the learning support coordinator?
- If the writing is illegible, will the student need to use a laptop in the classroom?

*How does a learner that has a skill deficit in all or any of the above areas feel?*

## Task 11.2

Let us experience what it feels like to have problems with these basic areas of learning. Read this aloud as quickly as you can:

Un derst an ding one spref er red learn in gsty lehas man y be ne fit sit hel psu sunder stand o ura reasof we akne ssesgi vin gust heop port unity tow orkon be com in gm orepro fic ien tint he ot hermodes an dith elpsus real izeour stren gthsw hich mig ht bead van tageou sin sit uati on s suc has deci din gup on o ur fut u re car e ers.

Write down one word that describes how you would feel if this was always the only way and speed that you could read.

Now, copy out these two sentences as quickly as you can: 'Take the xcvzyrsy and dhgtwsmk and mix. Leave to gtywrcvz for five minutes. Then take the kwvcxy and gfdhjk and add them to the xcvzyrsy and dhgtwsmk solution.' Now copy these two sentences with the hand that you do not normally write with: 'Has the resulting nkgyuqals changed ptysxvcz? What lktynvcdz has taken place?' How did you feel?

Words that others have used following the same exercises have included 'frustrated', 'useless', 'humiliated', 'disappointed', 'surprised', 'embarrassed'.

Unless we recognize and incorporate the individual needs of students within our classroom teaching, they may spend their entire education feeling as you did. Their self-esteem will be low and they will lose their confidence in learning. Whilst these students may have additional support, their needs must also be met within each lesson in the classroom where most of their education takes place.

# Preferred learning styles and preferred teaching styles

*Preferred learning styles*

There are striking differences in the way each individual takes in and processes information and, to improve their learning, students need to understand their individual learning style. Teachers also need to be aware of the preferred learning styles of their students and how these styles are suited to the subject taught. It is often students who have command of a broad range of learning styles who are the most effective learners for they have learnt how to learn.

Through understanding preferred learning styles we move the educational focus from the teacher back to the learner. Preferred learning styles, however, should not be used to stereotype or segregate learners. For example, many students with disabilities or disorders may have to access learning in defined ways such as having a personal reader or tape recorder, or receiving handouts in advance. Their access to learning must be treated with respect and sensitivity as this is their *only* learning style. Many learning disabled students do, however, use inappropriate learning strategies and, by introducing them to a range of learning techniques, we allow them to experience a positive approach to learning.

In understanding *learning* styles it is important to look at our preferred *teaching* style and assess if it is appropriate both to the changing needs of the student of the 21st century and also to the individual needs of each student. The student of today has grown up with the new media of films, television, videos, video games and CDs. This means that many do not enjoy passive learning. They learn best through *interacting* with their learning rather than through 'chalk and talk' teaching.

Learning styles are influenced by *perceptual preferences* with regard to learning. For example, *visual* learners have a visual preference for learning. They learn most effectively through written information such as handouts, diagrams, pictures, charts, information leaflets and posters. They may prefer to take notes even if handouts are provided.

*Auditory* learners learn most effectively through auditory stimuli – through the spoken word, by listening, reading aloud, taping notes.

*Physical/tactile/kinaesthetic* learners learn most effectively through being actively engaged in hands-on activities. They learn through practice and imitation. They will prefer to learn by doing something active with information, such as rewriting their notes. They will prefer lessons where they can move around and not have to sit for too long.

> The head cannot take in more than the seat can endure.
>
> (Winston Churchill)

Students who can engage all of these perceptual preferences are said to be using a *multisensory approach* to their learning. A multisensory approach can maximize the potential for learning. Many students with learning-related disabilities depend upon a multisensory approach in order to access learning, particularly those with dyslexia.

It is also important to understand learners' preferences with regard to the ways that they process information. *Global learners* like to have the whole picture before the individual pieces of information fall into place. They link ideas and information through an internalized conceptual map as they make connections between pieces of information. They have a 'right-brain' preference for learning. The right hemisphere of the brain specializes in visual–spatial and holistic processes. Those with dyslexia usually have a global learning preference. *Linear learners* process information best through steps that follow a logical sequence. They like a step-by-step build-up of information to analyse and process sequentially. They have a 'left-brain' preference for learning.

## Preferred teaching styles

How we approach our teaching will depend upon our prior knowledge and skills, our motivation, our preferred teaching styles and our ability to anticipate the needs of all students. It will also depend upon the institutional context within which we teach as well as upon our own preferred learning styles.

## Task 11.3

- Write down the learning styles that you accommodated in your last lesson and explain how you did so.
- What can you do to extend your range of teaching styles in your next lesson?

Compare your answers with the checklist below:

- I have asked students about their preferred learning styles.
- I have observed preferred learning styles.
- I help students extend their range of learning styles.
- I have introduced a variety of approaches students may use for set tasks.
- I explain the whole task and the intended outcome clearly.
- I help students break down large tasks into smaller chunks.
- I use auditory and visual stimuli with each lesson.
- I provide computerized instruction for students outside of the classroom.
- I include discussion and group work within each lesson.
- I encourage students to interact with text through highlighting main points.
- I assess students' abilities to make and take notes.
- I provide examples of 'good' notes.
- I provide writing frames to show students the language and structure features of the subject genre.

Teaching that uses a variety of approaches to intellectual study that extend, supplement or replace traditional styles can increase student opportunity for learning. Teaching the student to take a problem solving approach to learning as they think about learning promotes life long learning. Give the students the opportunity to reflect on strengths and weaknesses in order to monitor and enhance learning...

Education is an activity of mind, not a curriculum to be delivered.

(Fisher, 1998: 140, 142)

# Students with professionally diagnosed individual needs

'Name the condition; do not label the student.' Students with professionally diagnosed individual needs are not 'dyslexics' or 'epileptics'; they are 'students with dyslexia' or 'students with epilepsy'. This piece of advice, given to me many years ago, has always reminded me to keep the person, not the disability, disorder or challenge, uppermost in mind when teaching. It has also reminded me to have high expectations and respect for each individual.

The needs of students with special educational needs *must* be met through good practice within the classroom as well as through any additional support that is in place that they will accept. We must 'see people with disabilities and/or learning difficulties first and foremost as learners' (Tomlinson, 1996). The attitude of students with special educational needs with regard to accepting additional support will depend on their past experiences. They may have felt humiliated or resentful at having additional support. Their special need may have been just recently diagnosed, perhaps whilst at college. They may not understand how their special need affects their ability or style of learning. They may not have been offered additional support. They may refuse additional help within the college and, if so, will depend on teaching styles that incorporate their needs within the classroom. Learning support must be built into classroom practice.

## How do I find out about these students' needs within the classroom?

The learning support coordinator will have a list of individual students' needs. It may be on the special needs staffroom noticeboard. Seek out this information and highlight in your register the names of students with identified special needs. Many coordinators will also have prepared 'Implications for learning within the subject area' sheets, which outline how the disability will affect their learning, for example:

> Jo is dyslexic. He should not be asked to read aloud as this stresses him. He uses a laptop as his writing is illegible, and he will rely on clear handouts. He cannot copy accurately from the board due to his poor visual short-term memory. He has difficulties identifying errors on the computer screen and needs to print out work in order to correct it. He needs a tinted background for teacher-constructed Web site materials. Avoid the need to scroll when producing Web sites. Use large, clear font. His verbal and comprehension skills are accelerated. He has 25 per cent extra time in exams.

Many students will have special examination provisions such as extra time, a scribe, a prompt or breaks within the paper to aid concentration. Note this information and the implications for coursework, classroom tests and marking.

## Task 11.4

Think back to the last class you taught. Answer these questions:

- Were you aware of students identified as having a special educational need?
- How did you get this information?
- What were the implications for your teaching?
- How many students in your last class were dyslexic?
- How many had other learning-related disorders or disabilities?
- How many had additional support?
- What form did the additional support take?
- Did you need to refer any students for additional support?
- Did you know the procedures for referral for additional support?
- How did you facilitate learning for each individual student within the class?

## Good practice guidelines for students with professionally identified individual needs

It would not be possible to cover more than a limited range of needs within the context of this chapter. I have, therefore, confined the following to some conditions that I have personally encountered and taught within the last educational year. The implications for teaching are by no means exhaustive. Add some more ideas to each section.

### Dyslexia

> Dyslexia is a complex neurological condition that is constitutional in origin. It is a lifelong condition but the symptoms may diminish over time as various coping strategies are taken on board. The symptoms may affect many areas of learning and function, and may be described as a specific difficulty in reading, spelling and written language. One or more of these areas may be affected. Numeracy, notational skills (music), motor function and organisational skills may also be affected. However it is particularly related to mastering written language, although oral language may be affected to some degree.
>
> (Crisfield, 1996)

Those with dyslexia are often articulate and display their knowledge well through verbalizing. It is the mismatch between this ability and their poor spelling and reading fluency and accuracy abilities that alert us to the specific need.

For example, a student recently read the word 'diver' for driver', 'bread' for beard' and 'internal' for 'interview'. The same student spelt 'rember' for 'remember', 'scense' for 'science' and 'hoover' for 'however'. As students with dyslexia need to 'read back' in order to remember what they have written, they often miss sentence boundaries. Look out for this verbal and written 'mismatch' within the classroom as many students are identified as being dyslexic for the first time whilst at college.

### Some implications for teaching

Students with dyslexia may have difficulty in copying from the board, reading aloud, skimming and scanning, spelling and making notes. They may tire easily. Many need to word-process their work. Many need 'Read/Write' computer programs. Do not ask them to read aloud unless this has been agreed with the student. Do not expect them to silent-read for long periods as this activity stimulates the visual channel only. Do not expect accurate reading aloud to mean that comprehension has taken place as the act and effort of decoding each word mechanically can impair comprehension. Do not correct each spelling; choose a few target words to focus upon and encourage the use of a spell check. If spellings are so bizarre that they mar meaning, ask the student to write on every other line so that you can give the correct word clearly. Do correct in a pen of another colour. Agree on a marking strategy so that the student knows what to expect. Check that verbal instructions for homework are read correctly.

Encourage students with dyslexia to use highlighters, which may mean providing them with their own personal copies of texts. Help them with self-organization and planning. Those with dyslexia have difficulties sequencing ideas in writing; they will be helped by mind mapping in order to plan, and through the provision of writing frameworks that give them a 'sentence starter' for each paragraph. A mind map involves putting the central idea in the middle of a piece of paper and then extending it with subsections of related ideas before deciding upon the order in which to deal with the ideas. Problems with 'getting started' can often be allayed by brainstorming as all thoughts can 'flow' on to paper in random order prior to classifying the ideas and sequencing the thoughts.

## Dyspraxia

Dyspraxia results in difficulty in carrying out both familiar and non-familiar motor skills. The process does not become automatic; thus it remains a novel task. Those with dyspraxia will have poor fine motor skills, problems in remembering the shapes of letters, short attention span and poor short-term auditory memory.

### Some implications for teaching

- Improve memory and organization through providing time-budgeted tasks and lists of tasks to be undertaken.
- Check understanding of tasks through asking the student to repeat the instructions to you.
- Do not give an abundance of 'copying from the board' tasks.
- Allow access to a laptop.
- Be aware of difficulties that may arise in physically manipulative demanding tasks.
- Be aware of problems that could arise in PE tasks.

## Language-processing difficulties

Those with language-processing disorders may have problems in understanding the task, 'finding' the right word and reading fluently. They may have difficulties in following directions because they talk to themselves as the directions are given. This creates an internal interference that blocks effective processing of the external information.

### Some implications for teaching

- Give, clear, precise, sequenced instructions.
- Introduce new vocabulary.
- Allow extra time for students to locate the words they may be searching for in order to express themselves.

## Attention deficit hyperactive disorder

Students with ADHD display higher levels of inattention and overactivity in any setting. It is often linked with disruptive behaviour at the younger stages. Students with attention deficit hyperactive disorder will have difficulties with concentrating for long periods and with self-organization. Impatience may be displayed in, for example, searching for the correct answer in multiple choice questions. Poor handwriting is often exhibited and sitting still for any length of time will be a challenge. Reading without care may result in incorrect answers or in not understanding the task.

## Some implications for teaching

Lecture-type lessons will be difficult for those with ADHD. The lesson should incorporate a variety of teaching styles that include the opportunity to move around and talk to others or to watch a video extract. Verbal instructions may be better understood than written ones. A calm environment for teaching will be important.

## Asperger's syndrome

Asperger's syndrome is a developmental disorder affecting social relationships and communication. Students with Asperger's syndrome will have little or no skill in abstract thought, language difficulties with regard to a tendency toward literal interpretation, and idiosyncratic use of words. They often have an excellent memory, are creative in their thinking, work very hard and are independent in their actions and views.

## Some implications for teaching

Students with Asperger's syndrome will often find group work a challenge so whole-class and independent work should be built into the lesson. They will need to be reminded of and kept to the task regularly as they can become absorbed in amassing facts that appeal to their personal interest rather than in carrying out the task.

## Epilepsy

The grand mal form of epilepsy is the best-known typology. Those affected become unconscious, and their muscles stiffen and relax in convulsive movements. They will be dazed and confused and often wish to sleep after a seizure. Petit mal may go unrecognized as those affected experience brief interruptions to consciousness. They may look as if they are daydreaming and unaware of their surroundings. Temporal lobe epilepsy seizures involve a period of 'switching off' or clouded consciousness where certain repetitive movements may be made. Those affected will feel confused as they return to full consciousness.

The seizures are often controlled by medication but those with epilepsy may experience extreme anxiety and be generally of low spirits due to anxiety and the pressures that the epilepsy imposes. Those with epilepsy may have poor attention, concentration and memory. They will have an impairment of accuracy of eye movements that will affect their reading accuracy and comprehension. They will have impaired motor speed and, often, poor handwriting. They will find it difficult to take a problem-solving approach to learning.

## Some implications for teaching

- Build in rest breaks where students can sit back and listen for a while rather than 'perform' for a whole lesson.
- Ensure that computer screens and fluorescent lights do not flicker.
- Ensure that the lesson is summarized at the end to 'fill in gaps' that may have occurred.
- Allow extra time for reading.

## Obsessive compulsive disorder

Students with obsessive compulsive disorder are besieged by intrusive thoughts, images or impulses, and will lose concentration, find difficulty in 'getting started' and may be late or miss lectures. They may also suffer from depression and be taking medication.

## Implications for teaching

Students with obsessive compulsive disorder may be slow to react to instructions. Allow them time. Be prepared to repeat. Be prepared to give directions that take away choice, as they have great difficulty in making decisions, for example 'By the end of this lesson you will have completed task 1.' Time on task will be important.

## Teaching the hearing-impaired

Hearing-impaired students will need to sit where they can see the teacher's lips, and be given instructions in plain English. They will need to be given extra time for reading material. They may misunderstand words with more than one meaning – check understanding. Keep to one verb tense. Use an overhead projector rather than the board to write notes so that they can see your lips.

## Teaching those with English as a second language

Those with English as a second language also have individual needs. They will range in their command of speaking, listening, reading and writing. They may also be dyslexic. Their listening and speaking skills may mismatch their reading and writing skills. They may be asylum seekers or settled refugees who have suffered trauma, cultural shock and a disrupted education. They may be experiencing practical difficulties or racist attitudes and behaviour.

## Task 11.5

Return now to the checklist in Task 11.1 and fill it in again using a different pen. You will now feel confident in addressing the diversity of needs within the classroom and in giving students the opportunity to develop autonomy in their learning.

When the best leader's work is done, the people say, 'We did it ourselves.'
(Lao Tsu, Philosopher)

# References

Crisfield, J (1996) *The Dyslexia Handbook*, BDA, Reading

Fisher, R (1998) *Teaching Thinking: Philosophical enquiry into the classroom*, Cassell, London

Tomlinson, J (1996) *Report of the Committee on Students with Learning Difficulties and/or Disabilities* (The Tomlinson Report, also known as Inclusive Learning), FEFC, HMSO, London

# 12 The implications of the development of ICT for teaching and learning post 16

Hilary Street

## Introduction

The government has set challenging targets for the education sector in terms of the development and use of ICT as a learning and teaching tool. Many of these targets relate to the school sector pre-16.

Two targets are particularly important:

- By 2004, 75 per cent of school pupils will achieve level 5 or above in ICT at the end of Key Stage 3 as a milestone to the 2007 target of 85 per cent.
- By 2006, ICT should be the fundamental tool to enhance, extend and individualize learning opportunities (and the management of this learning) for 5- to 19-year-olds.

This is an important point for colleagues teaching in a post-16 environment to be aware of. Increasingly the students joining sixth form centres of FE colleges are likely to be highly computer-literate, used to ILT being used as a learning and teaching tool and comfortable with using the Web as a resource for their learning. Many of them will be used to relating online to their teachers, having assessment and feedback undertaken online and accessing work and lesson material from their home.

This has significant implications for staff teaching 16- to 19-year-old students. They are likely to expect the use of ILT to be an integral part of their learning experience. This chapter first summarizes the key aspects of ILT that teachers themselves need to be aware of, and then discusses the implications of those developments for the design of the learning and teaching of 16- to 19-year-old students. Specific examples are included throughout. The chapter concludes by providing examples of the use of ILT to support learning and teaching.

# How can the development of ILT help teachers and learners?

The development of ILT can help *teachers* in the following ways:

- Teachers are able to find high-quality teaching materials and resources using the Web and their own college intranets.
- Teaching can be designed to be more tailored to individual student needs.
- Teachers can share the workload of planning more effectively.
- There is more time for teacher talk and interaction with learners in the class as a whole group, small groups or individually because by effective use of interactive white-boards much of the material that needs to be written during the course of the lesson is already prepared.
- There is an increased variety of teaching methods that allows teachers to respond to different learning styles.
- There is the potential for ongoing contact for students when they are not in lessons.
- There is the potential for online feedback, assessment and marking.
- It can encourage and support more collaborative learning between staff in the same college and between staff across colleges.

The development of ILT can help *learners* in the following ways:

- Students have access to a wider range of current resources.
- Students are able to have more direct 'real-time' experiences, eg real-time conferencing with students in other parts of the country or world, and online discussions with other students.
- There is an increased variety of teaching methods that allows teachers to respond to different learning styles.
- There is the potential for ongoing contact for students when they are not in lessons.
- There is the potential for online feedback, assessment and marking.
- ILT can support the development of self-directed learning through the development of supported self-study units.

The National Association of Advisers for Computer Education (NAACE) and the British Educational Communications and Technology Association (BECTA) published a guidance note about ILT and noted that there were five key features of effective practice when ILT was being used and taught effectively:

- the development of learner autonomy;
- the development of increased capability;
- the creative use of ILT;
- an improvement in the quality of students' work when they are using ILT effectively;
- an increase in 'scope' – learning activities can be developed using ILT that would otherwise not be possible.

This contribution from Paul Norris of Farnham Heath School in Surrey shows the features in his development of the use of ILT to support learning and teaching in MFL:

- commenting text to help support vocabulary;
- hyperlinking between documents to link activities together;
- bookmarking longer passages to develop independence and confidence with literacy;
- show/hide to enable pupils to check their own answers and feel confident to work at their own pace;
- show/hide to provide pupils with writing scaffolds for longer pieces of written work;
- colour to highlight the different components of language and how they form structures in sentences;
- drop-down menus to make multiple choice more interactive;
- symbols to bring certain texts alive;
- hyperlinking to a specific site on the Internet in order to keep an activity on task and avoid wasting time searching ineffectively;
- animations to encourage creativity;
- sound to help pupil confidence without having to perform in front of the whole class.

Paul Norris believes there are benefits to students, because they are more motivated. Whilst it is difficult to quantify potential increase/decrease in performance based on assessment, observations in everyday classes, such as the following, are worth noting:

- *Keenness to get on with work*: an increase in motivation.
- *Taking more care with presentation*: the desire to get it just right.
- *Increased student autonomy*. Differentiation is easier for teachers so pupils have work that is appropriate. This in turn has a positive impact on their motivation.
- *Increased confidence*. They can work at their own pace with or without peers.
- *Supportive peers*. Students often solve technical problems before the teacher!
- *Longer concentration spans*. Many students will continue through break to finish something off because they are proud of their work.

## ILT and its implications for the teaching role

The development of easy access to ILT for both students and teachers has significant implications for the relationship between teachers and learners. Teachers will still have a crucial and central role in the learning process but it will be different.

Teachers need to:

- design the learning and teaching differently to take into account the potential of ILT and help their students learn how to navigate their way through the mass of information now available so that students can be discerning users;

- still 'teach' directly by giving direct input and, as well, they will have to integrate a wider range of strategies into their repertoire that draw on and use ILT – including the use of interactive whiteboards, online feedback, videoconferencing etc;
- develop their own competency in developing their own online learning materials and supported self-study materials and will need to develop the skills to do that.

## The creation of effective self-study materials

Writing effective self-study materials requires careful thought to ensure that they are effective tools for student learning. The following list highlights some of the things it is important to think about when designing self-study materials.

---

This is based on the work of Liz Whitelegg, a lecturer in the Centre for Science Education at the Open University with extensive experience of developing supported self-study materials, in particular in the APIL programme for A level physics.

- *What will the format be?* Will it be text only or multimedia (audiotapes, videotapes, TV programmes, CD ROMs, computer programs, Web-based resources, set books)? The material must look different from a textbook. Factors to consider are:
  - Small sections provide pace and enable attainable goals to be set.
  - Give an estimated study time for each section.
  - Self-contained sections allow for a 'pick-and-mix' approach.
  - Materials must be user-friendly.
- *Use of existing materials*:
  - Time and resources are limited so use some existing material as well.
  - Research what is available and then write a 'study guide' to provide active learning opportunities.
  Note: the OU ROUTES system is very useful for tracking Web-based resources.
- *Getting students on board.* If the idea of supported self-study is new for some students then they may be sceptical of unfamiliar methods, for example they may see it as 'breaking the pedagogical contract' if they have a 'transmission' view of knowledge and learning based on the assumption that the teacher 'gives them the facts'.
  - Self-study materials need to be introduced gradually and a mixed approach used.
  - Students need to be supported to develop the skills and self-discipline required for self-study.
- *The teacher's role in supported self-study*:
  - Acting as a facilitator to support students' learning.
  - Students working in groups according to level and pace of study.
  - Teacher working on a one-to-one basis with students.
  - Tutor running 'surgeries' for individual or groups of students.
  - Tutor needs to be monitoring individual student progress regularly – either face-to-face or online.

- *Elements of supported self-study materials*:
  - aims and objectives clearly stated at the beginning;
  - study plan given (length of study for each section, items needed);
  - margin notes and 'flags' to link to other materials;
  - introduction and overview to each section;
  - exercises followed by discussions in each section (questions, problems, quotes);
  - questions throughout the materials to check understanding;
  - bold terms defined in glossary;
  - dialogue between author and student (use of personal voice);
  - illustrations;
  - summary of each section and summary of all sections;
  - learning outcomes clearly stated and achievements checklist;
  - answers to exercises and questions in full.

## What ILT resources are you likely to find in your college?

You will already have had experience from your teaching practices of the sorts of equipment that are now routinely available at colleges, but the rate of development is not uniform. However, most colleges are likely to have some or all of the following:

- college-wide intranet;
- interactive whiteboards in some or all teaching rooms, and certainly some in each department (with PowerPoint projectors in the ceilings);
- a 'learning centre', which will house the majority of the college's computers for student use, with online access;
- videoconferencing facilities;
- computers in some or all teaching rooms;
- wireless technology allowing for a more flexible use of laptops.

## Task 12.1

Consider:

- Are you clear what facilities are available in your college or school?
- Are you clear how you can access support for your own professional development in ILT?
- Are you clear what technical back-up is available?

# What specific aspects of ILT have particular impact on the design of the learning and teaching?

## Interactive whiteboards

Interactive whiteboards (sometime known as 'Smartboards') are whiteboards that are wired electronically and can be connected to a laptop. They enable teachers to prepare all their lessons on a laptop, plug their laptop into the projector in the teaching room and work through the lesson on the whiteboard. It also means that teachers when designing their lessons can integrate video clips and sound whenever they feel it is appropriate. It brings presentations alive. It is also a great time saver during the lesson as the teacher can use, for example, grids, graphs and maps more easily with a whole class, and can manipulate and change data on-screen.

For example, in a history session looking at the battles of the First World War, a diagram showing the position of Allied and German troops before the Battle of the Somme could be on the screen and students could be asked 'What if?', eg 'What if the troops had been in different positions? How might the outcomes of the battle have been different?'

### Planning to use an interactive whiteboard

If you are using the whiteboard then it means it can be used interactively with the students – who can then add, amend and answer questions on the whiteboard as part of the session. It is important to think how you can use it interactively when you are planning for its use.

In a lesson on *Macbeth* the teacher might plan the lesson to focus on the relationship between Macbeth and Lady Macbeth. The teacher will prepare a lesson plan, which will be on computer and displayed to the class, enabling the teacher to give the class the 'big picture' overview of the whole lesson, complete with timings for each section. The teacher may have identified the particular page references where there are particular parts of a scene that give an insight into the relationship – these references will be on the computer and displayed straight away for the class, and individual groups of students will be assigned one of the page references to look up and read and present their views to the group. The teacher might have downloaded a scene between Lady Macbeth and Macbeth from one of the videos of the play – this will then be shown through the interactive whiteboard when the class have had their initial discussion; there will then be a class discussion on this. The teacher may have a number of quotes from the play that illustrate the relationship, and a list of words describing the relationship, and students can be invited to go up to the whiteboard and draw arrows between each quote and the description of the relationship. The lesson might end with another clip of an actress being interviewed discussing her view of the relationship between Lady Macbeth and Macbeth.

The homework will also be prepared and shown on the whiteboard and may include details of links to relevant Web sites.

In colleges that have an intranet this lesson would then be stored on the college's intranet and any student who was absent could access it from home, or any students could go over the lesson again in their own time at home or in the college learning centre.

### The genetically modified food example

If a biology, geography or business studies teacher were teaching the topic of genetically modified (GM) food, s/he could: put the lesson plan on the board and so give students the 'big picture' easily; include photos of genetically modified foods and GM farms; integrate some excerpts from news items about GM food; and, finally, do an interactive quiz with students about what they know about GM foods.

### The interactive whiteboard tablet

The technology has already developed further. There are now A6-size interactive whiteboard tablets available. They act as mobile whiteboards and can be used anywhere in the room. This means that the teacher does not have to be static at the front of the classroom when using the interactive whiteboard.

The *TES* 13 September and 11 October 2002 gave a complete analysis of the range of interactive whiteboards available and their different properties.

## Task 12.2

Consider the following:

- Have you been trained in the use of interactive whiteboards? If not, then are you clear who you would talk to at your college to arrange training for yourself?
- Do you know how many interactive whiteboards there are in your college and where they are situated? If there is not one in every teaching area do you know how to gain access to a room with an interactive whiteboard if you wish to use it in your teaching?
- How do you currently plan your lessons? Is the lesson planning shared with other colleagues? Do you all share your lesson plans and put them on a college intranet?
- Are there colleagues in your department or team who already use the interactive whiteboards for their lessons? Would it be possible for you to observe them giving a lesson where they are using the interactive board?
- Can you identify a module/part of one of the courses you teach where you would like to use the interactive whiteboard? How would you use the interactive whiteboard creatively?

## Videoconferencing

This is as yet a relatively underused ILT resource but it has enormous potential. The term 'videoconferencing' is used to describe the process whereby, using video cameras and a computer link, people in different places (different parts of the same college, different parts of the country, different parts of the world) can work and discuss something together at the same time. Such conferences need significant forward planning, clarity of purpose and often a conference 'manager' who will manage the technical side of the process.

Videoconferences offer a number of opportunities. Students who might be studying a minority subject on their own online can take part in such conferences at regular intervals to discuss an aspect of a course with other students who are also learning online. Students can have a videoconference with an 'expert' in a particular aspect of their subject or course, for example a scientist in a laboratory talking live to students about his/her current research, or a discussion with students in an economically developing country about the effect of the Kyoto agreement on their economy.

It is possible to subscribe to the international videoconferencing Web site www.Global-leap.com. There is a timetable of different topics to be discussed. They have to be highly organized with everyone online at the same time. A conference 'moderator' manages the process. Students and other participants have to be well prepared to ensure that they do not 'freeze up'.

Video cameras can now be put on computers so that students can see each other as well as their tutor if they are using videoconferencing for distance learning.

Another useful resource is 'Video-Conferencing in the Classroom', which has been produced by Devon County Council and launched at a global videoconferencing day organized by Global Leap in aid of the *TES*/UNICEF appeal to support the rebuilding of Afghanistan's infrastructure.

## *The genetically modified food example*

A group looking at the issue surrounding the development of genetically modified products might want to set up a videoconference with one of the farmers who is currently involved in the government trials, and/or two scientists who have been investigating the effect of GM foods.

## Darlington College

The college has established a 'telematics learning centre' at the Catterick campus. This is a videoconference suite with 150 computers. Each computer has a mini-cam attached, to facilitate one-to-one tutoring on distance learning courses. The Catterick campus is 20 miles from the main college at Darlington and the original intention was that students could attend their course at Catterick and pursue it in 'distance learning mode', tutored by staff at the main site.

The college has had to rethink its approach to the use of distance learning in this way as it is dependent on the existence of a large range of materials available on the 'learning platform' in the system, which the students can access. Originally the college used bought-in material but this is not always sufficient or bespoke enough to fit particular course needs. The college is now exploring generating in-house material.

The college has widened out its portfolio and now uses the centre more flexibly. It is used regularly for staff-to-staff conferencing between the sites and for videoconferencing calls.

In addition the telematics centre also has an interactive whiteboard, which has allowed teaching staff to develop their learning and teaching strategies further. In particular it means that the staff can bring up a live link on the interactive whiteboard during the lesson. The technology is also more user-friendly as the teacher does not have to be at a keyboard when using the whiteboard because of its touch-screen facility. The teacher can if s/he wishes teach from the front of the class.

Videoconferences are complex to organize particularly if you are trying to link with students or experts in another country. If you are interested in developing this as a learning and teaching strategy then it is best to start small and identify one videoconference that you want to organize in one year. The added value to the students' learning has to be very clear.

## Task 12.3

If your college does have or were to have videoconferencing facilities, which parts of the courses you teach would be appropriate for the development of a videoconferencing opportunity?

## The use of laptops

The use of laptops by teachers as part of the interactive whiteboard technology has already been discussed. However laptops when used by teachers and pupils together can be a very powerful resource for learning and teaching.

If a whole class has access to a laptop then the learning can be designed to encourage and enable the students to work straight on to their laptops, to e-mail and share their notes and the teacher's notes between the group and to prepare presentations for each other as part of the teacher's design of the learning.

### PowerPoint presentations

One of the most common uses of laptops as a learning and teaching tool is to enable the teacher and/or students to make PowerPoint presentations. Some examples are given here of how this facility can be used to support learning and teaching.

## *The genetically modified example*

In a science, English, citizenship, PSHE or geography lesson, a class may be divided into small groups and each may have to prepare a PowerPoint presentation on the use of GM technology. One group will be asked to present the benefits from a farmer's perspective, one from a pharmaceutical company's perspective, one from the perspective of an environmentalist who is against GM products, one from the perspective of the marketing director of a supermarket chain and one from the perspective of a government representative of an economically developing country.

Each group will be expected to construct a PowerPoint presentation for the whole class. They will share out the preparation and research and all members of the group will contribute to the final compiling and delivery of the presentation. Each presentation should last no longer than five minutes. A lesson is then given over to the five presentations. The teacher manages the process of the presentations, structuring discussion and questioning after each presentation. All students are then e-mailed each group's presentation and the teacher's comments on each one. Any gaps or misconceptions are addressed by the teaching and also given to the whole group.

Teachers themselves will obviously use PowerPoint presentation as one of their ways of teaching a whole group. PowerPoint presentations when designed properly can give a clear focus to a topic, help the presenter be precise and direct about the main points and enable a lot of material to be covered in a relatively short time. They are particularly useful for giving an initial overview of a whole module (the big picture) for the reasons given. They also allow for 'chunking' of material. A whole presentation can be prepared but can be given in small bites.

Another advantage of PowerPoint presentations is that if enough planning time is given they can be designed to appeal to visual, auditory and kinaesthetic learners as they can include pictures and photos, text and sound.

They also mean that students can easily have a printout of the presentation and have an easy reference tool in their notes.

## Eggbuckland College

Eggbuckland Community College in Devon have been piloting the laptops project with their pupils. The same process could be used with older students as well, and have a double use as one of the ways of accrediting key skills.

### The laptops project

The college decided to explore what would happen to learning and teaching if all students had a laptop with them in all lessons. At the beginning of Year 8 (2001/02) there was one tutor group where all the students had laptops. They were known as the laptop group.

## The mechanics of the process

For the college the challenge was how to use ICT to support collaborative learning between students. Traditionally in ICT suites the arrangement does not support collaborative learning. The primary laptop project had shown that once pupils were working with their own laptops then collaborative learning and working can follow.

The school identified a room for the laptop group where 'flexible learning' could happen – where the geography, space and size of the room and the type of furniture in the room made it possible to teach flexibly. All lessons would be taught in this room so it needed to be a science lab, classroom, lecture theatre and performance space, and capable of partitioning. As a learning and teaching research laboratory, it needed to be capable of supporting numerous modes of working.

## The vision for the laptop group

The deputy headteacher met with the subject teachers of the laptop group to explain the concept and in effect 'talk up' the project. He explained to staff that there was no requirement to use the laptops but that over time it was hoped that all staff would find a way of using the opportunity presented. All teachers in the laptop group were given their own laptops. The main concepts that the school hoped the staff would explore with the students were how the laptops could encourage different patterns of working across the group and how groups of students working together could be responsible for teaching the rest of the class.

## Protocols for laptop use

Such a concept and new way of working required new routines in the class to 'scaffold' the process, so detailed routines, procedures and protocols for the use of ICT in lessons had to be agreed, and insisted upon with the students. For example, 'Students all get up and line up outside between lessons', 'When anyone says "Can I have your attention?" all laptop lids will be closed', 'Unrequested use of the Internet results in removal of the network card.'

The deputy headteacher explained that ideally it would be good if each teacher could develop one module/unit of work each term that required both the teacher and the students to use their laptops.

## Managing the learning and teaching

The model that was adopted by all of the teachers in the end was to divide the students into small work groups and each group had to investigate for themselves part of the particular unit being studied and then teach that unit to the rest of the class. Not only were groups to teach it to the class but they would assess their work at the end, the main criterion being whether the rest of the class achieved the learning outcomes as a result of the teaching. This meant that the teachers had to be clear about both the learning objectives and the learning outcomes for the unit and discuss this with the students. It did not mean that the teachers did not teach. Although the styles differed, all teachers would set the scene for the unit with the students, and teachers would then use the PowerPoint presentations that the student work groups gave to enhance, support and clarify the learning.

For example, in a laptop science lesson the group had been learning about phagocytes and the immune system. A work group of three students gave a joint presentation about phagocytes, using PowerPoint and also acting out the process between them. The teacher took this, highlighted some key points that needed to be emphasized from the presentation, made some brief notes on the whiteboard from the laptop and then asked that group to e-mail their presentation to the rest of the group.

One of them explained it like this: 'We have a topic to research and then we make presentations in our groups – so half the tutor group do their presentations and then the teacher does the "ordinary stuff" and then the rest of the group finish their presentations.' And in answer to the question about whether they enjoy this way of working, students were quick to note that it made it easier to have all their notes on the laptop rather than in lots of files and books and bits of paper, and it was more interesting.

## Weekly review with staff and students

The laptop teachers meet weekly to discuss progress and sticking points and to refine the approach. The membership of this weekly meeting has now been extended to include students from the group as well. This is peer learning in action for both students and staff. The issues that have come up for discussion include students wanting to know how to support members of their group who are disorganized or finding the work difficult, and staff and students discussing the merits of different forms of assessment and what you do if you realize that some students haven't understood.

## Initial learning from the project

This project has shown that for the first time students were talking and thinking about how to engage others in learning. It has been a stimulus for the staff to think through strategies for addressing disengagement amongst students; it has supported the development of more innovative methods for assessment as staff and students have had to answer the question 'How do you know if learning has taken place?'; and it has required teachers to think through how, if something doesn't work, it can be done another way.

All the materials developed are put on the college's intranet.

During the year the laptop students have been having the same assessments made of their work and learning as other students in the year and there is no evidence to show that they have learnt less as a result of this way of working – but what they have done is develop a range of skills that their counterparts in the rest of the year have not had the opportunity to develop in the same way (collaborative working, research, presentation, assessment). They also have highly developed ICT skills – they have typing practice in tutor time once a week as well as discrete ICT.

The college has now used this project as part of its outreach work with other secondary schools. Three secondary schools are going to link with the college to enable teachers from those schools to teach with someone from the laptop group to develop their own practice in this area. The college already has links with the hospital school and provides them with all its resources to their laptops through its terminal services.

## The 'intelligent' use of the Web

The use of the Web as a teaching and learning tool is almost infinite – but it requires planning and skill to use the Web 'intelligently'. Teachers can use the Web as a source of raw material for work they are planning for their students and as a resource for their students to use.

Both teachers and students need to have been taught how to use the Web effectively: what search engines to use, how to do a key word search sensibly (including making the key word search as specific as possible so that the search is as specific as possible, and making judgements about the quality of the material located). These skills have to be taught to students by all their subject and course teachers – as the skills and knowledge required will vary from subject to subject.

### The genetically modified food example

Typing 'genetically modified food' into a search engine resulted in 371,000 sites being identified. If a teacher wanted to ask students to investigate aspects of GM food then it would be important to identify precisely what questions the students should be seeking to answer. The teacher might share the questions out amongst the students so that, working in pairs, each pair had to investigate two questions. The teacher would have undertaken an initial search and identified at least 10 sites that were known to be useful and reliable in terms of the source of the information.

A creative use of the Web is to post an article on the college Web site in the agreed location for your subject or programme and pose some questions at the end of the article. Students in the group are then expected to go online, read the article and post their responses to the questions asked. As other students answer the questions they comment on previous answers. The group ends up with a discussion document about the article that is then a learning resource for them all.

What can teachers do to help students use the Web effectively?

- Many teachers identify the most useful sites on a particular subject for their students and direct them to those first of all. They will incorporate the names of these sites into any teaching materials they produce.
- Many colleges now have an intranet and there will be links from the college's intranet to the useful Web sites.
- Teachers need to develop their own protocols with students about the use of Web-based material. For example, students may want to print off material for their own reference but they should not as a general rule cut and paste direct from the Web into their work; instead they should draw out the main points in their own words, and if quoting they should show this specifically.

## ILT as a learning and teaching tool in AS music and music technology

Rob Tucker, Head of Music at the Royal Latin School in Buckinghamshire, has used ICT to support the learning and teaching on AS music and music technology in a number of ways:

- He used it to administer an online learning styles questionnaire (see Chapter 5 for a discussion of learning styles).
- He used it to develop his own knowledge and understanding about ILT as a learning tool and to find out about Web-based learning environments by looking at university-based music technology Web sites.
- He designed a Web-based system of learning units, which included the resources for each task.
- He also put a pre-course study online, which students had to complete in the summer holidays prior to the start of the course as a requirement of entry to the course.

Two particular aspects of the work are described here: the development of Web-based learning units and the use of questioning as a learning and teaching tool.

### *Web-based learning units*

Students are under pressure of time and often over-rely on short cuts to complete their work, particularly when library access may be unavailable or the necessary resources are limited. I therefore designed a Web-based system of learning units, which included the resources for each task. Integrated links encouraged them to research a topic in different ways by looking at alternative sources/viewpoints. This meant finding the relevant information quickly without wasting time searching the wider Web. The site also included an interactive section, thus allowing students to consolidate their understanding by seeing and hearing actual musical examples and online questioning. Students were required to complete the work over the summer holidays as part of the entry requirement for the course.

The students were obviously enthused by the specific nature of the site, and the highly *immediate* form of learning instantly appealed, particularly because all the supporting knowledge for the questions could be found in one place and they were able to manage their study time wisely. There were two distinct advantages: (a) the confidence gained from a completely interactive medium and (b) the instantaneous retrieval and feedback of results from online question forms.

The only obvious disadvantage with the online questioning was that students sometimes felt they were being expected to find factual answers to thinking-based, open-ended questions even when a structure was provided to support them. They still needed the opportunity to be encouraged through group questioning and further discussion in their group sessions. For example, in ICT work 'How might the "save as" facility be used musically?' or 'Does a piece of music need a climax?' are both thinking questions. Online learning does not replace face-to-face work.

## The use of questioning as a teaching and learning tool

It became apparent developing this work that there was a need to create question units containing a carefully ordered balance between factual and thinking questions. The online forms that the students completed meant that the teacher could see the pace of completion, the order in which they answered the questions and the content itself. Feedback by e-mail invariably showed that the student simply needed reassurance: that it was OK to include more intellectual- (thinking-) based answers and that several different answers may be possible, depending on the musical subject/situation. In some cases, however, students made the assumption that factual-based questions inevitably require researching, whereas open-based questions do not. This suggests a need for a unit about how to respond to different sorts of question.

## The use of the intranet and Internet

All the question units were completed online. This saved time in monitoring of progress and provided feedback via e-mail as students accessed the system and sent each unit. It also meant the related study materials/links could be located in one place. Intranet-/Internet-based learning provides a pathway between homework and school-based written learning, for example an end-of-topic test completed online and sent by e-mail for marking. Certain question banks might be marked electronically. The marks are sent direct to the staff intranet for assessment and monitoring. Results are then instantaneously collated, aligned with the pupil's profile in other subjects and made available for reporting immediately. This might even take place online. This increases flexibility of the learning environment for students, provides instant feedback, reduces staff workload and gives students more ownership over their learning.

## The use of computers

It may seem strange to have a specific section about the use of computers *per se* in a chapter on ILT but it is important to consider the specific applications that have relevance for most subjects.

### Word processing

This is the most obvious use of the computer. Increasingly students will make their course notes on computer as they go through their course; some will make their lesson notes directly on to computer if they have their own laptop to use in the lesson. One of the most useful strategies to encourage students to do is to build up their own revision notes on each module as they go along, eg in modern foreign languages to build up their own vocabulary lists on computer as they go through the course – they can then classify the vocabulary in a range of ways. In history they might want to summarize the main dates/events/people in a database as they go along.

Any work that requires drafting should be done using a word-processing programme though teachers need to make it clear whether they need to see the interim drafts as well as the final product. This is particularly important in the development of coursework where verification could become a problem.

---

### *The genetically modified food example*

Topics such as this lend themselves to the use of word-processing or desktop-publishing programmes. Students can be asked to design a leaflet advertising a protest rally against the development of GM foods or to produce a leaflet from farmers involved in GM trials and putting the case for GM products.

They can 'script' and word-process an imaginary interview between the prime minister and a member of Friends of the Earth about the government's GM policy.

---

## PowerPoint

The benefits and uses of PowerPoint have been discussed earlier in this chapter.

## Spreadsheets

Spreadsheets are one of the functions that students (and teachers) need to be able to use. Almost all subjects and courses can find opportunities for the use of spreadsheets, particularly if graphs and the forms of charts are needed. For example, a business course may be looking at information about customer complaints and wanting to develop graphs about type of complaint, number of complaints at different times of year, etc. An economics course may be doing work on exchange rates or a science course may be looking at statistics about diseases in various parts of the world and their relationship to the death rates in different countries.

---

### The genetically modified food example

In the case of genetically modified food it would be possible to obtain statistics from the Department for Environment, Food and Rural Affairs about the GM trials and from the large food producers about the benefits of GM in terms of yield per acre and cost per acre. This information can then be presented in spreadsheet form.

---

## Databases

Again databases have potential in many courses and programmes. A database is simply a means of storing a large amount of information electronically, and in such a way that the data can be printed off and retrieved in a variety of ways and a variety of combinations and can be manipulated in different ways. They therefore offer flexibility in their use. For example, a GNVQ business course may develop a database about companies in the local area that includes information about geographic location, size of work force, age and gender of work force, focus of business and age of company. This information can then be analysed in a number of different ways. An English group may want to look at particular themes in the novels of Jane Austen and produce a database that shows the themes in relation to the various novels. A geography database might be based on climate and topography statistics.

## Desktop publishing

Again this is one of the most common applications that is useful for all subjects and courses because it is so versatile. This application enables students (and teachers) to produce documents in a variety of layouts and styles other than simply an A4 piece of text. Business students can produce a prospectus for a company, catering students can produce a menu for a restaurant in a range of different styles, drama students can produce publicity information for a play or a programme for a production, and history students are frequently asked to design the front page for a newspaper reporting a historic event as it happens.

Detailed examples of all of these applications in different subjects can be found on two Web sites: www.InteractiveEducation.ac.uk and the FELR Web site at BECTA http://ferl.org.uk. A summary of some of the examples included on those Web sites is given here. The full versions are available on the Web sites.

# Examples of the use of ILT to support learning and teaching

## From the Interactive Education site

### Sequences and series with Year 12 AS/A level students (by Leila King)

Students are learning about arithmetic and geometric sequences through using the power of Excel (spreadsheets) to formalize rules to generate sequences and their sums. Some of the teaching takes place in an 'ordinary' classroom and some in a room with an interactive whiteboard. The students have rapidly seen the links between inductive definitions in mathematics and spreadsheet formalisms.

### The golden ratio in art in Intermediate GNVQ

This is used in art with Intermediate GNVQ students in art and design and forms part of the students' key skills level 1 application of number requirements. Students learn to construct the golden rectangle using pen-and-paper techniques. Using the Internet and other software they then search for examples of paintings and investigate whether aspects of the paintings fit within a golden rectangle frame. They also investigate measurements within paintings such as distances between the various parts of the face. This enables a comparison to be made between different artists.

## From the FERL Web site

### Interactive online testing in AS/A2 sociology (by Chris Gardner at Cadbury Sixth Form College)

Cadbury College is a sixth form college in south Birmingham whose students are recruited from a wide variety of cultural backgrounds across the city. The sociology department has approximately 180 full-time students aged 16–19 following AS and A level sociology courses. The majority of students are female, and over half are from a mixture of ethnic minority groups. AS level has produced an increase in student numbers.

### The problem/issue identified

The department had used computer-based objective testing for two years in response to two problems: 1) retention problems in the autumn term of the first year – it had been our experience that students experiencing difficulties in the early part of the course were inclined to panic, particularly if they had initial problems with writing longer stimulus answers and essays; 2) large sets creating problems of additional marking.

The tests were designed to test basic knowledge and understanding and focused on sociological definitions, concepts and the overall structure of topics. A limited number of tests were piloted and the following year these were extended to provide sets of tests for three A level topics. We also introduced regular monitoring with paper tests, which students could practise in advance on computer. Tests were used for topics taught in the first year of A level.

## The use of Hot Potatoes software

At the end of the summer term 2000 we heard of Hot Potatoes software. The software is free, provided that it is used for non-commercial purposes and shared with others. It can be downloaded from http://web.uvic.ca/hrd/halfbaked.

There are different kinds of tests: multiple choice, short answer, ranking and matching exercises, jumbled sentences, gap-fill exercises and crosswords. Most of the tests export a paper version to Word, which can then be adapted for paper tests. The tests are written simply by inserting questions and answers into ready-made boxes. Appearance can be customized or, if preferred, left in a standard format. The tests produce versions for early and more recent Web browsers. They run on the Internet or on intranets. The software produces sophisticated javascript-based Web pages, which run equally well on Netscape and Microsoft browsers.

This met many of the problems we had encountered with the software we had been using. The department had developed an expanding intranet site, and Hot Potatoes tests could be integrated with existing material. The software was free.

## How the tests are used

Tests are being written for the new AS sociology course. They are available on the college intranet. Students practise the tests in non-contact time. Some tests were produced in advance of the new AS level course for September 2000, and others are being written as the first year of the new course progresses. Students do the tests online. They receive a score and some feedback. Some of the tests are then monitored by paper tests in class. Students are told about the paper tests in advance, and can practise them on the intranet.

## The changing role of ILT in AS/A2 geography (by Stuart Hitch)

Initially ILT resources were either bought in (eg GeogCal, Earth Science Software Consortium, Scamp 2) and integrated into the schemes of work, or limited to simple exercises such as basic Web enquiries, digital image folders etc.

More recently the department has progressed on to content-specific Web enquiries, structured enquiries targeted directly at the needs of the students but still providing a wide number of skills (AS/A level examples produced by the author can be found at www.sln.org.uk/geography and via the Web enquiries link). Simple to produce in Microsoft Word, these provide a number of differentiated tasks, often combining text, data and image handling with an assignment such as the production of a presentation, essay or case study using the available ILT facilities as the outcome.

These have proved popular with both staff and students as they are self-contained units, can be completed during lessons or set as homework, and prove useful when there are staff or student absences or as revision exercises. A downside of any Web-based enquiry is the transient nature of some of the Web sites and so relatively frequent updating may be necessary. It is also important, when developing such resources, that staff are aware of the specific content of the sites and of any bias, although this element could be built into the student exercise. Time remains the biggest, and often least considered, element in the development of such resources.

More recently resources have become more integrated, bringing together not only ILT but also more traditional resources such as course texts, video and fieldwork. Such units cover large areas of the course and may eventually be extended to cover complete modules in a move towards a more distance learning approach to the use of ILT. This has been brought about largely due to the increased content demands of the new AS specification completed by the department and the reduced teaching time allocated to AS/A levels.

## Coursework

ILT plays an increasingly important role in the delivery and completion of coursework. Students have access to an increasing number of home-produced, online virtual fieldtrips, past fieldtrip data sets and digital image folders. This allows familiarization with the field study area, vegetation, land use etc prior to carrying out the field course, thereby better preparing students for their field study. It is also a resource that can be accessed after the field course to provide follow-up activities. These virtual fieldtrips have proved particularly important when weather conditions have restricted data collection or when students have been absent through illness.

In terms of presentation, ILT has been both a blessing and a concern. It has clearly improved the quality and variety of presentations, made the statistical analysis of data and their graphing simpler and more effective, and allowed the integration of photos and data into text. It also makes the editing of the draft versions of the coursework much easier but has several major drawbacks.

Several students struggle with time management, spending hours making the presentation look superb at the expense of geographical content. There are those who have limited ICT skills and resent completing coursework using the computer and there is an increase in the number and variety of graphs etc showing the same data at the expense of detailed analysis.

A major issue has been the technical problems students have claimed associated with loss of files, hard disk crashes, printer problems, etc.

## New specifications

The new AS/A2 specifications demand increased use of ILT to the extent of including Internet-based research coursework and ICT skills. The reduced time many schools and colleges are being allowed to complete these specifications is leading to an increased use of ILT to support learning and not simply as an add-on. The integration of geographical learning through ILT with the key skills programme should allow students a relatively easy transition into this new way of learning whilst supporting both their geographical education and their key skills portfolios. As such, geography is in a very strong position to develop ILT and to use it as a marketing tool for the subject itself.

## The creation of a managed learning environment (MLE) in history (by Rob Johnson)

At Richard Huish College, Taunton, Somerset, the history department has been pioneering the use of information and learning technologies alongside traditional methods to enhance delivery, motivation and achievement. Department staff have constructed an effective intranet, authored their own software, designed and implemented a management system for the differentiation and tracking of students, and constructed interactive multimedia for pre-class study, presentations, online learning and assessment. Positive outcomes are already evident in results, work submissions, reading and responses to teaching and learning.

### Aims and objectives

There are two specific needs in the teaching of history: the mastery of essay writing and the ability to analyse documents. The first objective was to enhance the delivery of these skills. It was also noted that students were attending sessions ill prepared (particularly in the reading of essential texts), which needed to be rectified. There was also a desire to raise the level of student achievement. There was an increased demand for access to books because of a rising student population. It was also critically important to integrate ILT with existing offline learning.

### Rationale and solutions

The history staff were determined to maintain and improve their excellent standards of teaching and student achievement, whilst embracing the tools new technology had to offer. This meant that ILT was introduced gradually and tested at each stage. A number of levels of ILT now exist. At the lowest level, all handouts are word-processed and replicated online for absentee students. At the highest level, an MLE product was introduced to set work plans, test student knowledge and track progress and performance, and it was integrated with other learning materials.

### Phases of the project

1. *Staff training*. The first step in developing effective ILT resources and integrating them was staff training to level 3 key skill/CLAIT standard and mastery of basic authoring skills. This has been achieved through the determination of the staff and through IT training offered by the college.
2. *Use of interactive multimedia*. PowerPoint is a popular presentation tool used in history, but the history staff have developed their own interactive multimedia based on topics taught on the course. Self-test questions are interspersed between animated information with sound, music and colour. Advice on questions and study skills, and copies of staff presentations are all utilized by the students. Year 2 A level students have found these pre-class study materials useful for revision too. CD ROM is also used in presentations, projected by a plasma screen with Minimo technology, or with Smartboard. The results of using these technologies have been submitted to FERL.

3. *The use of an intranet.* The intranet has proven a powerful tool and assists in student access to resources. The site for history now contains: an interactive multimedia database, illustrations for use in projects, Web sites (filtered) of direct relevance to the course, interactive scheme of work, online student handbook, charter, information on the annual battlefield tour, exemplar essays, current work and study skills. The intranet also provides a bulletin board for student discussions. In addition, e-mail gives students access from home to make enquiries before and after lessons, or during revision periods. Mail groups have been created to speed up the dissemination of work and deadline reminders (Microsoft Outlook tells you when it has been read).

## Outcomes and benefits

Results have improved as a result of greater use of ILT, and the quality assurance results testify to the value added. Motivation and enthusiasm have increased; work submissions have improved. The MLE management system, constructed by a former history teacher, has been upgraded and offers differentiation, improved student tracking and assessment. Presentations are enhanced with the integration of video, CD ROM, paper-based work (document study) and essay writing.

## Task 12.4

Use Table 12.1 to think through how the various applications could be used to support the design of learning and teaching in the course you are currently teaching. The columns have been headed for a range of subjects but you could insert your own module topics.

**Table 12.1**  Using applications to support the design of learning and teaching

|  | *World War Two* | *Othello* | *Equilibrium* | *Refraction* | *Economic development of sub-Saharan Africa* |
|---|---|---|---|---|---|
| Interactive whiteboards |  |  |  |  |  |
| PowerPoint presentations |  |  |  |  |  |
| Videoconferencing |  |  |  |  |  |
| CD ROMs |  |  |  |  |  |
| The Web |  |  |  |  |  |
| Intranets |  |  |  |  |  |
| Computer applications: Word processing Spreadsheets Databases Desktop publishing |  |  |  |  |  |

# Further information

The full versions of the MFL example from Farnham Heath School, the Rob Tucker case study of music AS and the Eggbuckland Community College case study can be found in Secondary Leadership Paper 12, *ICT for Learning*. It is available for £7.50 from the NAHT Publications Section (tel: 01444 472472).

# 13 The personal tutor

Lin Le Versha

The role of the personal tutor is central to the achievement and social and personal development of each student. You are the first point of contact for students, their tutors and parents. You are the person who will listen to their problems and observe changes in their behaviour or demeanour that may indicate underlying difficulties at home or in the classroom. You will probably have a number of roles and tasks to perform and these may include:

- enrolling and undertaking the induction of students;
- overseeing changes to their course or programme;
- monitoring attendance and performance;
- acting as a 'learning coach' or mentor – helping students to set and meet realistic targets;
- delivering a tutorial programme;
- helping with higher education and careers guidance and education;
- writing references for students;
- taking responsibility for providing personal, emotional and social support;
- acting as first point of contact for parents;
- maintaining detailed records on students;
- acting as your students' advocate with their tutors.

## Enrolment, induction

As we have seen from Chapter 4, the role of the tutor in managing enrolment and induction is crucial in ensuring that students choose the correct course and then remain on it. You will receive support from specialists in this process and advice should be sought from careers departments and, if the student has individual learning needs, from the learning support department.

When selecting a post-16 course it is vital that the students should be given realistic, impartial advice, built on their previous achievements, which will provide breadth, coherence and a good progression route. Even more important, as many students will be moving from the familiar surroundings of school to the larger world of the college, they will need sensitive support and guidance. You will be the human face of the complicated procedures in the enrolment and induction process so make them as positive as possible.

*Ice-breakers* are useful induction activities when you have your tutor group together for the first time and most of the students are strangers to each other:

- In pairs ask students to discover two or three points about the other so that they may introduce their partner to the rest of the class, eg home town, number of pets, unusual hobbies, most exciting experience.
- In groups of three or four, each student will provide the group with two truthful statements and one false statement. The group will question the speaker to try to discover the lie.
- If you have space, ask students to move around the room finding somebody with whom they share a subject, a common holiday destination, or a favourite pop group or TV programme. You could use the grid in Figure 13.1. Each student moves around the room meeting as many other students as possible and asks them the questions on the grid, filling in their names in the appropriate squares.

It is these very early experiences that will determine whether students will make friends and settle on their new course or wander around the campus alone and begin to drop out of college.

Students need to feel part of their new environment, so a campus tour, meeting members of staff who may be helpful to them and making them aware of personal and study support services in the first few days will help them to establish themselves. Meeting other students who are in the year above them is another useful strategy at this stage. New students are able to ask these students questions that they consider too trivial for adults at this stage. It is also helpful to offer them the opportunity to meet second-year students in the same subject so that they can find out if that subject is what they are looking for. Too often students enrol on the non-National Curriculum 'ologies' – sociology, psychology, philosophy – without really understanding what the subject is about. The more effort that is put into providing advice and guidance at enrolment and induction, the fewer course changes and drop-outs there will be.

## Task 13.1

- Think of your experience of joining a new course, college or university. What activities made you feel welcome and enabled you to make friends? What could have improved the experience for you?
- You are now a personal tutor of a new tutor group. Consider what strategies you might employ to:
  - get to know your students;
  - get them to know each other;
  - get them to feel happy to speak to you.

| Has an elder brother or sister who came to college. | Has a dog. | Comes to college by train. |
| --- | --- | --- |
| Is studying one of the same subjects as you. | Is not wearing jeans. | Is addicted to *EastEnders*.  |
| Has a birthday in the same month as you. | Has not seen *Lord of the Rings*. | Has played in a sports team. |
| Lives in Cranleigh. | Plays a musical instrument.  | Knows where room 101 is. |

**Figure 13.1**  Who is who in the set? (Hewitt, 2002)

# Monitoring attendance and course changes

The importance of monitoring attendance and taking action to support students is a well-understood factor in retaining them in post-16 education (Martinez, 1997, 2000; Martinez and Munday, 1998). Colleges and schools will have various mechanisms to monitor attendance. Some systems rely on subject tutors to inform personal tutors of absence; others use central records to produce lists that are communicated to tutors using the management information system or displayed in the staffroom. As a result of the clear link between attendance and retention some colleges employ administrators to contact students or their parents within three days of their first absence or if a pattern of absence is emerging, such as a reluctance to attend on Monday mornings.

When students return from being absent it is the tutor's job to offer support and to use the opportunity to discuss any personal, domestic or academic problems. A one-to-one tutorial is useful at this stage to help students to produce an action plan so that missed notes and assignments can be realistically worked into the daily programme as students resume normal lessons. A follow-up session to check on progress is an effective way of ensuring that students have met their targets and provides the opportunity for discussion of any underlying issues.

Long illnesses, such as glandular fever, may result in the negotiation of a lighter timetable and a reduction of programme for students. Careful careers guidance to ensure that realistic progression routes are still possible should inform any changes to courses. If, however, students wish to make changes to their programme or course with no previous warning or reason, careful discussions should be held with students to explore the reasons for the change. Too often students will have problems with the teaching style or personality of the subject tutor rather than with the subject and this will be disguised in all sorts of excuses. Others may have been too ambitious in the load that they thought they could handle at enrolment and again individual tutorials will offer the opportunity to discuss the issues and to make action plans to ensure that they can cope with the demands of the new course.

# Setting targets

You may need to sit down with a student to negotiate an individual action plan following an illness or a change of course or as a routine part of the college tutoring system. Students should understand the purpose of setting the targets and how they will be monitored and supported.

- Targets should be SMART:
  **S**pecific;
  **M**easurable;
  **A**chievable;
  **R**ealistic;
  **T**ime-bonded.

- Students may be asked to consider their strengths in a subject and the areas that they would like to improve.

- Choosing one area for improvement, they should think about one or two actions they could undertake that would make a demonstrable difference to their performance before they come to each tutorial.
- At the tutorial explore the area identified. Ask questions such as:
  - What do you think you have to do to improve that?
  - How would that help?
  - How long will it take?
  - What help do you need to achieve it?
  - Do you need any resources to achieve it?
  - How will you know that you have achieved it?
  - What will the evidence look like?
- Formulate the target, the time and the evidence that will show the target has been met.
- You might present the information in a traditional action plan form (see Table 13.1).

**Table 13.1** Action plan

| Issue | Action | Time | Evidence |
|---|---|---|---|
| To improve my time management. | Keep a diary in which I will write the assignment and deadline, and show the study periods and evenings when I will complete it. | Keep diary for a month and show to the personal tutor once a week. | 1. Diary in use. 2. Report from subjects that work is handed in on deadline. |

In the example in Table 13.2 the student and personal tutor each have a copy of the targets negotiated with the subject tutors so that they can be monitored. It also provides the personal tutor with detailed information on how the student should be working to improve performance in each subject. As the personal tutor is the only person, apart from the student, to have the complete picture, it provides the tutor with the opportunity to act as a learning coach and have a real effect on the student's approach to learning.

## Task 13.2

If you received the set of targets opposite for one of your students, what issues would you discuss with that student? What advice would you give and how would you support the student?

Targets need to be monitored and students congratulated on their achievement or helped to analyse why they did not meet the target they set. It is useful to keep brief records of your meetings with each student so that you can manage this effectively. Students make progress if they set goals and achieve them, and your part in this process for some students is vital as a motivating force.

**Table 13.2**   Action plan for Jo Hynes

**Student – Jo Hynes**

| Subject | Target | Time-scale | Evidence |
| --- | --- | --- | --- |
| English | Annotations to be made in novel on theme and character following the lesson. | Every Wednesday evening October–December. | See me immediately before Wednesday lesson to show me the annotations you have made. |
| Law | Complete law diary each week for four weeks. | November. | Make presentation to group on the articles you have found. |
| History | Give in essay plans for the next two essays a week before the deadline. Arrange a tutorial with me to discuss the plans. | 17 November.<br><br>3 December. | Essays handed in on time and planned using appropriate structure. |
| Business studies | Using 'Business Today', do two additional case studies showing all your maths work. | November. | Two case studies with correct calculations evident. |

The monitoring process will also enable you to see if problems such as poor time management and organization are hampering progress, whether paid work is having an adverse effect on learning or whether the student is taking on an unrealistic workload. As we have seen from research into learning careers (Bloomer and Hodkinson, 2000 – see Chapter 4), the complications in students' domestic and personal lives often lead to them leaving individual courses or education altogether. It is the early awareness of problems that students may be experiencing beyond the course that enables tutors to suggest ways of managing the situation or to offer support services that can help to keep students in education.

# Tutorial programme

Many schools and colleges produce a common programme that all students follow and that is delivered by the personal tutor. In schools this is taught alongside the National Curriculum and is often known as personal social education and usually covers citizenship, and health and sex education. At 16-plus, the tutorial programme will probably cover induction activities, individual study skills and learning styles, revision and examination techniques and planning for higher education or a career. At 17-plus, application to higher education or employment will be a major feature, along with issues such as financial planning and living independently of parents. Teaching resources are usually provided for use in these sessions and a typical two years' programme might look like the one in Table 13.3.

**Table 13.3**   Tutorial programme

| Week Beginning | Lower Sixth | Upper Sixth |
| --- | --- | --- |
| 9 September | Parents' induction evening – invitation issued. Student profile completed. Basic skills test. | Interview Oxbridge, medics, vets and dentist candidates. Personal statements for UCAS. |
| 16 September | College quiz. Library induction. | Personal statements for UCAS. Starting electronic application UCAS. |
| 23 September | Individual interviews. | UCAS procedure – individual interviews. Completing practice UCAS forms. |
| 30 September | Individual interviews. | UCAS procedure – individual interviews. Completing practice UCAS forms. |
| 7 October | What are SMART targets? Individual discussions. | UCAS procedure – individual interviews. Completing practice UCAS forms. |
| 14 October | Time-management exercises. Individual interviews. | UCAS procedure – individual interviews. Completing practice UCAS forms. |
| 21 October | Review time-management exercises. Action: Plan half-term work to incorporate targets and work not up to date. | UCAS procedure – individual interviews. Completing practice UCAS forms. |
| 28 October | HALF-TERM | |
| 4 November | Learning style profiles. | Preparation for interviews. |
| 11 November | Team exercise based on learning profiles. | Preparation for interviews. Check subject targets. |
| 18 November | A citizenship topic. | Check subject targets. |
| 25 November | A citizenship topic. | Student self-assessment and individual discussions using it. |
| 2 December | Student self-assessment and individual interview using it. | CV writing. Individual discussions. Art applications. |
| 9 December | Individual interviews – using self-assessment. | CV writing. Individual discussions. |

| | | |
|---|---|---|
| 16 December | Individual interviews – using self-assessment. | Individual discussions. |
| 6 January | Careers work including a visit to the careers room to explore resources. | Individual discussions with students to review reports and holiday targets. |
| 13 January | Careers. | Standard job application forms. |
| 20 January | Careers. | Individual careers discussions. |
| 27 January | A citizenship topic. | Employment issues. |
| 3 February | A citizenship topic. | Employment issues. |
| 10 February | A citizenship topic. | Financial support for HE. Student loan form. |
| 17 February | Bereavement. Voting for college reps. | Financial support for HE. Student loan form. |
| 24 February | HALF-TERM | |
| 3 March | Bereavement/citizenship topic. | Legal issues. |
| 10 March | Bereavement/citizenship topic. | Accommodation/legal issues. |
| 17 March | Careers work – individual interviews. | Accommodation/legal issues. |
| 24 March | Careers work – individual interviews. | Individual interviews on revision. |
| 31 March | Careers work – individual interviews. | Individual interviews on revision. |
| 7 April | Careers work – individual interviews. | Individual interviews on revision. |
| 29 April | Exam and general admin. | Individual interviews on revision. |
| 6 May | Student services evaluation. | Student services evaluation. |
| 13 May | Subject evaluations. | Subject evaluations. |
| 26 May | HALF-TERM | |
| 2/9 June | Exams. | Exams. |
| 24 June | Careers individual interviews. | |
| 1 July | Careers individual interviews. | |
| 8 July | Careers individual interviews. | |
| 15 July | Careers individual interviews. | |

(Hewitt, 2002)

One group of 16–19 personal tutors at Godalming Sixth Form College produced the following list of the criteria of a good tutorial:

- The activities sustain interest, engage students and maintain a purposeful working atmosphere.
- The tutor is well organized and the lesson starts promptly.
- The classroom is appropriately arranged for the activity.
- The purpose of the activities is made clear to the students.
- The tutor communicates clearly and effectively with all students.
- The tutor ensures that all students are involved in the activity.
- The tutor ensures that students listen while others are making contributions.
- The tutor is aware of any learning difficulties the students may have.
- The tutor gives appropriate attention to equal opportunities, and cultural, spiritual and social issues as part of the programme of work.
- The tutor strives to create an environment of mutual trust to enable him/her to carry out the role of adviser in supporting his/her students on personal problems, fears and hopes.

## Task 13.3

- With a partner discuss what differences there are between the criteria above and those you might expect to use to judge a good lesson in any subject. Should there be differences between your roles as subject tutor and as personal tutor? If so, what are they and why should they be apparent in delivering the tutorial programme?
- Would you include other topics in the tutorial programme? Provide a short description of the area with reasons for its inclusion.

## Citizenship

Citizenship is now a compulsory part of the National Curriculum and it is an important part of 16–19 tutorial programmes and the student's experience. Bentley suggests that 'developing citizenship... is a gradual outward expansion, a series of learning experiences which encourages constructive encounters with the needs, values, rights and varying perceptions of others' (Bentley, 1998: 63). He illustrates this process in the diagram shown in Figure 13.2.

The work within the school or college can support this process of developing citizenship. Students can have direct experience by participating in the democratic process through student representative elections to school or college student councils. Most governing bodies are required to have a student member and students have the opportunity to serve on subject or course review groups where they will have the responsibility of representing the views of their peers.

Local issues that have a direct effect on the students can also be a way of providing them with an insight into local politics and help them to realize that their view can be heard. Lobbying for or involvement in the development of a skateboard park, a new sports centre or social facilities will provide them with opportunities to develop their communication

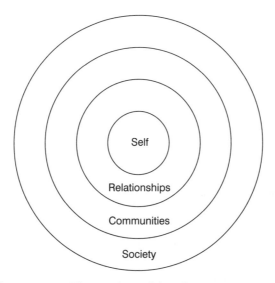

**Figure 13.2**    The process of developing citizenship

skills while appreciating the mechanics, policies and finances of local government. Some enlightened and innovative local councils are setting up student councils that work alongside the town council so that the young people in the area feel that they have a voice and an impact on the locality.

Conservation and community projects, often undertaken as part of the Duke of Edinburgh Award scheme, give students an insight into other organizations and ways of changing the society in which they live. Working in play schemes for younger children during the holidays or at weekends or participating in any local community project provides useful experience for building a CV but also for developing social awareness.

In the tutorial programme, political awareness sessions help students to understand the workings of Parliament, the concept of 'right' and 'left' in politics, the first-past-the-post and proportional representation systems, and our role in the European Union and the United Nations. The quizzes in Table 13.4 are stimulating starting points for discussions on politics and provide you immediately with an assessment of the students' knowledge and understanding and the basis for a research exercise in the learning resource centre.

Exploration of equal opportunities policies and issues in the college or the workplace will encourage debates on discrimination, disability and diversity (see Table 13.5). Discussion of the college charter can be a good starting point, with issues and suggestions made by the group then referred to the college council for action. The opportunity to discuss these core issues with a generation considered to be politically inert emphasizes the importance of the role of the personal tutor and the impact you might have on the citizens of the future.

**Table 13.4** Political awareness quizzes

*Elections, Parties and Policies*

1. List the political parties currently represented in Parliament.

2. When are general elections called?

3. There has to be a general election how often?

4. What is Britain's current voting system known as?

5. In 1997 Labour gained over half of the seats in the House of Commons, with what percentage of the votes?

6. What party is most in favour of proportional representation?

7. Give two arguments in favour of proportional representation.

8. Give two arguments against proportional representation.

9. Into how many constituencies is the UK divided?

10. In which constituency is Godalming and who is the MP?

11. How old do you have to be to vote?

12. Which party is most committed to free enterprise?

13. Which party believes the state should do more to help the underdogs in our society?

*Parliament and Government*

1. Name two kinds of members of the House of Lords.

2. Name two of the functions of the House of Lords.

3. What is the Queen's Speech?

4. What are backbench MPs?

5. Name two of the things that they are expected to do.

6. Give one argument for the House of Lords.

7. Give one argument against the House of Lords

8. Who becomes prime minister after a general election?

9. What is the difference between ministers and other MPs?

10. Name two government departments.

11. Name one of the Cabinet's functions.

(Kirby, in Hewitt with Dunnett and Kirby, 2001)

**Table 13.5**  An equal opportunities quiz

| *A few questions for starters:* | *True or False* |
|---|---|

1. The UK has some of the best equal opportunities legislation in Europe.

2. The Race Relations Act of 1976 is more about promoting racial harmony than about race discrimination.

3. The McPherson Report followed the inquiry into Stephen Lawrence's murder.

4. The Equal Pay Act of 1970 has made a significant change in the pay of women.

5. The Sex Discrimination Act of 1975 states that a man or woman cannot be treated differently because s/he is or is not married.

6. The 1995 Disability Discrimination Act gave disabled people new rights in employment and education.

7. Black people are more likely to be stopped by the police than white people.

8. At Godalming College equal opportunities means:
   i. Equal access to all courses.
   ii. Equal access to resources.
   iii. Equal achievement.

9. There is an equal opportunities statement in the college charter.

10. All students are entitled to a tutorial each term with their academic tutors.

11. The equal opportunities committee must have equal numbers of males and females.

*In your group define the following important equal opportunities definitions:*

prejudice
discrimination
harassment
victimization
racism

**Task** **13.4**

- Using the materials above as a starting point, write a lesson plan showing how you would use them in one tutorial and follow them up in the second session.
- Consider topics you would include in a tutorial programme to develop students' understanding of local and national government and their role in them as citizens.
- Many students feel that voting for an MP has little to do with them – how would you convince them to use their vote?
- What other experiences could you provide in the classroom to provide students with an understanding of their role as citizens?
- What activities would you suggest that the college or school should offer students to develop their understanding and experience of citizenship?

# Careers guidance and education

Although colleges and schools have excellent careers departments, they will need you to advise and support individual students in their applications to higher education, a gap year or employment. As we saw in Chapter 6, understanding the demands of higher education and the reality of living away from home is essential if your students are not to be part of the growing group of drop-outs in their first year at university. The tasks you may be asked to undertake as part of this process are:

- exploring opportunities available at 18-plus;
- developing an awareness of the local and national labour markets and higher education;
- developing individual career plans by helping students to make a realistic assessment of their strengths and aspirations;
- understanding an application process;
- completing the application form;
- supporting students in writing personal statements and letters of application;
- teaching students interview techniques;
- helping students to understand the rudiments of employment law;
- exploring financial planning, accommodation and legal issues.

So you will be a careers adviser, lawyer, life coach, bureaucrat, welfare officer and fortune teller or seer! Actually you will have a great deal of support from the organizer of your tutorial programme who should provide all the information you need and activities for you to undertake with your students. What you actually need is the ability to know your students well and to support them in setting realistic goals, and organizational skills to monitor their progress in the application process.

# Writing references

As you are more likely to know your students better than anyone else, you will probably be asked to write a reference for them for part-time work, full-time employment or higher education. Some of these requests may come several years after the student has left full-time education so it is important that records are kept so that the reference can be compiled even if you are no longer working in the school or college.

In compiling a reference for a student the following checklist may be of use:

- achievements prior to entry and in your institution;
- education history – list of schools or colleges attended with dates;
- subjects or course followed with dates;
- subject reports from tutors;
- extra-curricular activities;
- achievements outside education;
- personal qualities and skills;
- attitude to peers and tutors;
- punctuality and attendance rates.

In some cases it can be quite a juggling act to be honest while giving students the best chance possible in their quest for higher education and employment. Asking another tutor who knows the student to read your reference can provide you with an unbiased eye and assure you that you have been fair in your appraisal.

As a starting point, the students' self-assessment exercise in Figure 13.3 can provide you with a great deal of material for your individual discussions with students about their career plans.

This can lead to a careers action plan (see Figure 13.4) in which students agree targets with you and undertake research or action, which you are able to support and monitor. Both exercises provide you with a framework for individual work with your students.

**Self-assessment**

Whatever job, career, gap-year opportunity or course you apply for, you will be asked the question 'Why?' It is therefore important that this question is asked first, before you apply for anything. A realistic assessment of your characteristics, abilities, interests and potential is the first step on the road to a successful application.

**Strengths and weaknesses**

To begin with, let us look at the combination of characteristics that make you unique.

1. Look at the list below. Give yourself a score from 1 to 5 for each of the qualities listed, with a score of 5 = strong and 1 = weak.
2. Now select the six that most accurately describe your strengths and place your selection in the boxes at the bottom.
3. Try to indicate how you have demonstrated each stength by giving an example.

| | | | | | | | |
|---|---|---|---|---|---|---|---|
| Mathematical ability | | Confident | | Like working with figures | | Cope well under pressure | |
| Diplomatic | | Imaginative | | Flair for languages | | Good listener | |
| Can accept responsibility | | Able to analyse problems | | Can lead and motivate others | | Good colour sense | |
| Like challenge | | Cheerful and optimistic | | Can take decisions | | Can persuade and influence | |
| Like working in a team | | Want to get 'out and about' | | Determined | | Good in a crisis | |
| Organized | | Inquisitive | | Prefer to work alone | | Observant | |
| Able to express complicated information clearly | | Flexible and adaptable | | Can deal with the public | | Ambitious | |
| Rarely bored | | Logical | | Persevere | | Use initiative | |
| Like ideas | | Conscientious | | Like giving attention to detail | | Have physical stamina | |
| Like doing practical tasks | | Can express myself clearly on paper | | Can work quickly and accurately | | Good sense of humour | |

The six characteristics that most accurately describe my strengths are:

| Characteristic | I (have) show(n) this… |
|---|---|
| | |
| | |
| | |
| | |
| | |
| | |

*This information will not only help you in the next stage of your research, but will be useful when you discuss careers and next year's courses with your personal tutor and when you write your personal statement as part of your application for courses or employment.*

**Figure 13.3** Self-assessment exercise

**My Career Action Plan** (some ideas of goals that you might include on your action plan)

---

*My long-term career goal is:*

To become a primary school teacher.
To study medicine.
To get a job in the computer industry.
To set up a graphic design (Web design) company.

---

*Short-term goals towards my career goal:*

To pass maths GCSE.

To get at least a grade B in chemistry and biology AS.

To apply for an art foundation course.

---

*To reach the short-term goals I will need to set targets in:*

Revising AS topics.

Organizing work experience.

IT key skills.

Researching university courses.

Coursework for biology.

Art project work.

(Dunnett, in Hewitt with Dunnett and Kirby, 2001)

*Tutor signature:*

*Date:*

**Figure 13.4**   Career action plan

## Task 13.5

- Consider the two time lines in Figure 13.5. Write a list of how their direct experience would help each newly qualified teacher in supporting his/her students in planning their career.

| Part-time employment in three shops | | Term work in a bar Holiday work in offices | |
|---|---|---|---|
| 16 Took GCSEs | 18 Gap year after A levels<br><br>Worked in offices<br><br>Spent six months in USA | 19–22<br><br>University – lived in residence then a shared house | |

| 18 | 22 | 25–40 | 41 |
|---|---|---|---|
| Left school Jobs in marketing | Got married Worked in advertising | Had two children Part-time work as childminder Took OU degree | PGCE/A |

Figure 13.5  Time lines for two newly qualified teachers

- Consider your life so far. Draw a time line from 16 to the present time, plotting your career and experience. Make a note of what you can offer your students through direct experience and what you may have to research or ask others to provide to enable you to cover the topics listed in the section on careers guidance and education above.
- Complete the self-assessment (Figure 13.3) and use it as the basis of discussion with a partner on the way in which your life and career decisions have been made.
- Produce your own action plan for your teaching career over the next 10 years, setting yourself realistic short- and long-term goals.

# Providing personal, emotional and social support

Once again, you are not expected to be an expert or professional counsellor in this area of your work and you should be supported by those who are. Your job is to act as a first point of contact for students and to refer them on to those who can provide professional support. You will, however, need to have good interpersonal skills and sensitivity to cope effectively with the demands of this aspect of your role.

The first rule when students approach you in need of such support is: NEVER PROMISE CONFIDENTIALITY. You have no idea what students are about to tell you and keeping certain disclosures confidential could bring you into conflict with the college or school or even the law. In his discussion of confidentiality, May (1999) observes that tutors keep their doors open while counsellors shut them. Counsellors working within the institution while observing the b aries of confidentiality will have to decide what information should be given to who how this will affect the counselling relationship. Their decision will be taken with the support of their professional code of conduct but your role does not equip you for this so the safest way of approaching the problem is to say to the student, 'I cannot promise to keep what you tell me confidential but you and I will decide together who should share it if that is necessary.'

You need to understand what the counselling service can offer and when it is the right time to refer a student to the counsellor. This disengagement can be difficult if you have formed a good relationship with the student. You need to:

- respond – listen to the student so that you may evaluate the action or support that is needed;
- agree an appropriate plan of action with the student;
- communicate with others who may be able to offer appropriate support to the student.

Active listening is the first step in offering support to students. You need to find an appropriate place and time. If you are about to teach a lesson when a student approaches you, make an appointment later so that you have time to listen without distraction. Find a space where you will not be interrupted and where you can both be comfortable, and then listen to what the student says and how s/he says it.

Communication does not consist of words alone but tone of voice and body language play a large part. Mehrabian (1971) broke down communication into:

- 7 per cent verbal;
- 38 per cent vocal, including tone of voice, inflection, pauses;
- 55 per cent non-verbal or body language.

Often students have difficulty in finding the words to describe their feelings and with experience you will become practised at spotting the 'subtext' or the message beneath their words (see Table 13.6).

Such conversations are typical with young adults who are in need of help yet avoid confronting the problem. You can try to reflect their feelings in the hope of breaking down the adversarial tone: 'I can see you're angry now I've mentioned your weight loss. Would it help if you talked to me or the counsellor about it?'

Another approach could be to use prompt questions to move the student into the area you would like to discuss: 'You tell me that you haven't been on a diet so how do you feel about losing so much weight?'

Your careful use of non-judgemental questions and prompts could move the student to confronting a situation or taking action. It is the student's problem and, although you can offer support, it is the student who will have to find a solution.

Help the student to sort out the problem by breaking down the mass of issues into single points that can be approached one by one. This does not diminish the student's problem but may offer some strategies to approach parts of the problem. At the end of the conversation summarize the points that you have agreed and make a note of them so that you can review them with the student at a later meeting.

Students may come to you with problems with their subject or a particular tutor (see Table 13.7).

**Table 13.6**  Text and subtext

| Text | Subtext |
|---|---|
| *Tutor*: How are you? | I'm worried about you. |
| *Student* (averting head): Fine. | I don't want to talk to you. |
| *Tutor* (trying to make eye contact): You have been looking very pale recently. I was worried that you might be unwell. | You're looking anorexic. |
| *Student* (moving away): No, I'm fine. | It's none of your business. |
| *Tutor*: It's just that two of your friends and one of your tutors had mentioned to me that they were worried about you as you seem to have lost a lot of weight recently. | Please talk to me. |
| *Student* (with defiant tone and aggressive stance): I've not been trying to lose weight. | Leave me alone. |
| *Tutor*: OK. Perhaps we can have a longer chat next week when we go through your UCAS form – as long as you're all right. | Help! Where do I go next? I'll leave channels open and find out what to do from the counsellor. |
| *Student*: Yes, I'm fine. I've told you. | Go away. |

**Table 13.7**  Student having problems with a tutor

| Text | Subtext |
|---|---|
| *Student*: I hate Mrs Jones. She's always picking on me. | I'm thinking of dropping business. |
| *Tutor*: I'm sure it's not as bad as that, James. | This is the second comment I've heard about her picking on students – but I mustn't let him know that. |
| *Student*: Yes, it is. She shouted at me when I came into the class this morning. | I'm going to tell you before she does. |
| *Tutor*: What time did you arrive? | Late again? |
| *Student*: I was late because of the train strike. At least I got here – loads didn't. I'm going to give it up because she isn't a good teacher and she hates me. | She's not going to change my mind. |
| *Tutor*: But you were doing so well at the last review. What has happened? | Move him away from the personal – has he got behind with work? |

*Student*: The marketing topic was OK but when we moved on to case studies the maths was impossible. She wouldn't help and now she's screaming at me every time I go in without the work.

I can't do the maths. I need help.

*Tutor*: Have you thought about going to see Mr Gant for help with the maths? I could introduce you to him at break. You may only need a couple of sessions. How do you feel about that?

If I can get you to Mr Gant in learning support he will give you confidence and help you to overcome the problems.

*Student*: If you think it would help…

Maybe – I don't really want to go down to two subjects.

*Tutor*: What about Mrs Jones? Why don't you go and see her and ask for a tutorial to help you with the assignment? Imagine I'm Mrs Jones. What do you think you might say?

With that expression no wonder she shouts – try to be polite. Let's try some coaching.

*Student* (hesitantly): I'm having real problems with this work and I wonder if you would be able to help me, please.

I wish she'd listen to me like you do.

*Tutor*: Great! She really wants you to succeed. Tell her you're getting extra help from Mr Gant and she'll know you're serious. Now what have we decided?

Get him to go and do it today so I can see him tomorrow before it has gone too far – now summarize action and close.

*Student*: We'll go to see Mr Gant at break and I'll see Mrs Jones straight after.

I can manage this but if she shouts again…

## Resources

A useful book providing practical advice on ways in which tutors can support students is *Counselling Skills for Teachers* by Gail King (1999). It will provide you with advice and guidance but it should not replace the professional support of a counselling service.

Your might find the following list of contact numbers and Web sites useful for your own research or to offer to a student who may not wish to make direct contact with a counsellor. Students who are confident using text messages and chat rooms on the Internet may prefer this as a way of discussing their problems rather than face-to-face contact.

Counselling services and helplines include:

| | |
|---|---|
| Al Anon | 020 7403 0888 |
| Childline | 0800 1111 |
| Cruse (bereavement care) | Local number |
| Eating Disorders Association | 01603 621414 |
| Health Information Service | 0800 665544 |
| Lesbian & Gay Switchboard | 020 7837 7324 |

| | |
|---|---|
| National AIDS Helpline | 0800 567123 |
| National Drugs Helpline | 0800 776600 |
| Samaritans | Local number |
| Victim Support | 020 7735 9166 |
| Youth Counselling Service | 01276 676048 |

Key Web site addresses include:

| | |
|---|---|
| Childline Web site for children | http://www.childline.org.uk |
| Computers in Mental Health | http://www.ex.ac.uk/cimh/ |
| Connexions Service | http://www.connexions.gov.uk |
| Depression Resources List | http://www.execpc.com/ corbeau/ |
| Go Ask Alice | http://goaskalice.columbia.edu/ |
| Health Education Authority Web site for children aged 14–16 | http://www.mindbodysoul.gov.uk |
| International Society for Mental Health Online (ISMHO) | http://www.ismho.org/ |
| Internet Mental Health | http://www.mentalhealth.com/ |
| Learnfree Parents Service | http://www.learnfree.co.uk |
| Mental Health Net | http://www.mentalhelp.org.uk |
| Metanoia | http://metanoia.org/ |
| NetPsychology – Exploring Online Delivery of Mental Health | http://netpsych.com/ |
| Psych Central (formerly Grohol's Mental Health Page) | http://psychcentral.com/ |
| The Student Counselling Virtual Pamphlet Collection at the University of Chicago | http://ujs.bsd.uchicago.edu/scrs/vpc/virtulats.htm |
| The Samaritans | http://www.samaritans.org.uk/ |
| Trust Study for Adolescence (TSA) | http://www.tsa.uk.com |
| TSA Youth Counselling Network | ycn@tsa.uk.com |

## Task 13.6

In pairs, work on the following role-plays with one of you playing the tutor and the other the student. If you have a third member of the group, that person could act as observer, noting your body language and the 'tutor's' response to it:

- A student comes to tell you that she is pregnant.
- A student asks you to intercede in a conflict with his politics tutor who has accused him of copying an assignment from the Internet.
- A student comes to tell you that the reason she is behind with her work is that her parents expect her to work in their corner shop every evening until 10 pm.

# Working with parents

In most schools or colleges you will provide parents with reports on students' progress. You may attend parents' consultation evenings where you will discuss your students' progress with or without the student present and, if there is cause for concern beyond these routine types of contact, you may need to have a meeting with the student and parents.

Schools and colleges will have routines and procedures that you will be advised to follow when coming into contact with parents. Many will expect supporting evidence to be produced for use in the meeting. These may include:

- accurate records of student attendance and performance;
- evidence of the standard of a student's work;
- evidence of target setting or action planning with the outcomes;
- any contract that has been agreed between you and the student with evidence to support it;
- any involvement of senior members of staff.

Most of the time you will find that parents are supportive and appreciative of your time and effort. Occasionally you will have to deal with a parent who wishes to complain about you, the college or another member of staff and then it is essential that you have the documentary evidence described above.

The need to keep accurate records that support your argument will be needed at the meeting. Too often students tell their parents what they think they want to hear rather than the truth, which might be uncomfortable when it is revealed. So a meeting with the student, parents and a member of senior staff is a way of facing the problem and working out a solution together. The purpose of the meeting should be to find a way forward that is in the student's best interests and the 'agenda' or shape of the meeting could be structured thus:

- Calmly state the problem as you see it, providing evidence.
- Listen carefully to their response.
- Provide further evidence to support your case or accept that you or the college is at fault.
- Negotiate a way forward or plan of action that you, the student and the parent(s) accept.
- Arrange a review date or another meeting as appropriate.
- Send a letter to the parent(s) outlining the plan of action and relevant dates for action as agreed.

Parents can often appear to be unfair or unreasonable in their expectations of you and the college but you need to remember that it is the student who matters most and you should do your best to put the student's future at the core of all that you do.

## Task 13.7

In pairs discuss your responses to these letters from parents and the action that you would take:

Dear Tutor

I would like to complain about the amount of work David's art tutor expects him to do. Each week for the last six weeks David has spent three evenings working until midnight and all day Sunday on his art. This means that he has little time to play cricket or to do work in any other subject.
    I hope that you will be able to sort this out.

Yours truly
B Smith

Dear Tutor

I would like to ask your permission for Vanessa to visit her grandmother in Australia for a month. She will miss the last week in November and the last three weeks of the autumn term in December. She will make up all the work she has missed when she returns.

Yours truly
A Minor

Dear Tutor

As my wife and I have now separated I would like to receive a second copy of all documents to parents sent to my new address above. I am afraid that I shall be out of the country for the next parents' evening so I would be grateful if you could arrange for me to meet Jane's tutors when I am next in your vicinity on 23 February.

Yours truly
C Mann

Dear Tutor

As you know we hope that George will be able to go to Cambridge University to study anthropology. We would like to come in to meet you to discuss his application as soon as possible. I would also be grateful if you would be able to have a word with his geography teacher who has predicted George grade B. He does need all his predicted grades at A if he is to stand a chance of getting an interview.

Yours truly
A Brent

# ... a final word

Many tutors come into post-16 education as passionate evangelists for their subject and reluctantly agree at the interview to undertake the role of personal tutor in addition to their subject tutoring. Often untrained and unprepared, they face their tutor groups apprehensively only to find that their jobs as personal tutors are as important as those they perform in the subject departments. Through their good work the students can complete their course and progress to higher education or a career confident of knowing how to survive and succeed in the world of work or study and to play their part as citizens in the society of the future.

# References

Bentley, T (1998) *Learning Beyond the Classroom*, Routledge, London

Bloomer, M and Hodkinson, P (2000) Learning careers: continuity and change in young people's disposition to learning, *British Educational Research Journal*, **26** (5), pp 583–97

Hewitt, V, with Dunnett, W and Kirby, A J (2001) Tutorial programme, Unpublished, Godalming College

Hewitt, V (2002) Tutorial programme, Unpublished, Godalming College

King, G (1999) *Counselling Skills for Teachers*, Open University Press, Buckingham

Martinez, P (1997) *Improving Student Retention: A guide to successful strategies*, FEDA Report, FEDA, London

Martinez, P (2000) *Raising Achievement: A guide to successful strategies*, FEDA, London

Martinez, P and Munday, F (1998) *9000 Voices: Student persistence and drop out in further education*, FEDA Report, **2** (7), FEDA, London

May, R (1999) Doing clinical work in a college or university, in *Clinical Counselling in Further and Higher Education*, ed J Lees and A Vaspe, Routledge, London

Mehrabian, A (1971) *Silent Messages*, Wadsworth, Belmont, CA

# 14 Improving performance – external monitoring

Lin Le Versha

A major force in the 1990s in all age ranges and sectors of education was the desire to improve standards. Educational provision from playgroups and nursery schools to degree courses is now subject to a series of inspection systems where targets are set and monitored and league tables and reports are produced that show comparative levels of achievement between providers at every stage.

In 16–19 education there are four processes you will experience that will monitor your performance and have as their impetus the desire to improve standards. These are:

- the quality improvement processes of your college school;
- the target setting and monitoring by governors;
- the monitoring of self-assessment and target setting by the local Learning and Skills Councils;
- 16–19 inspections by OFSTED.

In some of these processes you will be directly involved, while in others you will only be aware of them taking place from a distance but they will still have an effect on your practice.

## Quality improvement processes

Your school or college will have its own processes for improving the quality of its provision and in which you will be involved. The processes described below summarize the quality assurance processes evident in most 16–19 schools and colleges:

- *Strategic planning.* All tutors should be involved in consultations on what is included in the strategic plan, the strategic priorities that are set and how these should be achieved in the development plan. The strategic plan may be produced to cover a three- or five-year period with annual updates or it may be part of an annual planning cycle. Strategic priorities are usually set annually along with the development plan.

- *College charter.* The charter, which all students should receive, will include service standards that are set and monitored. It could include detail on enrolment processes, the provision of learning and tutorial support, the speed at which work should be marked and returned to students, and administrative processes such as the time it will take for a UCAS or employment reference to be produced. All charters should include a procedure for making complaints about the teaching or services provided.

- *Targets and performance indicators.* Targets are set annually for recruitment, attendance, retention and achievement for each subject. There may be generic targets, such as a college target for attendance, but most of them will be specific to the department and the course so that particular contexts are taken into account such as the quality of the intake.

- *Annual reviews and self-assessment.* Each year you will be involved in a self-assessment of your department or course. The process of self-assessment will identify the strengths and weaknesses of the department, set an action plan for the next academic year and review the actions carried out in the last year. More detailed discussion of this process is undertaken later.

- *Observation of teaching and learning.* You will find that your teaching and your students' learning may be observed by several people including your NQT mentor, your head of department, senior managers and inspectors. This process is also discussed later.

- *Monitoring and tracking of students.* All students are monitored and tracked from recruitment to their destination when they leave the college. Information on their learning programme, their attendance, their performance on internal assessments or reports, and their achievements on external assessments will all be recorded on the management information system (MIS).

  Managers have access to the MIS so that they may take action to intervene if, for example, the retention of a course drops below the target. Student support managers or tutors will use it to monitor a student's attendance or performance so that support may be offered and you may use it to discover details on a student such as individual learning needs, patterns of attendance or entry results.

- *Student evaluations.* Students now make routine evaluations of the teaching and the services they receive. They may be asked to comment on the quality of:
  - their enrolment and induction;
  - the variety of teaching styles they experience;
  - the support they are given in completing assignments;
  - the speed at which assignments are returned to them;
  - the usefulness of the comments they receive on marked work;
  - the value of tutorials;
  - the careers guidance and support they receive;
  - the standard of the cleaning in the rooms they use;
  - the provision of recreational facilities.

  The list is endless! You will find that there is an annual cycle of seeking student views on a variety of topics through questionnaires, focus groups, course review groups and individual interviews. The analysis of these surveys should be fed back to students along with the action that will be taken as a result.

- *Moderation of assessed work.* You will probably find that, after you have set and marked a few assignments, a moderation exercise will be undertaken with your head of department or another tutor who has experience of teaching your course. You will be given the opportunity to look at each other's marking and grading of assignments, and the awarding of marks will be compared with the criteria of the examination board or the department.

To establish what a piece of A-grade work looks like and to distinguish between an E and a D is a useful exercise even for the most experienced tutors, and ensures that standards of marking across the department are consistent. Such procedures take place annually if coursework is being submitted for external examinations.

If you teach on VCE courses you will find that there are well-established internal verification procedures that originated in Intermediate and Advanced GNVQ courses. Regular meetings are held between tutors and an internal verifier to ensure that standards of assessment are consistent within and between departments offering the award. An external verifier will then assess a sample of portfolios to check that the moderation and verification procedures in the college are rigorous and robust.

- *Appraisal.* Each year you will experience an appraisal or review. You may be observed teaching as part of this process and you will have an individual interview with your line manager or head of department. In the meeting you will review your performance, experience and achievements of the previous year and set targets for the next academic year. These may be numerical targets on retention and achievement rates for your course(s) or they may be actions that you will undertake.

Your appraiser should provide clear expectations of your performance for the next year and offer you support or opportunities for the personal and professional development you need to meet those expectations. If, for example, your head of department would like you to produce a scheme of work and resources for a new examination specification then you should be offered an appropriate course run by the examination board.

## Task 14.1

- Look at the areas covered above and decide how each could change your approach to teaching. Put your responses in a grid like that in Table 14.1.

Table 14.1   Quality processes and their effects on teaching

| Quality Process | Effect on Teaching |
| --- | --- |
| Appraisal. | Agree to teach a new examination course. |

Now with a partner compare lists and put the quality processes in rank order – the process that will have the most direct effect on you first and the one that will have the least effect last. Would this rank order be the same if you were a head of department?
- Consider your classroom practice. Think of two processes that you could undertake to assure you that you are teaching to the right standard and that your students are learning. Who can you involve in the processes and how would you carry them out? (See Table 14.2.)

**Table 14.2** Quality processes and standard of teaching

| Quality Process | Who Is Involved? | How Would You Do It? |
| --- | --- | --- |
| Evaluation with students to check on learning. | Students in class. | At the end of a topic ask students to answer the following on a pro forma: Which areas have you understood and could teach to someone else? (Provide a list of areas covered.) Which areas would you like someone to explain to you? |
| | | Next lesson divide into pairs so one can explain a topic to another. |

- Consider the ways in which personal and professional needs might be met using the checklists in Table 14.3. Look at the development need in the first column and link it with one or more of the range of strategies in the second column.

**Table 14.3** Development needs and strategies

| Development Need | Strategy to Meet It |
| --- | --- |
| Get to know a new subject specification. | Observe lessons in other departments. |
| Improve classroom management. | Visit another college to observe an alternative approach. |
| Develop group work in class. | Apply for a course run by the examination board. |
| Improve range of questioning styles. | Apply for a course run by a commercial company on a particular topic. |
| Monitor student learning. | Observe a colleague's lessons. |
| Monitor student attendance and completion of work. | Ask a colleague to mentor you. |
| Understand ways of supporting students with individual learning needs. | Sign up for a distance learning course in the subject. |
| Produce more interactive materials for students to use for e-learning. | Team-teach with a colleague. |
| Develop your role as a personal tutor. | Visit a local school or university. |
| Improve your ICT skills. | Take an additional professional qualification. |

- Now consider your personal and professional needs at the moment. Discuss with a partner ways in which you will meet them, how long that will take and how you know that you have been successful, using a grid like that in Table 14.4.

Table 14.4  Meeting needs

| Issue | Action | Time-Scale | Outcome |
|---|---|---|---|
| To understand and apply assessment criteria for coursework. | Attend examination board briefing session on coursework assessment. | September–December | Report to department on grading of assignments and criteria for awarding grades. |
| | Ask colleague teaching course to show me examples of top, middle and lowest grades in previous coursework and look at sample of my assessment. | October

March | The assessment of my group's work in line with department and external criteria. |

# Governors

You will probably meet members of your governing body at your induction or when governors come to visit your department. Most governors are linked to the curriculum through subjects or faculties or take responsibility to cover cross-college areas such as careers, learning support or estates and premises.

Governors are responsible for:

- maintaining the mission, values and educational character of the college;
- ensuring that the strategic plan supports the development of the mission of the college and the funding council's framework;
- maintaining a strategic overview of the curriculum and quality issues;
- ensuring that targets are set for the curriculum that will lead to quality improvement and meet the requirements of the funding body;
- ensuring that the financial management of the college is sound and that resources are used according to agreed policies and procedures in support of the strategic plan;
- overseeing the admission, assessment, examination and discipline of students and the procedures for providing learning support;
- ensuring that policies and procedures meet all legislative requirements for health and safety.

There is a fine but crucial dividing line between 'governance' and 'management'. Governors should, for example, be involved in the appraisal of senior managers in the college. They are not, however, expected to be involved in the implementation of the targets, only in monitoring the outcomes at the next appraisal. Governors will approve the policy on equal opportunities but they have no say in how it is to be implemented. This is left to the management of the college.

All governors are volunteers and receive no payment for the work that they do in supporting and monitoring the operations of the college. Governors can often provide a refreshing view of an issue based on their personal expertise and experience but they must not perform in a professional capacity. Solicitors, architects or marketing managers may be useful to inform debate on certain topics but they are not permitted to offer professional advice in their role as governors.

## Task 14.2

- If you are in a college or school find out which governor is linked to your subject area and what he/she has seen on visits.
- What activities would you suggest that governors might undertake to help them become familiar with the members of staff and students without getting involved in management of the school or college?

## Self-assessment and target setting

Annual self-assessment reports have been produced in colleges since 1997, when the Further Education Funding Council introduced them as the basis of the inspection framework (FEFC, 1997). The introduction of self-evaluation meant that quality improvement systems had a much greater effect on the work of the tutor by increasing individual accountability and introducing graded lesson observation.

Colleges were expected to produce self-assessment reports for each subject or curriculum area and grade them using a 1–5 scale, with grade 1 as the highest score. The reports had to provide evidence for the judgements that were being made and include lesson observation grades (on the same five-point scale), data on the achievement and retention of students and value-added information. Cross-college reports were produced and similarly graded to provide information for the seven areas of inspection:

- the mission of the college;
- the curriculum;
- student support and guidance;
- resources;
- quality;
- management;
- governance.

The development of this inspection framework had a direct effect on the tutor in the classroom. Each department became accountable for its examination results and retaining the students that it had recruited. Individual tutors were expected to explain why their examination results were above those of their colleagues and what they had done to maintain high retention levels. Obviously those with lower achievement and retention results were also called to account! The classroom door, which had been pushed open by appraisal systems in 1991, was opened wide by the requirement to provide evidence of what was happening in the classroom.

The accuracy of the self-assessment report was the subject of the opening paragraph in each section of the inspection report. It was, therefore, important to ensure that classroom observation grades were realistic, robust and reflected the standards expected by inspectors and that strengths and weaknesses in the area were identified accurately and acted upon. All tutors were expected to participate in this process within their subject department and in any cross-college area in which they worked.

The demise of the FEFC and the introduction of the Learning and Skills Council (LSC) and the Common Inspection Framework (OFSTED) in April 2001 led to a change of emphasis. The self-assessment process has continued and is now monitored by the LSC and, although used in OFSTED inspections, these now concentrate primarily on teaching and learning and the experience of students in colleges.

## Self-assessment

The LSC in *Raising Standards in Post 16 Learning* (2001) outlines the self-assessment process it expects colleges to follow and the local LSC to monitor. The rigour of the process is stressed along with the need to involve all tutors and students in the college. The report has to follow a similar structure to that used by the FEFC of identifying strengths and weaknesses and has to produce grades for each area of provision on the five-point scale used by OFSTED (see 'Inspection' below). Again any disparity between the grades awarded by the college and by the inspectorate will indicate a flawed quality assurance process. Although the college can present the report using its own structure, that structure is expected to 'be similar to that of published inspection reports' (LSC, 2001: 17).

The self-assessment report then leads to a development plan that will show what action is being taken to improve provision by building on strengths and addressing weaknesses. Each action is linked to a target for improvement with clear outcomes that will indicate that the action has been successfully completed within a given time-scale.

The local LSC (LLSC) monitors the self-assessment process. A copy of the self-assessment report and the development plan are sent to the LLSC and, through two or three visits a year, progress on the plan is checked. More frequent visits will be made if there is concern about the performance in a college.

## Target setting

The LLSC will also monitor the targets set for recruitment, retention and achievements by the college. They are expected to be realistic, lead to improvement and to be set with reference to benchmarks. For example, if you are teaching A level English you would refer to national statistics for the number of students who pass the subject and how many achieve grades A–C and would set your targets accordingly.

You may refer to specific benchmarks for your sector and use as a guide the pass rates and high grades achieved by schools, sixth form colleges and tertiary or general further education colleges. The LSC has plans to produce benchmarks on:

- value-added data;
- recruitment;
- retention;
- participation rates;
- student destinations;
- student satisfaction;
- health and safety;
- value for money.

An example of a departmental self-assessment report is given in Figure 14.1.

## Task 14.3

Look at the self-assessment report in Figure 14.1 and discuss the following questions with a partner:

- What is the value of including more than one year's data?
- How good is the department at setting realistic targets?
- What do you learn about the department from the 'success rate' figure?
- Do you think the strengths and weaknesses are supported by the data?
- What would you suggest they should do about the concerns expressed in the student survey?
- Do you think that the review of last year's action plan has led to improvements? What are they? Which do you think have been the most effective?
- Are the actions for the next academic year going to lead to improvements? If you were running the department, which two or three actions would you take as top priority?
- Can you think of any other actions not included in the report that could lead to improvements in the department?
- What grade would you award the department and why? Use the 1–5 grading scale for departments where 1 is excellent, 2 is good, 3 is satisfactory, 4 is unsatisfactory and 5 is very weak.

**Departmental Self-Assessment Report: September 2004**   SUMMARY PAGE

Area of provision: Geography | Submitted by: RB | Grade:

| Subject | No. at start | No. completed | Number achieved | Success rate % | Value-added index 2003 | 2004 |
|---|---|---|---|---|---|---|
| Geog AS | 113 | 100 | 95 | 84% | 0.01 | 0.04 Significant |
| Geog A2 | 55 | 55 | 55 | 100% | 0.02 | 0.04 Significant |

**No. of lessons observed at each grade**

| Grade: | 1 | 2 | 3 | 4 | 5 | 6 | 7 |
|---|---|---|---|---|---|---|---|
| Learning | 1 | 6 | 3 | | | | |
| Teaching | 2 | 7 | 2 | | | | |
| Attainment | 1 | 4 | 5 | | | | |

High means grades A–C at A level, A*–C at GCSE. Starters/Retention is from 1 Oct. Success rate is % of starters who passed.

| Subject code | Trends and targets | Attendance | Retention | Pass rate | High grade |
|---|---|---|---|---|---|
| | Actual value 2001/02 | 87% | 92% | 89% | 56% |
| | Actual value 2002/03 | 89% | 96.2% | 90.2% | 57.2% |
| Geography AS | **Actual value 2003/04** | **85.8%** | **88.5%** | **95%** | **77%** |
| | Target set for 2003/04 | 90% | 90% | 90% | 65% |
| | New target for 2004/05 | 90% | 89% | 95% | 68% |
| | Benchmarks 2003/04 | 90% | 88% | 90% | 60% |

| Subject code | Trends and targets | Attendance | Retention | Pass rate | High grade |
|---|---|---|---|---|---|
| | Actual value 2001/02 | 89% | 80% | 92.5% | 56% |
| | Actual value 2002/03 | 89% | 82.1% | 95.2% | 57.8% |
| Geography A level | **Actual value 2003/04** | **87%** | **100%** | **100%** | **81.8%** |
| | Target set for 2003/04 | 90% | 90% | 95% | 65% |
| | New target for 2004/05 | 90% | 95% | 95% | 70% |
| | Benchmarks 2003/04 | 90% | 90% | 92.5% | 63.5% |

**Student survey results**

Three strongest categories:

1. Homework based on clear instructions.
2. Satisfied with progress.
3. Satisfied with overall quality of teaching.

Three weakest categories:

1. Returning work takes longer than 10 days.
2. Involvement of students in lessons not high enough.
3. Student-tutor relationships need to be improved further.

**Figure 14.1** Departmental self-assessment report

| Area of provision: Geography | Collated by: RB |
|---|---|
| **STRENGTHS** | **EVIDENCE** |
| **Students' achievements**<br>Excellent AS and A level results above national benchmarks and targets.<br>High grades above targets.Improved performance over three years.<br>Significant value-added score. | Results analysis. |
| **Learning and teaching**<br>Well-planned, well-structured lessons with a variety of methods used.<br>Good student response. | Lesson observation sheets and notes.<br>Peer observation programme and minutes of meeting.<br>Student evaluations and minutes of student focus group meeting. |
| **Assessment and monitoring of learning**<br>Continuous, accurate assessment across both courses.<br>All staff use common mark schemes provided by AQA.<br>Moderation meetings effective in ensuring all tutors mark consistently. | Tutors' mark books.<br>AQA moderators' reports.<br>Action plans following moderation meetings. |
| **Management of the curriculum**<br>Choice of modules responsive to student need and improved results.<br>Programme of workshops effective in improving student performance.<br>Allocation of tutors to modules develops strengths but also develops new subject expertise. | Examination records.<br>Improved results: 4.8% increase in pass rate and 24% in high grades.<br>Appraisal record with requests and attendance at courses. |
| **Student experience (support, enrichment, guidance, progression)**<br>Individual tutorials each term effective in developing individual performance.<br>Field courses effective in providing evidence for physical geography module.<br>Increase in students progressing to geography courses. | Tutorial records, increase in performance grades and value-added score.<br>100% attendance on course.<br>14% students on geography-related degree course. |
| **Resources**<br>Enthusiastic, well-qualified tutors.<br>Departmental intranet established.<br>Specialist texts used to good effect. | All tutors attended at least one geography course.<br>RB trained on Dreamweaver and established site.<br>New set of texts. |
| **Equal opportunities**<br>Visually impaired student successful.<br>Applications to access fund meant that all students attended field course.<br>Additional support for dyslexic students effective. | Dan Griffiths achieved Grade B, one grade above ALIS prediction.<br>Access record - seven applications made.<br>11 students received additional support from Jenny Martin. |

**Figure 14.1**  Continued

| Area of provision: Geography | Collated by: RB |
| --- | --- |
| **WEAKNESSES/AREAS FOR IMPROVEMENT** | **EVIDENCE** |
| **Student achievements** | |
| AS module A3 and A2 module A6 producing lower marks. | Examination results. |
| **Learning and teaching** | |
| Variety of approaches needs further development. | Student survey and focus group. |
| **Assessment and monitoring of learning** | |
| Some marked work not returned within 10 days. | Student survey showed one group had work returned late. |
| **Student experience** | |
| Some students unhappy with tutor-student relationship. | Student survey and focus group. |
| **Resources** | |
| Intranet not sufficiently developed. | Student survey. |
| Use of Internet and ILT in classroom needs improvement. | Lesson observations. |

REVIEW OF PREVIOUS ACTION PLAN

| Area of provision: Geography | | Collated by: RB |
| --- | --- | --- |
| **Priorities for action determined a year ago** | **Outcome** | **Evidence** |
| 1. Additional support for students at risk. | Jane Freeman provided a session for all students on essay writing. | Notes from sessions. |
| | One additional tutorial provided for each student identified. | Tutorial record sheets. |
| 2. Intranet development. | RB attended Dreamweaver course – September. Intranet site launched December. Used by 2/6 groups. | Staff development records. Site available on college intranet. Lesson notes and observations. |
| 3. Schemes of work. | Reviewed and updated with all tutors and incorporating method of teaching and learning. | Schemes of work and lesson observations. |
| 4. Fieldwork. | Wider programme developed but hit by poor weather so activities restricted. | Fieldwork log and student notes. |
| 5. Variety of teaching methods. | Wider range observed in lessons but still needs improvement. | Lesson observation notes. |

**Figure 14.1** Continued

**ACTION PLAN FOR 2004/05**

| Area of provision:Geography | | | Collated by: RB | |
|---|---|---|---|---|
| Issue to be addressed | Action to be taken | By whom | Expected outcome (SMART target) | Target date |
| Additional support for students in modules A3 and A6. | Study guides to be produced for each module to support activities in lessons. | RB, HG | Improvement in grades for modules. | August 05 |
| | Maths department to provide training session for geography tutors on how to cover maths content in module. | | A3 increase of 7% high grades. | |
| | Interactive material to be put on intranet. | | A6 increase of 8% high grades. | |
| Improved variety of teaching methods and greater involvement of students. | Peer observation to analyse methods and suggest new approaches. | All tutors | Lesson observation sheets comment on increased variety of teaching methods. | Oct 04 |
| | Each tutor to observe lessons in two other departments. | | | Nov 04 |
| | Visit to two other geography departments following same syllabus to observe lessons. | RB and KM | Student survey results improve by 10%. | Feb 05 |
| | Further focus group to ascertain student views on improvements to be made. | RB and CS | | Nov 04 |
| Develop fieldwork to support shift for some students to module A7. | Provide workshop to encourage students to design own investigations. | RB | Improve module results by 8%. | August 05 |
| | Design new fieldwork task and report sheets. | CS | | |
| | Provide additional opportunity for one day's follow-up visit to collect additional data. | RB | | |
| Improve use of ILT and intranet. | All tutors to attend Dreamweaver course. | All | Intranet used by all students. | July 05 |
| | All tutors to produce one lesson plan for each module incorporating ILT and share with department. | | Use of ILT judged as useful and effective in student survey and focus group. | |

**Figure 14.1** Continued

# Inspection

All schools and colleges in England and Wales are subject to inspection as part of a four-year cycle. From 2001, under the Learning and Skills Act 2000 all post-16 education in colleges will be inspected according to the Common Inspection Framework (CIF). Schools with sixth forms have modified arrangements as a part of their inspection process and a report of the inspection is now sent to their LLSC.

OFSTED has been given the responsibility for inspecting provision for 16- to 19-year-old students in sixth form and further education colleges while the Adult Learning Inspectorate (ALI) has powers to inspect post-16 work-based training and adult education. When a college offers courses requiring OFSTED and ALI inspection, this should be undertaken during the same week. Her Majesty's Chief Inspector of Schools in England (HMCI) has the responsibility for publishing the reports on the provision, undertaking joint college and area inspections and ensuring that OFSTED and ALI inspectors follow the CIF.

## What happens in an inspection?

The purpose of inspection is to analyse the 'efficiency and effectiveness of the provision of education and training in meeting the needs of students' (OFSTED, 2002: 3). The inspection should:

- provide an independent account of the quality of teaching and learning;
- encourage improvement by highlighting good practice and identifying strengths and weaknesses;
- inform the DfES and LSC of the quality of post-16 education;
- promote a culture of self-assessment;
- encourage continuous improvement;
- maintain high quality and standards.

The four-yearly inspections will:

- analyse the achievements of the learners – taking account of three-year trends;
- inspect the quality of teaching and learning;
- make judgements on the range of the curriculum offered and the extent to which it is educationally and socially inclusive;
- explore the extent of the support provided for students;
- inspect provision for students with learning difficulties and/or disabilities;
- comment on the effectiveness of management and leadership;
- comment on quality assurance processes and improvement;
- comment on the value for money offered by the college.

The inspection is managed by the reporting inspector, who has a team of subject inspectors supporting him/her. The financial systems of the college are inspected by an auditor at the same time as the inspection of education provision. The college is able to appoint an internal nominee to join the inspection team to ensure that the evidence represents the college fairly.

The subject inspectors observe lessons for four days during the inspection week in the classroom, the workplace or the community. They evaluate student work, the effectiveness of college documents and policies, and student records, particularly of those with special educational needs.

Lesson observations are at the centre of the inspection. An inspector may observe tutorials, group and individual activities, students working in resource areas, on work experience or on fieldwork, enrichment and extra-curricular activities in addition to the sessions in classrooms and laboratories. When an inspector enters the classroom s/he will ask to see the tutor's register or mark book, a plan for the lesson and any other relevant documentation. S/he will stay in the lesson for a minimum of 30 minutes and may talk to individual students, look at their work or ask to see their notebooks or folders.

The inspector provides brief verbal feedback to you following the lesson or later in the day and comments on 'what went well, what was less successful and what could be done more effectively' (OFSTED, 2002: 14). Three grades are awarded for learning, teaching and attainment on a seven-point scale. You are not told the specific three grades awarded for the lesson but they will be presented as a profile of grades awarded to the department or area as a whole.

The lesson observation grade profile is:

- Grade 1 – excellent;
- Grade 2 – very good;
- Grade 3 – good;
- Grade 4 – satisfactory;
- Grade 5 – unsatisfactory;
- Grade 6 – poor;
- Grade 7 – very poor.

Student views on the teaching, learning and support provided in a subject area play an important part in assessing the effectiveness of that area. Chatting to students in lessons, meetings with groups of students, and discussions and analysis of formal evaluations will inform the inspector's judgement.

In addition to lesson observations you may also be asked to meet an inspector to discuss your role within the department and the way in which college policies and procedures are carried out. In any feedback session your comments should not be identified individually.

In your department you will have a collection of documents in a subject file, which the inspector will examine. Most of this paperwork you will have as part of your normal departmental documentation and you should not need to create it especially for the inspection. This will include:

- CVs and job descriptions for staff in your department;
- department, course or subject self-assessment reports;
- student evaluations or course reviews with the actions taken as a result;
- course and subject specifications and schemes of work;
- samples from a range of students' assessed work;
- samples of student records including tutorial records, action plans and learning plans;
- staff development undertaken by members of staff in the department;
- college and departmental policies.

The inspectors will be looking for evidence to answer the following seven key questions during the inspection and the notes below provide you with an indication of the ways in which they will look for this evidence:

1.  *How well do learners achieve?* This is an analysis of achievement and retention rates in relation to benchmarks, the value-added score of students and the extent to which target setting encourages high standards to be met.
2.  *How effective are teaching, training and learning?* Judgements are made on how well the area meets individual needs and course requirements, the progress and attainment of learners, the quality of teaching and enrichment activities.
3.  *How do resources affect achievement and learning?* This question explores the adequacy and suitability of staff and how effectively equipment, accommodation and learning resources are used in a subject.
4.  *How effective are the assessment and monitoring of learners' progress?* The rigour and use of assessment as a formative part of the planning and learning processes are evaluated.
5.  *How well do the programmes and courses meet the needs and interests of learners?* This is an evaluation of the extent to which courses meet learners' ambitions and potential, satisfy external requirements and are responsive to local needs.
6.  *How well are learners guided and supported?* This question covers individual guidance on entry to and exit from the college, the extent to which individual needs are met and the accessibility and quality of individual support.
7.  *How effective are leadership and management in raising achievement and supporting all learners?* This summative question attempts to draw together judgements from all inspectors and the auditor on the leadership in the college, the effectiveness of the governors, how improvement is achieved through quality assurance and self-assessment processes, and the extent to which equal opportunities are promoted in the college.

At the end of the inspection week the subject inspector will give formal feedback to the head of department or the manager responsible for the subject area. In addition to the grades awarded for lesson observation, the inspector will provide a list of strengths and areas for improvement in the subject area and an overall grading for the area on a five-point scale (the subject area grade profile):

*   Grade 1 – outstanding;
*   Grade 2 – good;
*   Grade 3 – satisfactory;
*   Grade 4 – unsatisfactory;
*   Grade 5 – very weak.

Feedback will then be provided to the principal, senior staff and governors on each area inspected and on the leadership and management, and the adequacy of the college. Arrangements will be made, if necessary, for reinspecting subject areas or the entire college between 12 and 18 months later if they are not judged to be satisfactory.

Following the euphoria and exhaustion that permeates most staffrooms in the wake of an inspection, the college produces an action plan to address the weaknesses identified in the inspection and this is monitored by the local LSC.

**Task** **14.4**

Go to the OFSTED Web site www.ofsted.gov.uk. Find two inspection reports that include the area in which you teach. Look at the strengths, areas for improvement and the text; then compare the two departments, making suggestions on what you would include in the action plan to improve their performance.

# Lesson observation

As a newly qualified teacher, you can expect that your teaching will be observed by a variety of people and for a variety of purposes, which could include those shown in Table 14.5.

**Table 14.5**   Purposes of observation:

| Observer | Purpose |
| --- | --- |
| NQT mentor | To support you in developing particular aspects of your teaching, eg group work, classroom management.<br>To assess your performance as part of the DfES induction year. |
| Head of department | To offer development points on particular aspects of your teaching.<br>To gather evidence for the departmental self-assessment report.<br>To explore different approaches in the area, eg use of electronic whiteboards.<br>As part of your appraisal to identify areas for development. |
| Other tutors | To disseminate good practice between departments.<br>To develop policies in the college, eg guidelines for managing coursework. |
| Senior managers | To assess you as part of the induction year.<br>To collect evidence for the college self-assessment report.<br>To check that grades awarded in classroom observations are consistent across the college. |
| Inspectors | As part of an OFSTED inspection. |

## *Preparing for a classroom observation*

The purpose of the lesson observation will determine the preparations you make for it. Lessons observed as part of your personal and professional development will be different from those for inspection both in the role of the observer and in their outcomes.

For all lessons you will need to provide the observer with:

- the scheme of work and the place of the lesson you are teaching in it;
- a lesson plan incorporating your learning objectives, the activities you and the students will be undertaking, an idea of the time you will spend on each activity, the resources you will use and any assignment or work the students will do (for a more detailed discussion of lesson planning, see Chapter 8);
- copies of handouts, textbooks or other resources you will use.

For lessons where you are to be observed as part of your personal development you should meet the observer some days before the lesson to discuss the areas on which s/he will focus. These could include:

- questioning techniques;
- group work;
- tutor input;
- use of IT in the classroom;
- organization of practical work;
- individual involvement of students;
- managing males and females;
- classroom management;
- pace of teaching;
- balance between teaching and learning;
- the range of activities;
- managing individual learning;
- differentiation;
- managing coursework or assignments;
- providing feedback to students.

In fact any area of work in the classroom may be selected as the focus for a classroom observation. In discussing the lesson you may cover its context, aims and objectives, the activities that will be seen and when the observer may have the opportunity to chat to students or look at their notebooks or files. At this point mention any students who have learning difficulties or individual needs or whose behaviour may need explanation.

The position of the observer in the room is important as s/he should be able to see your teaching and also observe the students' learning. A seat at the front of the classroom against one wall allows the observer to see you at the front of the class and the students' faces without being in the direct line of your vision constantly. Even the most experienced teachers are nervous when their teaching is observed but by careful preparation you can make the observer part of the process.

If you are being observed for appraisal, self-assessment or inspection you may not know exactly when you will be visited. The observer will expect to receive a lesson plan, your attendance register and your mark book when s/he enters the classroom. Explanation of the context and of the performance or behaviour of particular students will usually have to wait until the feedback.

## Feedback

If the observation is part of your personal development then you can expect a detailed feedback session where the observer will go through the lesson commenting on what s/he has observed and making suggestions on how you might improve your practice. You will be able to discuss strategies that you may employ in the future and agree an action plan as a result of the lesson. This may involve changing your approach to planning or to classroom practice. To support you the observer might suggest that you observe other tutors' lessons to see how they manage that particular area of work. It is useful to observe lessons from other subject areas, for when you are not fully conversant with the content you are able to concentrate solely on the management of teaching and learning.

Feedback from a formal observation will be brief, concentrating on a summary of the strengths and areas for improvement in the lesson observed. At this point you should have the opportunity to comment on the context of the lesson or the effects of individual students on the lesson.

The sheet in Figure 14.2 was filled in during an observation of a lesson.

## Task 14.5

Using the observation sheet in Figure 14.2, discuss with a partner: 1) the grades you would award for the lesson and your reasons for doing so; 2) the action plan you would develop if you were the tutor and the support you might need in achieving it.

**Teacher Observed: Kate Jenkins**　　　　　　　　　　　　　**Observed by: F Barry**

| Subject/level/year: A2 Drama | Date: 4 November |
|---|---|

Context - Following theatre visit to see *Romeo and Juliet*, lesson to prepare students to write a review to compare 21st-century with 16th-century production.

---

**How effective was the learning of all learners?**
*Strengths*
All students used framework for producing notes effectively.
All students produced notes for the review.
Students engaged and able to recall examples from the play to support their views.
Collaborative learning evident in pairing of students.
Students used technical terms with confidence.

*Weaknesses*
Not all students had made notes following the production so relied on others in the lesson.
Not all students contributed to the discussion.
Position of students in the room meant that they could not see whiteboard.

---

**How well did the teaching promote the learning of all the learners?**
*Strengths*
Variety of activities maintained student interest and used resources well.
Framework for making notes and for analysing the production effectively used.
Subject knowledge and ability to communicate enthusiasm for play excellent.
Good use of questions to elicit initial response; then follow-up questions challenging.
Excellent comments made to students while doing pair work to keep them on task.

*Weaknesses*
Did not offer differentiated activities despite great range of abilities in the group and level of preparation for the lesson.
Did not reprimand late student. Poor punctuality appeared routine.
Instructions not always clear, and obviously not understood by students.
Allowed three students to dominate question-and-answer session, and four students not involved in discussion.
Poor timing of activities curtailed student involvement and participation.
Insufficient copies of production notes for students meant that their learning was impeded.

---

**How well did all the learners achieve?**
*Strengths*
By the end of the lesson all students had notes incorporating key points in the production.

*Weaknesses*
Failure of some students to do the preparatory work meant they were unable to complete the set design section of their notes.
Working notebooks were not used sufficiently by all students.

---

**Summary comments** (it is important that the grades reflect the evaluations in the text above)
Lively lesson enjoyed by most of the students.
Some students played little active part but achieved the objective of producing the notes.
Lack of resources slowed the pace and impeded learning.
Differentiation strategies not fully developed.

**GRADES:**　　**Learning**　　**Teaching**　　**Attainment**
**1** (excellent) **2** (very good) **3** (good) **4** (satisfactory) **5** (unsatisfactory) **6** (poor) **7** (very poor)

---

**Figure 14.2**　Feedback from lesson observation

The following checklist is produced for observers by the External Quality Review (EQR) Consortium. This is a group of 20 colleges in the south of England, supported by three consultants, who organize peer reviews between colleges to support their quality improvement processes. As part of the training, the reviewers use the *aide-mémoire* to consider what they should observe in the classroom and what makes a good lesson. It also provides an excellent checklist for you to use when you are being observed. EQR videos, used in training tutors to observe lessons, may be in your college or school and these provide excellent examples of ways in which lessons may be observed and the ways in which feedback is given.

## Aide-mémoire for lesson observation

How effective is the learning of all learners?

- Learners understand the purpose of the lesson and what they are expected to achieve.
- Learners are confident, and know how well they are doing and what they need to improve.
- The interests of learners are engaged and sustained and they participate well.
- Learners build on and develop previous learning and make progress at least appropriate to their capacity.
- Learners, as appropriate, demonstrate a capacity for working independently and collaboratively.
- Learners have access to and make effective use of appropriate learning and IT resources.
- Learners respond to feedback from their teachers that enables them to make progress.
- Learners apply effort to succeed with their work, work productively and make effective use of their time.
- Learners complete tasks and activities successfully.

How well does the teaching promote the learning of all learners?

- *Planning and preparation*:
  - The lesson is well prepared and well structured and takes account of the learners' needs.
  - The teacher has clear and appropriate aims and objectives, which are explained to the learners.
  - The lesson builds on previous learning.
- *Techniques/approaches*:
  - The teacher demonstrates sound, up-to-date knowledge of the subject.
  - The teacher gives clear explanations and instructions and the lesson is appropriately paced.

- The activities used are appropriate and effective and challenge and inspire learners.
- The teacher, as appropriate, makes good use of opportunities for independent and group learning.
- Basic and/or key skills are developed and applied systematically.

● *Attention to individual needs*:
- Learners experience a variety of teaching and learning strategies during the course.
- Equal opportunity issues are handled appropriately.
- The teacher takes account of the ability range in the class and the work is sufficiently challenging for all learners.
- Learners, as appropriate, are encouraged to draw on their own experience.

● *Managing the learning process*:
- The lesson starts promptly.
- The teacher promotes good working relationships that foster learning.
- Learners have a schedule with key dates for assessments etc so they can be helped to plan their study.
- The teacher uses accommodation, equipment and support staff to best effect and promotes safe working practice.

● *Assessment and feedback*:
- The teacher checks regularly learners' progress, corrects mistakes and gives prompt feedback to help them succeed.
- Learners are set a regular pattern of tasks, homework and assignments.
- Teachers assess work fairly, return it promptly and show how learners can improve.
- Criteria for assessment/marking are explicit.
- The progress of individual learners is monitored carefully, records are kept and learning plans are regularly updated.

To what extent do learners attain the expected standards?

● Learners acquire knowledge, skills and understanding appropriate to the syllabus and the stage of the course.
● Learners acquire appropriate key skills and the skills of critical evaluation, research and analysis.
● Learners attend regularly and are punctual.

(Furniss and Nicholls, 2001)

Your work as a personal tutor or as a subject tutor providing individual tutorials may also be observed. If you are delivering the tutorial programme you will inevitably include many of the suggestions above as examples of good practice in teaching a lesson. There are, however, other facets that observers would be looking for in a tutorial not necessarily found in a subject lesson:

- The tutor provides appropriate accommodation where the student and tutor may talk privately.
- The tutor creates an environment of mutual trust so that s/he is able to offer support to the student and the student feels able to ask for that support.
- Any actions agreed at a previous tutorial are reviewed.
- Any guidance given is impartial.
- Guidance is positive and linked to realistic and achievable targets.
- Students are provided with information or directed to appropriate resources.
- Targets set are SMART and will lead to improvement.
- Action to be taken by the student and/or the tutor is summarized and agreed by both.
- Information on the tutorial is recorded and stored appropriately.
- An appropriate appointment to follow up the tutorial is made.

You will be involved in improving your own performance as well as contributing to the improvement of the quality of what the college offers. This is a constant process of self-assessment, action planning and review. The more formal systems will be on paper and open to external scrutiny. The informal evaluations will be undertaken by you in the classroom, in daily discussions with your colleagues or in quiet reflection during your journey, at your desk or even in the bath!

You will be part of a profession that has at its core the desire to improve the quality of every aspect of the education and experience of its students. Standards may be set for you by external agencies, and complex systems may be introduced to improve the quality of your subject area but you, as the teacher, know that in the final analysis it is you who will make the difference in the classroom. It is through your constant striving to improve the experience of your students that standards will be raised and the quality of learning improved. You will learn to reflect on your practice and to improve it and in the process you may well agree with the wisdom of Socrates, who, centuries before quality assurance was heard of, declared 'an unexamined life is not worth living'.

# References

Furniss, B and Nicholls, S (2001) EQR handbook, Unpublished, EQR Consortium
Further Education Funding Council (FEFC) (1997) Circular 97/12, FEFC, Coventry
Learning and Skills Council (LSC) (2001) *Raising Standards in Post 16 Learning: Self assessment and development plans*, DfES, London
OFSTED (2002) *Handbook for Inspecting Colleges*, HMI 464, OFSTED, London

# Index